Supreme Hubris

SUPREME HUBRIS

HOW OVERCONFIDENCE IS DESTROYING THE COURT—AND HOW WE CAN FIX IT

• • •

AARON TANG

Yale
UNIVERSITY PRESS
New Haven and London

Published with assistance from the Louis Stern Memorial Fund.

Yale University Press books may be purchased in quantity for educational, business, or promotional use. For information, please e-mail sales.press@yale.edu (U.S. office) or sales@yaleup.co.uk (U.K. office).

Set in Gotham and Adobe Garamond types by IDS Infotech Ltd.
Printed in the United States of America.

Library of Congress Control Number: 2022950685
ISBN 978-0-300-26403-6 (hardcover : alk. paper)

A catalogue record for this book is available from the British Library.

This paper meets the requirements of ANSI/NISO Z39.48–1992 (Permanence of Paper).

10 9 8 7 6 5 4 3 2 1

For SS

As a wise man once wrote, you don't need many heroes if you choose carefully

Contents

Supreme Hubris

Introduction

In a battle of confidence, few could rival the late Antonin Scalia. The lone child of Italian immigrants in New Jersey, Scalia went from humble beginnings to a distinguished (if controversial) career as a law professor, government lawyer, and Supreme Court justice. He was the smartest person in every room he walked into, and he knew it.

The first time I met him, in the fall of 2013, he was holding court with a group of new law clerks in a stately reception room on the Supreme Court building's second floor. Hand-picked from a wide pool of applicants by the justices themselves, the clerks are recent law school graduates hired for one-year terms to assist the justices. Six of the Court's current members are former Supreme Court law clerks.

Only two years out of law school, I had just started my year as a clerk to Justice Sonia Sotomayor. It was a dream job, and I was beyond nervous. Palms sweaty, I joined the group of captivated twenty-somethings who'd formed a circle around Scalia, drawn in by his lively manner and his commanding baritone voice.

One of the clerks asked Scalia for advice on how to succeed in our new positions. Expecting a platitude in response, we were stunned by his answer. "Some of my clerks get stuck thinking cases at the Supreme Court must be hard," he cautioned. "Is it constitutional to execute a seventeen-year-old criminal?" He placed a palm over his furrowed brow, mocking a look of deep consternation. Then he threw up his hands. "Of course it is! I've already said it's ok to execute a sixteen-year-old!"[1] "See? Lots of cases are easy as can be. Easy, easy, easy!"

That was not my experience in my year clerking at the Supreme Court. It was not my experience at all.

Sleepless nights are a part of the job. Sometimes clerks have to stay up through the night to review last-minute requests filed by death row inmates to block their executions.[2] The clerks go home only after a Court official sends an email declaring "all clear"—a jarring way to learn that a person has died. A few of the clerks keep late hours to mirror the working patterns of their bosses. And each June, as the Court nears the end of its term, clerks pull all-nighters to meet pressing opinion deadlines.

My first sleepless night happened for none of these reasons. It was, rather, entirely self-inflicted.

One of the main responsibilities law clerks have across all the justices' chambers is to draft bench memos for major cases. The nature of these memos varies from one chambers to the next, but the general idea is for clerks to analyze the arguments on each side of a case to aid the individual justices in preparing for oral argument.

Most of the work of writing a bench memo involves reading the briefs filed in the case, distilling each side's best arguments, and making a recommendation about who should win. The clerks' recommendations count for very little. It is vastly more common for the justices to persuade their clerks to take a different view of a case than the other way around. Given the clerks' youth and their lack of Senate confirmation, this is as it should be. Still, the stakes don't feel low for the clerks themselves. Handing one's work to a sitting Supreme Court justice is a big deal.

I had a bench memo due to Justice Sotomayor in a few days, and I was at a loss. The problem wasn't that the case was particularly controversial or high stakes. In truth, it was one of modest importance, the kind of nonpolitical dispute over an arcane federal statute that only a few practicing lawyers even know about.

The problem was the way I'd gone about drafting the memo. I'd begun by reading the petitioner's brief—the written argument filed by the party that lost in the court below and is therefore asking the Court for relief. I'd found the brief's opening pages so convincing that I felt sure the Court should rule in the petitioner's favor. So for the sake of efficiency, as I finished reading the rest of the brief, I began outlining a memo with that outcome in hand.

When I picked up the opposing brief filed by the respondent—the party that had won in the lower court—I expected to find arguments with holes so glaring that my memo could easily (and cleverly!) exploit them. What I found instead was a set of arguments every bit as persuasive as the petitioner's. I began to doubt my initial reaction.

Somebody had to lose, though, so I had to choose a side. I'm only mildly embarrassed to admit that I succumbed to the sunk cost fallacy. Unable to discern a clearly superior legal argument and with a host of other memos still to complete, I looked at the screen in front of me and saw the outline I'd already drafted. I clenched my teeth and started typing. The result was a fifty-page memo recommending that my boss rule for the petitioner.

As I lay down to sleep that night, though, doubt overtook me. Was I really sure? Had I been more lazy than lawyerly? What if my memo was so obviously wrong that my judgment would never be worthy of trust again? I snuck out of bed, drove back to the Supreme Court building, and opened a new Word document. (In those days, law clerks were largely forbidden to work remotely out of concern for information security.) By the end of the next day, I'd written a second fifty-page memo recommending the exact opposite outcome.

But the toughest part was still to come. Which memo to hand in? After agonizing until the last minute, I finally placed the second memo, the one siding with the respondent, on the justice's desk. I don't remember sleeping much that night, either.

This dynamic, it turns out, is true of many of the cases at the Supreme Court. The Court's own guidelines ensure that simple cases rarely make it to the Court to begin with. Supreme Court Rule 10 limits the Court's review largely to important legal questions on which lower court judges are "in conflict"—meaning they disagree, often intensely.[3] The roughly sixty cases that qualify each year are thus so difficult—so *close*—that it's often impossible for a fair-minded person to read the briefs on each side of a case without thinking both are right. True, some cases have such loaded political implications that it's hard to approach them evenhandedly. But if there was such a thing as a magical truth serum, it would force us to admit that even in many of these hot-button cases, our preferred *policy* outcomes aren't necessarily the correct *legal* outcomes. With apologies to the late Justice Scalia, cases at the Supreme Court are anything but easy. They're hard, hard, hard.

Yet the Supreme Court never admits as much. The justices issue opinions so confident that one wonders how anyone could disagree with them. In fact, regardless of where they fall on the political spectrum, today's justices routinely shrug off the complex legal disputes before them as "easy cases."[4] And they do so even though those disputes typically produced divisions among dozens of lower court judges, not to mention the justices themselves. The case I found so difficult that I drafted dueling bench memos is a perfect example. The complexity that kept me up all night apparently did not trouble the justices. In a breezy opinion that admitted no uncertainty, the Court ruled unanimously for the respondent. I had handed in the right memo after all. But I'd done so more out of luck than skill.

• • •

When Daniel Kahneman speaks, people listen. A Nobel Prize winner and longtime professor of psychology at Princeton, Kahneman is one of the founders of behavioral economics, the study of how psychological biases afflict human judgment. The sunk cost fallacy is a common example.[5] Sometimes it produces costs that are merely annoying, like a day's wasted effort on an unnecessary bench memo. Other times it leads to tragic human suffering, such as during the later period of the Vietnam War when U.S. officials pointed to the prior loss of life to justify an escalation of commitment.[6] Another prominent idea from behavioral economics is confirmation bias, the troubling tendency people have to search for evidence to support their existing beliefs. Confirmation bias is largely responsible for turning our Twitter feeds and the cable news networks into echo chambers—a major source of today's dangerous political polarization.[7]

To Kahneman, however, neither of these powerful psychological traps is the most damaging of all cognitive biases. That dubious honor belongs to overconfidence.[8]

Overconfidence bias is misplaced faith in one's own ability. A common example is how three-quarters of Americans claim to be better-than-average drivers. The statistic may seem harmless enough. But research shows that overconfident drivers fail to appreciate the danger of behaviors such as speeding, driving under the influence, and driving while using a phone—all of which produce an increased risk of injury and death on the road, both to themselves and to others.[9] Overconfidence bias is damaging, in other words, because it acts as a force multiplier. By blinding us to our other biases and shortfalls, it amplifies their dangers.

This book is about how overconfidence bias afflicts a small group of exceedingly important people: the nine justices on the United States Supreme Court. It is a book of two halves. The first half is about the *problem* with today's Court. I describe how recent damage to the

Court's institutional credibility threatens profound consequences for the American people and show why overconfidence bias is the root of this threat. It is overconfidence, I argue—not the more commonly diagnosed evil of partisanship—that underlies what many have called a "legitimacy crisis" at the Court.[10]

Supreme Court justices have always been partisan, after all, in the sense of displaying loyalty to a given political party. The greatest chief justice in our nation's history, John Marshall, was a longtime political operative for the Federalist Party. He was President John Adams's sitting secretary of state when Adams nominated him to be chief justice in January 1801, *two months after Adams had lost the presidential election of 1800*. The modern-day equivalent would be if President Donald Trump had nominated Secretary of State Mike Pompeo to the Supreme Court after losing the presidential election of 2020—and gotten him confirmed by the Republican-controlled Senate. From day one, in other words, the Supreme Court has been a partisan institution. It has always been a part of our politics, not above it.

Yet the Court was not always overconfident. At certain points, most prominently during the New Deal settlement that lasted for a short period after 1937, the justices have been quite humble. They did not pretend to have the power to discover singular, legalistic answers to the difficult constitutional questions that divided American society. Instead, they trusted in the wisdom of the democratic process, deferring to the will of people's elected representatives and upholding minimum wage, maximum hour, and other economic regulations. Not coincidentally, these moments of judicial humility were accompanied by widespread public trust in the Court.[11] And this trust persisted despite President Franklin D. Roosevelt's appointment of several fiercely loyal—indeed partisan—justices. Without the amplifying effects of overconfidence, partisanship was still present at the Court; it just wasn't nearly as destructive.

Correctly diagnosing what is wrong with today's court matters. It matters because focusing on the wrong problem will beget the wrong solution. For example, after diagnosing partisanship as the primary source of the Court's legitimacy crisis, many on today's political left have called for "rebalancing" the Court, which is code for expanding it by adding more liberal justices. As a political progressive, I can certainly sympathize with the desire for a Court that reliably reaches more liberal outcomes. The trouble is, while many on the left may earnestly believe that an intervention of this kind represents an answer to the overtly partisan process by which Republicans came to hold their current supermajority on the Court, those on the right will view it quite differently: as partisan escalation that must be met with further retaliation. A Court that grows from nine to thirteen to still more members each time Washington's balance of power changes will quickly lose what's left of its institutional credibility. Packed courts foreshadowed the decline of democracies in Hungary, Venezuela, and Turkey. That is not a path to be taken lightly.

We see a vastly different picture, however, once we understand the problem of overconfidence bias and how it overtook the Court. Perhaps surprisingly, the Court's confidence began rising for the most noble of reasons at the most critical of times: during the Civil Rights movement. The Court's humble posture in the years following the New Deal made sense when the nation faced the dire challenges of the Great Depression. Yet even as the American economy recovered, a deeper rot remained in the form of pernicious racism. That left the Court with a dilemma. The deferential approach it had taken so successfully in the New Deal era would leave it powerless to strike down segregation laws, poll taxes, and other forms of state-sanctioned racial discrimination. The result was enormous pressure on the justices to claim special insight into the single, correct meaning of the Constitution so that they could override these laws. For good reasons, the justices did exactly that.

Once unleashed, however, this newfound willingness to strike down laws by finding them incompatible with the meaning of the Constitution suffered from a new challenge. How would the Court distinguish between constitutionally permissible and impermissible laws in contexts other than racial discrimination, such as personal privacy, criminal procedure, and religious freedom? Over time, the justices and legal academics developed grand constitutional theories to fill this void. One prominent philosophy is living constitutionalism, a view Justice William Brennan captured roughly when he described "the ultimate question" in any given case as, "What do the words of the text mean in our time?"[12] A competing approach is originalism, or the philosophy of interpreting the Constitution's text in accordance with its meaning at the time of enactment. Although the two theories are opposites in many respects, both are the same in a crucial respect. Both offer the justices a seductive power: a tool for using the Constitution to announce a single, correct answer to society's most difficult disputes.

Freed from deference to legislatures and emboldened by these high theories of constitutional interpretation, Supreme Court justices soon felt comfortable opining definitively on far-ranging matters of constitutional law. And our overconfident Supreme Court was born. Gone now are the days of the justices granting "every possible presumption" in favor of upholding a law even when they hold "views inconsistent with the [law's] wisdom," as the Court wrote in 1937 in a major case involving the minimum wage. Today's justices no longer humbly defer to the judgment of elected lawmakers in hard cases where the Constitution is unclear. Nor are they likely to defer to the collective wisdom of the justices who have come before them. Their opinions assert instead that there is just a single possible legal answer, and they evince no doubt in their ability to uncover what it is.

Consider, for example, Justice Samuel Alito's majority opinion in the most important Supreme Court decision in a generation: *Dobbs v.*

Jackson Women's Health Organization. The question in the case was whether a Mississippi law banning abortions after fifteen weeks (except in the case of a medical emergency or severe fetal abnormality) violated the Constitution. The Court had previously answered that question on two occasions, in 1973 and 1992, holding first in *Roe v. Wade* that the Fourteenth Amendment enshrines a right to abortion until the fetus can survive outside the womb (at roughly twenty-four weeks in pregnancy), and then reaffirming that basic rule in *Planned Parenthood v. Casey.* Then, as now, abortion was a hotly contested issue in our pluralistic society, involving a difficult balance between women's reproductive autonomy and the state's interest in protecting the unborn fetus. Yet of the fifteen justices who cast votes in *Roe* and *Casey* (Justices Byron White, Harry Blackmun, and William Rehnquist were on the Court for both cases), eleven voted to strike that balance in favor of the right to abortion, including eight who had been appointed by Republican presidents.

In *Dobbs,* however, a five-justice majority tossed *Roe* and *Casey* aside in an opinion that dripped with overconfidence. Suddenly, the reasoning that had earned the support of a bipartisan supermajority in *Roe* and *Casey* was, according to *Dobbs*'s newly constituted majority, "exceptionally weak." Writing for the majority, Justice Alito concluded that all of those earlier justices—from Thurgood Marshall to Sandra Day O'Connor, and Warren Burger to Anthony Kennedy—were not just wrong but "egregiously wrong." Never mind that the "most important historical fact" that Alito relied on to reach this conclusion—the claim that twenty-eight out of thirty-seven states had banned abortions throughout pregnancy when the Fourteenth Amendment was adopted—was no fact at all. (Among other mistakes, Alito counted two states as banning all abortions even though they permitted surgical procedures, he ignored contrary state Supreme Court rulings, and he even cited a Virginia law of 1848 that was repealed in 1849.)[13] To Alito and the other self-assured members of his majority, it was not they but the eleven justices who voted to uphold the right to abortion in *Roe* and *Casey* who had strayed "far outside the bounds of *any reasonable interpretation*" of the Constitution.

A similar degree of excessive confidence characterized the Court's ruling in a case from 2008 called *Kennedy v. Louisiana*. The issue in *Kennedy* was whether the Eighth Amendment's ban on "cruel and unusual punishments" forbids states to impose the death penalty for the crime of aggravated child rape.[14] In answering "yes," the Court found it decisive that just six states at the time of decision permitted such punishment—a fact the Court deemed "evidence of a national consensus" against the death penalty for child rapists. But in truth, this consensus was far from settled: in the decade before *Kennedy* was decided, elected lawmakers in five states had actually enacted new statutes authorizing the death penalty for child rapists in certain gruesome circumstances.[15] Perhaps the majority was correct to deem the death penalty "cruel and unusual" despite this emerging political development. Or perhaps not. My point for now is that the question was closely contested, with reasonable legal arguments on both sides. Yet the five-justice majority forged ahead with unbridled certainty in its own wisdom. "In the end," the justices proudly declared, the "acceptability of the death penalty" must be decided based on "our own judgment."

A humble Court would openly acknowledge the limits of its own judgment. It would admit when the constitutional questions that divide our people are genuinely difficult. And it would write careful opinions that acknowledge the good-faith arguments—and interests—on both sides of these hard cases. Sadly, today's Court writes blockbuster opinions in language so strident that it undermines tolerance among our already divided people when it should be building it.

All of this can seem deeply disheartening. What hope do we have against such a powerful psychological bias? Yet it turns out that a clear-eyed diagnosis of the Supreme Court's overconfidence problem can open the possibility of a more hopeful solution. That is the subject of the book's second half.

If the heart of the Supreme Court's legitimacy problem is not partisanship alone but the dangerous way in which overconfidence bias has amplified it, then the Court's future doesn't hinge solely on the unlikely prospect of some grand détente between two warring political factions that agree on virtually nothing. When spurred on by a great enough dose of public pressure, our justices have held their overconfidence in check before. If Americans care enough to exert similar pressure today, perhaps the justices can find some humility again.

There are signs the public may be ready to do its part. Never before have so many Americans expressed a lack of confidence in the Court: just 25 percent reported a "great deal" or "quite a lot" of confidence in the Court in June 2022, the lowest number Gallup has recorded in fifty years.[16] Indeed, many believe the Court has become so nakedly political that it is beyond saving. Calls to pack it, strip it of power, or ignore it altogether are thus increasingly common.

As radical as these proposals may seem, the truth is that they stem from legitimate public concern—and are now a very real part of the conversation surrounding the Court. But if these calls actually succeed in saving the Court, it will be through a different route: not by actually packing or ignoring it but by creating the conditions necessary for the Court to get serious about saving itself. And the way for it to do so may be closer at hand than many realize. Quietly and against all odds, it turns out that the Court has stumbled upon a way to dial down the temperature in the blockbuster cases that divide our society. Rather than rely exclusively on legalistic arguments over the law's original meaning, uncertain modern-day values, or a mystifying web of precedents, the Court has sometimes ruled instead with an eye toward doing as little harm as possible. And it has done so in an ingenious way: by ruling against the side with the greatest ability to minimize its own harm using the other options at its disposal. I call this the *least harm principle* of judicial decision making.

Consider, for example, the Supreme Court's divergent decisions in two of its highest-stakes cases in 2020: *Trump v. Vance* and *Trump v. Mazars*. Both cases involved efforts by President Trump's political opponents to obtain his private financial records, including his elusive federal tax returns. In *Trump v. Vance,* the Court considered whether a New York State prosecutor could subpoena Trump's financial records from his private accounting firm. Those subpoenas threatened to expose the president and his associates to significant criminal and civil punishment under New York law.[17] (As of this writing, they had produced evidence that led to a five-month prison sentence for Trump's longtime CFO, Allen Weisselberg.) So the president sued to block them.

Remarkably, three conservative justices—Chief Justice John Roberts and Justices Neil Gorsuch and Brett Kavanaugh, the latter two of whom Trump himself had appointed—voted with the four liberals to rule against Trump. How did a bipartisan supermajority reach this result? They did not purport to uncover some single correct answer to the dispute in the Constitution's vague text or history. Instead, they humbly acknowledged the important interests on both sides of the case before comparing each side's ability to avoid the harms of an adverse ruling. Writing for the majority, Chief Justice Roberts recognized that politically motivated states might harass a president by issuing burdensome subpoenas in bad faith. Yet he also noted that several state law and constitutional protections already exist to protect against such harassment. By contrast, Chief Justice Roberts reasoned, denying New York access to the subpoenaed financial records would leave the state powerless to investigate and hold criminals accountable for their wrongdoing. Because New York had less ability to avoid the harms of an adverse ruling, the Court ruled in its favor.

Now consider *Trump v. Mazars,* a case that concerned identical subpoenas issued by Democrats in Congress for the stated purpose of drafting potential legislation on topics ranging from money laundering to terrorism. The lower courts had rejected Trump's pleas to block the subpoenas, but the Supreme Court disagreed.

Just as in *Vance,* the Court based this ruling on a direct comparison of each side's ability to protect its interests if it were to lose the case. Unlike in *Vance,* however, that analysis in *Mazars* cut in favor of Trump. In another opinion written by Chief Justice John Roberts—and joined by six justices, notably including all four liberal justices—the Court reasoned that President Trump should prevail insofar as congressional Democrats had better options for avoiding the harms of an adverse ruling. Rather than rely on the president's private financial records as a case study for money laundering and terrorism legislation, the Court pointed out, Congress could subpoena nonpresidential sources for information that would be just as helpful. A ruling against President Trump, by contrast, would leave not just him but all future presidents powerless to avoid intrusive congressional demands for any personal medical, educational, or financial record, no matter how private.

In more than a dozen recent cases, the Court has applied the least harm principle to reach a sensible result on critical issues, ranging from LGBTQ rights to immigration and religious freedom to juvenile justice. These decisions follow three common steps. First, the Court considers whether the legal question before it is genuinely difficult in the sense that both sides possess strong arguments. If so, the Court refrains from deciding the case solely by relying on its usual lawyerly tools because doing so would create a real risk of error. Second, the Court accepts both sides' good-faith descriptions of the severe harms they would suffer if the Court were to rule against them. This means that the Court cannot rule for one side simply by discounting what the other side has at stake. Finally, because these other avenues for deciding the case are so difficult, the Court rules on a different basis that is more tractable. It considers each side's options for avoiding the harm it would suffer in defeat, and it rules against the side with the greatest ability to do so.

By candidly recognizing the reasonable arguments and significant interests on both sides of a case—and by signaling to the losing side how it can still protect its interests after defeat—the least harm principle avoids decisions that create all-out losers. That, in turn, enables the Court to shore up its public image. For the least harm principle creates losses that feel temporary, and thus tolerable, precisely because it reminds losing groups of their power to respond in more productive ways than assailing their opponents or the Court itself.

There are signs that this approach may be effective. In August 2020, after a year in which the Court decided a slew of major cases (including *Vance* and *Mazars*) using the least harm principle, the Supreme Court's public approval rating reached its highest level in more than a decade, 58 percent. Even more significantly, this approval crossed partisan lines: healthy majorities of Democrats (56 percent) and Republicans (60 percent) alike supported the Court's work.[18]

Alas, the Court has undergone dramatic change since 2020. After the death of Justice Ruth Bader Ginsburg and her replacement by Justice Amy Coney Barrett, Chief Justice Roberts (a stalwart conservative and yet the common denominator in many of the Court's least harm rulings) is no longer at the Court's center. The result is a conservative majority that has taken an approach largely insensitive to the immensely harmful consequences of its rulings. On cases implicating the most pressing issues facing our nation—from abortion to guns and voting rights to climate change—the Court has ruled instead based on its overconfident assessment of the law's one-and-only meaning.

Take, for example, the Court holding in *Brnovich v. Democratic National Committee* that Arizona could enforce a pair of voting restrictions that disproportionately burden minority voters, despite the Voting Rights Act's prohibition against laws that "result in" abridgment of the right to vote "on account of race."[19] In reaching that result, the Court left rural Native American voters (among others) facing severe obstacles to voting, including lack of access to polling places and mailboxes often located hours away. The Court instead accepted Arizona's bare assertion that its voting barriers were needed to reduce vote tampering and fraud. Yet at no point did the Court consider that Arizona could protect against those harms just as well using commonsense regulations such as tamper-resistant ballots and criminal prohibitions against actual fraud. That is precisely the kind of consideration that the least harm principle turns on. By ignoring it, the Court missed an opportunity to minimize the adverse effects of its decisions.

Decisions like *Brnovich,* which was decided on the last day of the 2020–21 term, are a part of a broader pattern. In an earlier case, *Shelby County v. Holder,* the Court struck down a long-standing requirement that states and political subdivisions with a history of racial discrimination must "preclear" changes to their voting systems with the Department of Justice to ensure that they do not disproportionately burden minority voters.[20] The Court's decision in *Shelby County* inflicted maximum harm on the losing side because it left minority voters virtually powerless to ensure equal access to the polls. Yet a ruling in the other direction, in favor of voting rights, would have left a reasonably escapable harm for states and political subdivisions. The Voting Rights Act granted them a right to "bail out" from, or escape, the preclearance requirement entirely—an alternative they could trigger by showing a panel of judges that they'd refrained from racial discrimination in voting for ten years.

Cases like *Vance* and *Mazars* on the one hand, and *Dobbs, Brnovich,* and *Shelby County* on the other, reveal an important choice facing today's Supreme Court. It can employ the least harm principle consistently across its docket, ensuring that the losers in monumental cases retain meaningful options for protecting their interests. That would lead to a world in which progressives and conservatives each suffer defeats that they can redress. Both sides would have reason to keep playing by the rules of our democratic order, and neither side would have cause for an all-out assault against the Court.

Or the Court's conservative supermajority can continue to overconfidently pursue an ideological vision of the Constitution supported by a minority of Americans, an approach that will create losers with few options other than to assail the Court itself. In that world, in which progressives are unable to protect rights as fundamental as the right to vote, a serious effort to pack the Court or strip it of power may come to seem the lesser of two evils.

The Court is going to have to choose—and fast. A number of important cases are set to come before it in the coming years implicating voting rights, the right to obtain abortion care across state lines, Congress's power to codify a statutory abortion right, and whether businesses have a free speech right to discriminate against LGBTQ customers. When the Court decides these cases, will it admit the limits of its own knowledge and rule in the least harmful way possible? Or will it plow ahead overconfidently, earning the public's lasting distrust?

In this book, I explain why the Court should choose the first option. By naming the least harm principle and describing how it has already been used with success, I hope to offer a promising path forward in this dire moment for the Supreme Court's legitimacy. What

America needs most isn't a more liberal Court or a more conservative one, and it certainly isn't a packed one. What we need is a Court that delivers decisions both sides of our political divide can live with. What we need, in other words, is a *less harmful* Supreme Court. This book offers a vision of what such a Court might look like.

PART ONE
The Problem

• • •

These days it seems nearly everyone has something they'd like to fix about the Supreme Court.[1] Democrats worry about the Court's conservative bent.[2] Republicans fear that it isn't as conservative as advertised.[3] Democrats, Republicans, and independents alike think the Court should just get out of politics.[4] Progressives and libertarians want to change the "poisonous" process by which justices are appointed and confirmed.[5] Even a bipartisan group of senators bemoans the Court's troubling lack of public transparency.[6]

Keeping track of everything that's gone wrong can be overwhelming. One is tempted to wonder whether the Court might be beyond repair.

At moments like these, it can be helpful to return to first principles and ask, What kind of Supreme Court does our society need? Only by having a clear goal in mind can we begin to form a coherent plan of action.

More than anything else, what America needs is a Court that can protect against the dangerous deterioration of essential democratic norms. Yet a disturbing decline in public confidence has left the Court ill-equipped for this crucial task. Figuring out why the justices have lost the public's trust is therefore the essential place to start. For without an accurate diagnosis, any effort to fix the Court is doomed to fail.

1

Distrust and Democracy

At its best, the Supreme Court of the United States is an important guardian of our democracy and a powerful force for good. Sometimes it fulfills this role in the most direct manner, by safeguarding vital political rights such as the right to vote. That's what the Court did, for example, when it announced the fundamental principle of "one person, one vote," and when it struck down racially discriminatory voting restrictions.[1] It has likewise upheld the essential right to political dissent even when that dissent is expressed by the least popular speakers—such as communists in the 1960s or neo-Nazis in the 1970s—and in the least popular ways, such as by burning the American flag.[2]

The Court has also issued powerful decisions protecting the rights of historically marginalized groups to equal and inclusive treatment across aspects of our society. In doing so, it has defended the pluralism and diversity on which our democracy thrives. *Brown v. Board of Education* is one obvious example; the Court's more recent recognition of the right to marriage equality in *Obergefell v. Hodges* is another.

At other times, the Court has stood up against corrupt officials to ensure their accountability to the people who elect them. When Richard Nixon tried to cover up his role in a foiled scheme to break into the headquarters of his political opponents at the Watergate office building, it was the Supreme Court that finally put the nation's collective foot down. In a unanimous opinion, the Court ordered Nixon to make public a series of secret tape recordings revealing his complicity in the cover-up. Just two weeks later, Nixon resigned from office.

But what happens to our democracy—and our nation—when the Supreme Court is not at its best? What happens when the Court loses the trust of the American people? If the Court continues down the path it has taken these past few years, we won't like what we find.

I grew up learning about the Court at its best. As the product of public schools in a small town in Ohio, I witnessed no shortage of America-boosting. My teachers were fervent in presenting the United States as a shining beacon of freedom. My parents, immigrants from Taiwan, were committed to the prospect of political and cultural assimilation in their new home country. One of the proudest moments of my childhood happened in the fifth grade, when the school principal called me to his office to tell me that a friend and I had been chosen to raise and lower the American flag each day. For a full year, I started and ended every school day at a towering flagpole in front of the building, looking up to the symbol of my family's adopted home.

That was also the year I discovered passages in my social studies textbook celebrating the Supreme Court as the declarer of American truths and champion of our most cherished liberties. I remember reading about the awesome power of judicial review, the final authority vested in the Supreme Court—not the president or Congress—to tell us "what the law is."[3] And I remember learning how the Court—not the president or Congress—ostensibly ended our nation's sordid history of racially segregated public schooling—a history in which, as a ten-year-old, I had only the vaguest sense that my own heritage would have left me excluded.[4]

I was hooked. So hooked, that when I later taught U.S. history in a St. Louis middle school after graduating from college, I would happily preach the same, flag-waving vision of the Supreme Court to my eighth graders. And when I started law school in the fall of 2008, I did so at the most hopeful of times for a young progressive: in the middle of Barack Obama's first campaign for president. After winning office, President Obama nominated Sonia Sotomayor to be the first Latina justice on the Supreme Court the very next year. History was happening, and progressives were on the right side of it. By the time I graduated, three years later, it's hard to say which was bigger: my inflated optimism about the Court or my student loan balance.

I know exactly where I was the day my optimism began its descent into reality. On Saturday, February 13, 2016, my wife and I were staying at a rental house with friends in San Diego. It wasn't much of a vacation, as we'd both woefully underestimated the challenges of traveling with an infant. We'd spent much of the weekend cooped up in a bedroom, taking turns desperately rocking our ten-week-old son, trying to coax him to sleep. That's where my son and I were—me, shushing like a maniac, and him, wailing his protest—when my phone buzzed on the table. I looked down to see a CNN alert. Antonin Scalia had died.

My jaw dropped. The man had seemed indomitable when I'd seen him at the Court, his passion for the law exceeded only by his supreme confidence. I'd thought he'd serve for another decade and enjoy a longevity like that of his former colleague John Paul Stevens, who retired from the Court at ninety.

Maybe it was the thought of Scalia's wife, their nine children, and the more than two dozen grandchildren he'd left behind. Maybe it was our shared love of America and our mutual interest in the Constitution, despite our very different political beliefs. Maybe it was the sleep deprivation. In truth, I'm still not sure what it was. But I cried.

I didn't see it coming at the time, but Scalia's death triggered years of all-out political warfare over the Supreme Court.

One month after Scalia's passing, President Barack Obama nominated Judge Merrick Garland to fill the newly vacant seat. The chief judge of the D.C. Circuit Court of Appeals, Garland was widely respected across the political spectrum—so much so that just two days before his nomination, Republican senator Orrin Hatch had praised him as a "fine man" whom Obama could "easily name," with the implication that he would quickly win Senate confirmation. But Obama "probably won't do that," Hatch continued, "because this appointment is about the election. So I'm pretty sure he'll name someone the [Democratic base] wants."[5]

Obama's choice to nominate Garland was surprising in several respects. Not only was he a more moderate judge than many had expected, but he was also, at sixty-three, considerably older than Obama's prior Supreme Court nominees, Sonia Sotomayor and Elena Kagan, who were fifty-five and fifty, respectively, at the time of their appointments. Garland also would not have added diversity to the bench.

Yet Obama's decision reflected a deliberate strategy. Knowing that his nominee's fate would run through the Republican majority in the Senate, he sought to take any plausible ground for objection off the table. Too inexperienced? Garland had served for nineteen years on the D.C. Circuit. Justice Clarence Thomas, by contrast, had served on that same court for barely a year before his nomination by President George H. W. Bush. Too young? The two most recent Republican appointees to the Court at the time—Chief Justice John Roberts and Justice Samuel Alito—had been in their fifties when nominated. Too liberal? No one could say that about Garland. Indeed, Senator Hatch had previously described him as a "consensus nominee" who would earn bipartisan Senate support.

But too late.

That, it turned out, was Garland's problem. Although nearly eight months still remained until the presidential election of 2016, Republican Senate Majority Leader Mitch McConnell quickly declared that Garland would not receive so much as a hearing in the Senate. Appearing on *Fox News Sunday* just four days after Garland's nomination, McConnell was unequivocal. "In the middle of this presidential [election] year," McConnell announced, "the American people need to weigh in and decide" on the next Supreme Court justice—"not this lame duck president on the way out the door."[6] The reason for McConnell's unprecedented stance was not hard to guess: confirming even as moderate a nominee as Garland to the Court would shift its balance from five-to-four conservative to five-to-four liberal, giving the Court a majority of Democratic-appointed justices for the first time since 1970.

Everyone knows what happened next. Despite losing the popular vote by nearly three million votes, Donald Trump defeated Hillary Clinton in the Electoral College. In 2017, when President Trump nominated Judge Neil Gorsuch—a highly respected conservative jurist on the Denver-based Tenth Circuit Court of Appeals—Democrats in the Senate invoked the filibuster. Senate Republicans responded by "going nuclear," eliminating the filibuster for Supreme Court nominees along a strict party-line vote.[7] The Senate confirmed Gorsuch by a margin of fifty-four to forty-five, and McConnell's gambit paid off: the conservative majority at the Court would live on.

Even after Gorsuch's confirmation, the left's hand-wringing over the Supreme Court was fairly muted. Some of this was because of the Democratic Party's long-standing, inexplicable failure to appreciate the Court's political and practical significance.[8] Some owed to the fact that adding Gorsuch to the Court simply maintained the status quo; liberals had survived, more or less, with Scalia on the Court, and it was hard to see how Gorsuch would make things worse. But mainly, the left's cautious optimism about the Court rested on the presence of Justice Anthony Kennedy at its center.

Born and raised in Sacramento, California, Kennedy had an eminent career as a jurist, first on the California-based Ninth Circuit Court of Appeals and then on the Supreme Court. His entire tenure was marked by civility and moderation. Kennedy's genteel tone stood out even as his colleagues used increasingly acerbic language, often exchanging personal jabs in dueling majority and dissenting opinions. Kennedy alone had a strict rule against answering arguments raised by dissenting justices in response to his majority opinions—a policy that continually frustrated his clerks. When Justice Scalia accused Kennedy of engaging in a "judicial Putsch" in his marriage equality ruling and added that if he ever joined such an opinion, "I would hide my head in a bag," what did Kennedy write in response? Absolutely nothing.

While unstinting civility was the defining feature of Kennedy's demeanor among colleagues and friends, his public persona was quite different. Frequently hailed as a "swing" vote in major cases (though he privately preferred the term "median" justice), he left a legacy of stark contrasts.[9] One of the most consequential opinions of his judicial career was his majority opinion in *Citizens United,* which unleashed a torrent of secret corporate spending on elections. Yet liberals were ready to throw parades in his honor over the opinions he wrote in favor of LGBTQ rights.[10] Kennedy's abortion jurisprudence showed similar contrasts. He surprised onlookers by voting to reaffirm *Roe v. Wade* in the Court's landmark 1992 decision in *Planned Parenthood v. Casey*. Yet later in his career, he voted to allow a number of burdensome abortion regulations.[11]

On balance, Kennedy was a deeply conservative jurist and person. One analysis showed that across 537 "close cases" decided during his tenure, Kennedy voted with the conservatives 71.3 percent of the time.[12] Yet it was still his opinions on gay rights that stood out to many liberals. The fresh memory of his marriage equality ruling in 2015 may be why some on the left gave a collective shrug when Justice

Neil Gorsuch occupied Justice Scalia's seat two years later. Kennedy had saved the left before, the thinking went, and he would do so again. Except Kennedy himself had very different plans.

It is sometimes hard to know how Supreme Court justices think of themselves. Because our Constitution grants them life tenure (at least "during good behaviour," as Article III puts it, only half-threateningly), the justices need not define themselves for the public the way a candidate for office must. So it was not clear to many Americans just how Justice Kennedy viewed his judicial legacy in the moments after Donald Trump's surprising victory. Did he remain the rock-ribbed Republican who'd voted conservatively for decades in decisions like *Citizens United?* Or had he perhaps moved so far left that he'd come to define himself more by his marriage equality opinion in *Obergefell?*

Justice Kennedy, it seemed, was on the fence again. This time, though, he held the swing vote on his own legacy. Lawyers and public intellectuals on the left did what we'd done for decades: we used public media in an effort to persuade Kennedy directly. In December 2016, I published an open letter urging Kennedy to stay on the Court through the Trump presidency in order to protect rulings like *Obergefell* and *Casey*. The *Washington Post*'s Ruth Marcus argued in another open letter in February 2017 that retirement "would be terrible for the country at a moment that demands healing." The *New York Times* editorial board repeated these themes the following year.[13]

When Kennedy rebuffed these pleas and announced his retirement in a note to President Trump on June 27, 2018—the final day of a term that saw him vote for a landslide of conservative victories, including in cases involving a Christian baker's refusal to make a cake for a gay wedding and Trump's decision to ban individuals from several predominantly Muslim countries from entering the United States—his action spoke volumes. Kennedy still identified as a conservative. And by letting Trump choose his successor, he had ensured that the Court would remain conservative as well.

Kennedy's vote had been decisive in prominent liberal causes from abortion to gay rights to affirmative action, and his continued presence on the Court insulated these liberal victories against subsequent overruling. Now that he was retiring, the left fretted, would *Roe* be on the chopping block? *Obergefell,* too? This was worlds apart from trading Scalia for Gorsuch—one dyed-in-the-wool conservative for another. Once Kennedy was gone and presumably replaced by someone farther to the right, the Court's new median vote would belong to Chief Justice Roberts.

The son of a steel plant manager and the graduate of a Roman Catholic boarding school in Indiana, Roberts was, according to his Harvard Law School classmates, a "conservative in the old-fashioned sense."[14] After clerking for Chief Justice William Rehnquist, a Nixon appointee whose seat he would later fill, Roberts went on to work for the Reagan era Justice Department. There he coauthored a controversial memo criticizing the Supreme Court's ruling in *Plyler v. Doe,* which held that the Equal Protection Clause guarantees undocumented children the right to a tuition-free public education. After stints in private practice and the Office of the Solicitor General—the elite cadre of lawyers who represent the federal government before the U.S. Supreme Court—Roberts served a short term on the D.C. Circuit before being named Chief Justice by President George W. Bush.

Few can boast conservative credentials more sterling than those of Chief Justice Roberts before he joined the Court. Fewer still can match his conservative record afterward. By one measure, the Chief's voting pattern in close cases before 2018 was even more conservative than Scalia's and Clarence Thomas's. He voted for the conservative position in 82.4 percent of cases decided by a five-justice majority.[15] Only Justice Samuel Alito had a higher percentage.

And yet the right never quite trusted him. The Chief had bucked the conservative establishment from time to time by casting occasional votes to join the liberals. The most notable instance was his decision to preserve the individual mandate that was a key part of President Obama's signature legislative achievement, the Affordable Care Act.[16] That vote had elicited nasty attacks from movement conservatives, leading him to joke that he was fleeing to Malta (where he was scheduled to teach a legal course) because it was "an impregnable island fortress."[17]

Yet votes like this were the exception. It was Roberts who in 2007 had written an opinion deeming it unconstitutional for public school districts even to *voluntarily* pursue racial integration because "the way to stop discrimination on the basis of race is to stop discriminating on the basis of race."[18] It was Roberts whose opinion gutted a crucial provision of the Voting Rights Act in *Shelby County v. Holder*—a ruling that has since enabled voter suppression efforts such as Georgia's infamous law against handing water to people waiting in line to vote.[19] And it was Roberts who had dissented from Kennedy's marriage equality ruling with an ominous warning that the Constitution "had nothing to do with" same-sex marriage. The Chief had spent much of his adult life laboring to prove to his fellow conservatives that he was no "squish," and Kennedy's retirement seemed unlikely to change that.[20]

President Trump's decision to nominate Brett Kavanaugh as Kennedy's replacement converted liberals' worry into full-on panic.

Kavanaugh's educational and professional background tracked those of the Chief to an eerie degree. After graduating from law school, Kavanaugh, like Roberts, clerked for the Supreme Court justice—Kennedy—whom he would later replace. Also like Roberts, Kavanaugh would go on to work as a lawyer in the Justice Department during a Republican administration. He served as associate counsel in Kenneth

Starr's Office of the Independent Counsel when it investigated President Bill Clinton's affair with Monica Lewinsky. He also assisted President George W. Bush's legal team in its efforts to stop the Florida ballot recount in 2000. After serving stints in private practice and in Bush's White House, Kavanaugh was appointed (again like Roberts) to the D.C. Circuit, where he served until his elevation to the Supreme Court.

Liberal pushback was swift. The day Kavanaugh was nominated, Senators Bernie Sanders, Cory Booker, and others addressed a crowd of protesters on the steps of the Supreme Court, all to the sound of "Hell no on Kavanaugh" chants. Senator Jeff Merkley of Oregon called Kavanaugh "a nominee who wants to pave the path to tyranny."[21]

Yet all of this furor on the left was nothing compared to what was to come. Two months after his nomination, Christine Blasey Ford made the bombshell allegation that in the summer of 1982, a drunken Brett Kavanaugh had sexually assaulted her at a high school party.

Virtually all Americans know that the Supreme Court has a profound impact on their lives. Yet fewer than half can name a single sitting Supreme Court justice.[22] One prominent explanation for this divergence is the private nature of the Court's work. Cameras are strictly forbidden in the building, including at oral argument. The justices do not campaign for office, and they make infrequent public appearances. Unlike elected officials who very much want to be in the news, Supreme Court justices generally don't want to be known. And most aren't.

The privacy that normally shrouds the individual justices made Ford's testimony about Kavanaugh, offered during a televised hearing before the Senate Judiciary Committee, all the more remarkable. "I was pushed onto the bed and Brett got on top of me," Ford testified. "I yelled and tried to get away from him, but his weight was heavy. I believed he was going to rape me," Ford recounted. "Brett put his hand over my mouth to stop me from screaming," Ford continued. "It was hard for me to breathe, and I thought that Brett was accidentally going to kill me."[23]

A number of sexual trauma experts weighed in on the credibility of Ford's testimony. Sherry Hamby, a clinical psychologist with more than twenty years of experience with sexual violence, declared that Ford "gave one of the most credible accounts I have ever heard from a victim." Patricia Resick, a professor of psychiatry at Duke University, noted that certain gaps in Ford's account, including her uncertainty as to the exact house address and failure to report the assault at the time, are "typical response[s]" to sexual trauma.[24]

Kavanaugh was unequivocal in his response. "I've never sexually assaulted anyone. Not in high school, not in college, not ever," he told the Senate Judiciary Committee. But his remarks went far beyond rebutting the factual accuracy of the allegations. "This whole two-week effort," he told the judiciary committee, "has been a calculated and orchestrated political hit, fueled with apparent pent-up anger about President Trump and the 2016 election" and "revenge on behalf of the Clintons." But, he warned, "what goes around comes around."[25]

For Kavanaugh, what came around was a seat on the Supreme Court. Ford's testimony did nothing to change the outcome: by a fifty to forty-eight vote that mirrored the Republicans' two-vote advantage in the Senate, Kavanaugh became the 114th justice to serve on the Supreme Court of the United States.[26] The strikingly partisan nature of the final vote echoed the broader reaction among the public: whereas 76 percent of Democrats said they believed Ford, the exact same percentage of Republicans said they believed Kavanaugh. Rather than revealing any deep truths about his qualifications or the societal problem of sexual violence, the entire saga merely confirmed our existing political disagreement.

Of the many casualties caused by Kavanaugh's confirmation process, none was more significant than the hit to the Supreme Court's public image. In a CNN poll conducted shortly after the vote, 73 percent of all Americans—including 78 percent of women—responded that it was a "problem" that two of the Court's nine justices (Kavanaugh and Clarence Thomas) had faced "accusations of sexual harassment or assault during their confirmation process."[27] Another poll showed that the confirmation battle had worsened the growing distrust in the Court's ability to rule independently: the percentage of Americans who believed that Kavanaugh's confirmation would make the Court "more politically motivated" outstripped those who believed the opposite by a four-to-one margin.[28] Yet still the deepening politicization of the Court was not over.

The second time I cried in front of my son was on a hot California afternoon in September 2020, for almost the same reason as the first. My son, then nearly five years old, was happily splashing in an inflatable pool in our backyard when my phone buzzed in my pocket. Another news alert.

Ruth Bader Ginsburg had died.

I burst into tears. My son looked up in surprise, saw me, and without yet knowing why, started bawling, too. Six months into a pandemic that had forever changed our lives, it was Ginsburg's death that finally broke us.

For a flickering moment, as the nation began to mourn Ginsburg's passing and celebrate her legacy, it seemed possible that our nation's elected officials might put the Supreme Court's public image above raw politics. Chief Justice Roberts lamented that "our nation has lost a jurist of historic stature." Republican Senator Rand Paul tweeted about Ginsburg's "legacy of thoughtful public service" and "life of great accomplishment." Even President Trump issued a respectful statement describing the civil rights icon as a "titan of the law" who was "renowned for her brilliant mind."[29]

Then Mitch McConnell spoke. In a statement issued just hours after the news broke of Ginsburg's death, McConnell barely tried to bury the lede. After briefly praising Ginsburg's "intelligence and determination," McConnell quickly pivoted to his main point. "President Trump's nominee will receive a vote on the floor of the United States Senate."[30]

On September 26, just eight days after Ginsburg's death, Trump nominated Judge Amy Coney Barrett, a judge on the Chicago-based Seventh Circuit Court of Appeals, to fill her seat. Political observers and journalists around the country opened their calendars and began to count.

Thirty-eight days.

That's how many remained until the presidential election of 2020. In 2016, after Scalia died, McConnell had declared 237 days too short a period to grant Judge Merrick Garland a hearing. His reasoning had been simple: "We think the important principle in the middle of this presidential year is that the American people need to weigh in and decide who's going to make this decision."[31] Four years later, we were again in the middle of a presidential election year in which the people would soon weigh in on who should fill a Supreme Court vacancy. This time, though, McConnell geared up for one of the fastest confirmations in history.[32] The hypocrisy was breathtaking.

None of this was Barrett's fault, of course. Like Kavanaugh, Gorsuch, and Roberts, Barrett had excelled in law school and clerked at the Supreme Court (in Barrett's case, for Justice Scalia). Like Kavanaugh, she had worked on the team of lawyers who represented George W. Bush in the *Bush v. Gore* election litigation. Barrett then entered the legal academy, earning accolades for her scholarship and teaching at Notre Dame Law School before her appointment to the Seventh Circuit in 2017.

Compared to the Kavanaugh hearings, Barrett's nomination was a yawn. It was clear that she was brilliant, eloquent, and highly qualified. It was also clear that she would steer far away from any definitive statement about the law that might cause her political difficulty—a policy she traced to none other than Ruth Bader Ginsburg. As Ginsburg put it at her own confirmation hearing, in 1993, "A judge sworn to decide impartially can offer no forecasts, no hints, for that would show not only disregard for the specifics of the particular case, it would display disdain for the entire judicial process."[33]

Ginsburg earned a now-unimaginable ninety-six yea votes against just three nos. Barrett's vote was closer. She was confirmed by a margin of fifty-two to forty-eight; only Republican senator Susan Collins voted against her party. Regardless of the final Senate split, however, all sitting justices have equal power in the form of their one among nine votes. With Barrett on the bench, six of those votes now belonged to Republican appointees with conservative judicial philosophies.

For many Republicans, it was a watershed moment. Conservatives had worked for years to fill the Court with jurists dedicated to overturning the right to abortion, outlawing affirmative action, and expanding gun rights. Now they had more than enough votes to do just that. Mitch McConnell thus celebrated Barrett's confirmation as a "huge success for our country."[34]

But independents and Democrats were less sanguine. An ABC News poll showed that 61 percent of independents and 90 percent of Democrats opposed confirming a replacement for Ginsburg before the 2020 election.[35] As numerous commentators argued, the rush to confirm Barrett, coupled with the Republican Senate's overt hypocrisy in denying even a hearing for Merrick Garland, threatened a legitimacy crisis at the Court.[36] *Politico*'s John Harris said of the Court, "We don't even bother pretending it's above politics anymore."[37]

But if the right's political maneuvering precipitated the crisis, many on the left seemed more than willing to accelerate it. Moments after Barrett's confirmation, Representative Alexandria Ocasio-Cortez fired off a three-word tweet: "Expand the Court."[38] The *New York Times*'s Jamelle Bouie wrote a column with a provocative headline: "Down with Judicial Supremacy!"[39] The *Week*'s Ryan Cooper agreed with Bouie in language even more blunt: "The simplest and easiest way to get around potentially tyrannical right-wing justices" is to "just ignore them. . . . The president and Congress do not actually have to obey the Supreme Court."[40]

Viewed against the backdrop of the heroic Supreme Court I'd learned about growing up, the Court's public image had completed a shocking transformation. Distrust of the post-Barrett Court had grown so prominent that influential writers were openly proposing outright defiance of Supreme Court rulings with which they disagreed.

This idea was not terribly original, to be sure. Racist public officials across the state of Arkansas had once tried the same gambit, ignoring the Court's command in *Brown v. Board of Education* to desegregate public schools. Fortunately, President Dwight Eisenhower called in the military to enforce the Court's ruling.

But what would have become of the Supreme Court—and the rule of law—if he hadn't? Suddenly, amid drastically different circumstances, public intellectuals on the left seemed open to finding out.

If any doubt remained over the significance of replacing Justice Ginsburg with Justice Barrett, it was dispelled in the final weeks of June 2022. During that time, the Court issued a startling stretch of decisions that lurched the law far to the right on gun safety, church-state separation, the rights of Native peoples, and climate change. But the most jaw-dropping ruling by far was on abortion.

The Mississippi law at issue in *Dobbs v. Jackson Women's Health Organization* was actually relatively modest, at least in the context of more aggressive red state abortion bans such as Texas's "fetal heartbeat" law, which bans the procedure after six weeks in pregnancy.

Mississippi's statute, by contrast, banned abortions only after fifteen weeks in pregnancy, and it included exceptions for cases of maternal medical emergency and severe fetal abnormality. Indeed, the Court's decision to review Mississippi's somewhat more measured ban was likely no accident; the conservatives ostensibly decided to grant review in *Dobbs* because it offered a more slow-paced vehicle for them to roll back abortion rights. Thus, when the State of Mississippi filed its petition for certiorari seeking the Court's intervention in June 2020, it was purposefully restrained in what it asked for. "[T]he questions presented in this petition," the state made clear, "do not require the Court to overturn *Roe* [*v. Wade*]."[41] Instead, all Mississippi sought was a ruling that it could ban *some* abortions before the fetal viability line announced in *Roe*, at roughly twenty-four weeks in pregnancy.

Four months after Mississippi filed its petition, however, Justice Barrett replaced Justice Ginsburg on the Court. This change meant that the state could be far more aggressive in its arguments because it had a one-vote cushion: even without the more incrementalist chief justice, there were enough votes to overturn *Roe v. Wade* altogether. And so when the time came for Mississippi to file its merits brief in July 2021, the state abandoned its previously restrained posture. There, on the opening pages of its brief, was the argument plain for all to see: "This Court should overrule" *Roe* and *Casey*. Only as a backup argument much later in its brief did Mississippi suggest as an alternative that the Court could uphold the state's fifteen-week ban even if it left in place *Roe*'s basic recognition of a right to abortion.

The real question in *Dobbs,* then, was not whether Mississippi would win the case but rather on which ground. Would the Court take the maximalist path of holding that the Constitution protects no right to reproductive autonomy whatsoever, greenlighting states to ban abortion at any stage in pregnancy? Or would it take the comparatively more restrained path of allowing Mississippi's fifteen-week ban, without eliminating the right to terminate a pregnancy at an earlier point? Even the latter route would be a major departure from settled precedent, to be sure. But many pregnant individuals would not notice the difference: roughly 96 percent of abortions in the United States occur before the sixteen-week mark, and the Mississippi abortion clinic at issue had an internal policy of offering the procedure only through sixteen weeks' gestation.[42]

Anxious onlookers expected an answer at the end of June, as is the Court's custom for deciding each term's most contentious cases. In an unprecedented development, we got a preview of the answer on May 2, when *Politico* published a leaked draft of what would become Justice Alito's majority opinion. Never before had a working opinion draft been leaked for public consumption, and the fallout was severe: the justices complained in public, the Court launched an investigation, and law clerks scrambled to consult lawyers in response. All the while, the Court's public image as a neutral arbiter above the rough and tumble of ordinary politics lost even more of its luster.

When the Court eventually issued its final opinion on June 24, Justice Alito had retained his majority. His opinion decisively rejected the minimalist approach first suggested in Mississippi's petition for certiorari and instead declared that *Roe* and *Casey* were "egregiously wrong" to recognize *any* right to abortion.

I will discuss the extreme certitude with which the majority reached that conclusion in the second part of this book, but for present purposes the key is to see how the ruling in *Dobbs* continued a course of events that deeply undermined public trust in the Court. Thousands of protesters took to the streets in massive demonstrations across the nation, in places as diverse as Washington, D.C., New York, Missouri, North Carolina, Oklahoma, and Michigan.[43] A Pew Research survey found that Americans who disapproved of the decision outnumbered those who approved it by a margin of 57 percent to 41 percent. And commentators on the left reacted by renewing calls to retaliate against the Court itself. *New York Times* columnist Jamelle Bouie, for example, urged Congress to "strip the court" of its power to decide cases. "The Supreme Court," Bouie argued, "is the final word on nothing."[44]

In truth, the Barrett, Kavanaugh, and Garland fiascos—and the Court's decision to overrule *Roe v. Wade*—merely added kindling to a raging fire. The Court's public legitimacy had been falling for years before 2016, for reasons having little to do with any individual nomination controversy or case. McConnell's hypocrisy, the ugly public battle over Kavanaugh's confirmation, and the unprecedented elimination of a decades-old, individual constitutional right were not themselves the sea change. They simply accelerated a longer-running trend. The truth is, the Court was already losing our trust.

One should not read too much into any single public opinion poll. A momentary expression of confidence in the Court or approval of its performance is not necessarily a statement of opinion concerning the Court's *legitimacy*. In theory, a survey could report disapproval of how the Court is handling its job without implying that the public doubts the broader legal and political legitimacy of the Court's decisions. But that is a tight needle to thread. Over a long enough time horizon, survey data revealing levels of confidence in the Court's performance can tell us something about the public's belief in its legitimacy.

Long-term trends in polling data are particularly instructive. With respect to the Supreme Court, Gallup poll data suggest that during a sizable period of recent history, the Court actually enjoyed widespread confidence among the American people. Between 1984 and 1988, for instance, most Americans reported a "great deal" or "quite a lot" of confidence in the Court. Reasonably high levels of trust were common throughout the 1990s and early 2000s (see figure).[45] Since then, however, the Court's public ratings have turned upside down. The num-

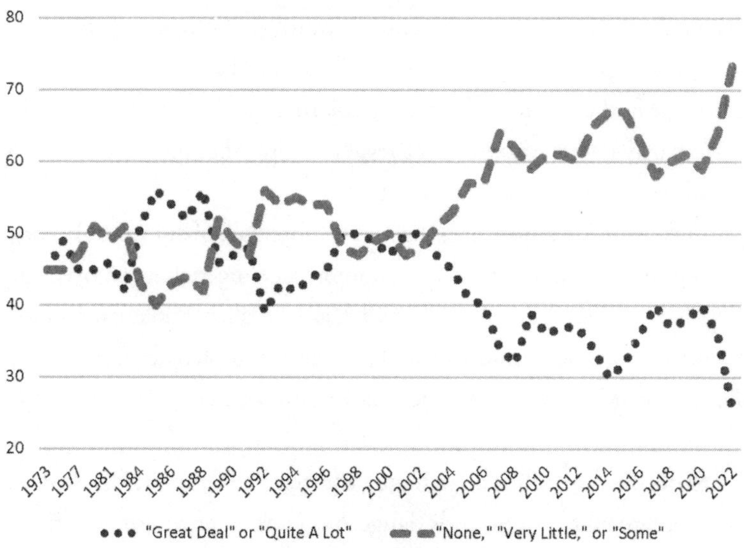

How much confidence do you have in the Supreme Court?
Data from Gallup, "Supreme Court," https://news.gallup.com/poll/4732/supreme-court.aspx.

bers fluctuate from year to year, but the overall trend is that since 2006, the proportion of Americans reporting a "great deal" or "quite a lot" of confidence has never exceeded 40 percent.

Since 2000, Gallup has also asked respondents roughly twice a year whether they "approve or disapprove of the way the Supreme Court is handling its job."[46] Across the eighteen polls conducted between 2000 and 2010, the Court's approval rating averaged 55.1 percent. Its approval even exceeded 60 percent five times, in 2000, 2001, 2002, 2006, and 2009. Intriguingly, the Court's high popularity in 2001 and 2002 suggests that it suffered surprisingly little fallout from its controversial decision in *Bush v. Gore* to halt Florida's recount of votes in the presidential election of 2000.

Yet since 2010, the Court's approval has plummeted. Between 2011 and 2017, it averaged a mere 45.9 percent—and never once reached 50 percent.[47] (The Court's approval skyrocketed, miraculously, to 58 percent in 2020 before falling back to 40 percent in 2021. I'll argue in the second half of this book that the short-lived upturn in 2020 partly reflects support for a legal principle that the Court used to decide several major cases that year.)

Taken together, these data suggest that for much of our recent history, at least until the mid-2000s, the Supreme Court generally enjoyed the public's confidence—but that this faith has since fallen. Public trust for the Court is on a long-term downward trajectory that predates Amy Coney Barrett, Brett Kavanaugh, Merrick Garland, and the end of *Roe v. Wade*.

This decline in public legitimacy matters.[48] Rampant distrust in the Supreme Court portends dangerous consequences for American democracy.

To see why, it's important to first identify the significant positive influence the Court exerts when it is the object of public trust. As Harvard professors Steven Levitsky and Daniel Ziblatt argue in their book *How Democracies Die,* functioning democracies depend on two critical norms, or "guardrails," that stop people from trying to overthrow the entire system whenever they lose a policy debate or election. The first norm is *mutual toleration,* or the acceptance of our political opponents and their victories as worthy of our respect, even when we disagree with them. The second is *forbearance,* the conscious choice to refrain from using one's "institutional prerogatives to the hilt, even if it is technically legal to do so," out of concern that "such action could imperil the existing system."[49]

A trusted Supreme Court plays an essential role in preserving both of these norms. Indeed, it can be thought of as a guardrail to the guardrail norms themselves. With respect to mutual toleration, when the Court is viewed as a faithful referee, its decisions leave losing groups feeling that they've gotten a fair shake. This is crucial, because when losing groups trust that the rules are not tilted against them, they are more likely to respond to their defeats by acting through the usual channels of democratic politics than by assailing the legitimacy of their opponents or fighting to overthrow our democratic system. And with respect to forbearance, when individual justices vote for outcomes that run against their own political preferences, the Court serves as a valuable institutional role model for putting the common good above narrow partisan advantage.

But when the Supreme Court is viewed with distrust, its ability to protect these essential democratic norms breaks down. Rather than acknowledging the legitimacy of their defeats and working within the democratic process, groups that lose before a Supreme Court they believe is rigged are more likely to make war against the system itself.

The prospect that this may happen in the United States is no longer a hypothetical. Incited by a president who routinely attacked the integrity of his political opponents and the judiciary, a mob of insurrectionists violently stormed the U.S. Capitol building on January 6, 2021, refusing to accept the legitimacy of Donald Trump's defeat. Yet just four weeks before this stunning antidemocratic turn, on December 11, 2020, the Supreme Court had issued a unanimous one-page order rejecting a last-ditch legal effort to overturn the results of the election.[50] Technically, the Court did so on the ground that the challengers—Texas and other red states that had voted for Trump—lacked standing, or a judicially cognizable interest, to challenge "the manner in which another State conducts its elections."[51] But it could not have escaped the Court's notice that every single claim of election fraud that the Trump campaign alleged across dozens of lawsuits in eight battleground states had been decisively rejected for lack of credible evidence.[52] In theory, these decisions—and the Supreme Court's ultimate refusal to intervene—should have closed the curtains on ill-founded claims that the election was "stolen." But two days after the Court's ruling, a staggering 82 percent of all Trump voters continued to believe that President Joe Biden's victory was illegitimate.[53]

Why didn't Trump's supporters accept his defeat? Some of the answer owes to the uniquely destabilizing effects of a presidential election loser who refused to acknowledge reality and peddled unsupported conspiracy theories instead of fact. But demagogues who try to bring down democracies invariably evince a reckless disregard for the truth. What is just as remarkable is that so many Trump voters placed more faith in a demagogue's lies than in the Supreme Court's unanimous refusal to overturn the election. Even with three of the demagogue's own appointees voting against him, the Court could not persuade Trump's supporters to respond to defeat in the usual way: by peacefully supporting their candidate in the next election.

Perhaps we should have seen this coming. For years, losing groups on both sides of the political spectrum have railed against adverse Supreme Court decisions in ways that sap the foundational trust the Court depends on in dire moments. In 2015, for example, a Republican former governor of Arkansas, Mike Huckabee, declared in response to the Court's same-sex marriage ruling in *Obergefell v. Hodges* that he would "not acquiesce to an imperial court any more than our Founders acquiesced to an imperial British monarch. We must resist and reject judicial tyranny."[54] President Trump sounded a similar alarm after the Supreme Court rejected his attempt to revoke DACA, an Obama era policy protecting law-abiding undocumented immigrants who arrived in the United States as young children. "These horrible & politically charged decisions coming out of the Supreme Court," Trump wrote on Twitter, "are shotgun blasts into the face of people that are proud to call themselves Republicans."[55] Such reactions are not limited to the right. Speaking from the steps of the Supreme Court building in 2020, Democratic New York senator Chuck

Schumer threatened two justices by name over their likely votes in a pre-*Dobbs* abortion case: "I want to tell you, Gorsuch. I want to tell you, Kavanaugh. You have released the whirlwind and you will pay the price. You won't know what hit you if you go forward with these awful decisions."[56]

Responses like these send a clear message to the American people. When the Supreme Court issues a major decision you don't like, don't abide graciously by the ruling or register your disapproval at the ballot box. Instead, accuse the Court and its justices of raw partisanship and even tyranny—the kind that must be overthrown like an "imperial British monarch."

No wonder the Supreme Court's refusal to overturn the election of 2020 had so little effect on the violent mob on January 6, 2021. The mob was simply acting on the hostile rhetoric our leaders have deployed against our institutions of government, including the Court itself.

Violent insurrection isn't the only way for a democracy to collapse. A more common way is democratic backsliding, where authoritarian leaders are elected and then start to erode democratic institutions—including judicial oversight and free elections—from the inside. On this path, too, the loss of public trust in the judiciary is an ominous sign. And it frequently results from efforts by the party in power to pack the courts with loyal justices who will support the party's political aims.

From an American constitutional perspective, there is nothing unlawful about this. Article III of the Constitution says there must be a Supreme Court, but it is silent as to the requisite number of justices. Congress is free to change the Court's size—and it has done so seven times. Three of those occasions were for largely apolitical reasons, to add an additional justice to oversee the growing number of Circuit

Courts of Appeals as the nation added states in the early nineteenth century. The other four were overtly partisan. The first two took place in the early days of the Republic and canceled each other out so quickly that the Court's size never actually changed.[57] (Though the episode still carries meaningful lessons that I'll discuss in the next chapter.) The third and fourth took place in the unusual circumstances that followed the assassination of President Abraham Lincoln.[58]

Because of the unique circumstances surrounding the election of 1864—held in the midst of the Civil War—Lincoln, a Republican, had selected a Democrat from Tennessee, Andrew Johnson, to be his running mate on a "unity ticket." After Lincoln's death, congressional Republicans grew worried that the new southern president would appoint justices who would undermine their national priorities, in particular Reconstruction efforts in the South. So they reduced the number of seats on the Court from ten to seven.[59] When Republican candidate Ulysses S. Grant won the presidency in 1868, Congress restored two of those seats, essentially transferring two vacancies from Johnson to Grant and bringing the number of justices to nine, where it has remained ever since.

What is most notable is that the Democrats voiced no opposition to the Republicans' addition of two seats during the Grant administration. As Professor Joshua Braver explains, the reason is simple: the Democrats, like the Republicans, "had deserted Johnson" politically.[60] Neither party wanted him to fill the vacancies that would eventually fall to Grant, so no one objected when Grant got to fill them. American history thus provides little cautionary precedent on the dangers of partisan court-packing.

There are, however, plenty of instructive examples from other countries. Consider Venezuela. In 1958, the nation began a forty-year period of largely stable democratic governance characterized by credible elections.[61] The economy, however, fluctuated wildly with swings in global oil prices, and government corruption grew increasingly problematic. Promising to alleviate poverty and crack down on corruption, a former military officer named Hugo Chavez rose to prominence and, after a pair of failed coup attempts, won the presidency in 1998. Venezuela's democracy has eroded ever since, both under Chavez and his hand-picked successor, Nicolas Maduro, culminating in 2018 in a presidential election in which opposition parties were forbidden to participate. Today, both Maduro and opposition leader Juan Guaido claim to be president.[62] Court-packing was a critical step in reaching this outcome: to prevent adverse rulings by the Venezuelan Supreme Court, Chavez expanded the court from twenty to thirty-two members in 2004. For the next nine years, "not a single Supreme Tribunal ruling went against the government."[63]

Other regimes have followed a similar playbook. In 2010, Turkey's prime minister (and future president) Recep Tayyip Erdoğan championed a successful effort to increase the size of Turkey's constitutional court from eleven members to seventeen. Freedom House, a nonprofit think tank, recently rated Turkey "not free" on its Freedom in the World scorecard. Hungarian president Viktor Orbán reduced judicial oversight over his rule, including over election administration, by expanding the nation's highest court from eleven to fifteen members in 2011.[64] When Orbán's party won large majorities in 2018, independent election monitors noted that "the party had used the resources of the state on a very large scale to bolster its chances of winning."[65]

What these examples have in common is an effort by the party in power to use court-packing to capture the referees in future legal disputes. None of the authoritarian leaders openly admitted that this was their motivation, of course. As Levitsky and Ziblatt point out, they used coded phrases, saying that they wanted to "clean up elections" or "improve the quality of democracy."[66] But once stocked with loyal judges, the newly constituted courts approved restrictions on political freedoms and opposition leaders, undermining the prospect of free and fair elections.

To be sure, progressives who support expanding the Court today do not see their proposals as a step toward authoritarian rule. In their view, more liberal justices are needed for the opposite reason: to protect our democracy, including from conservative attacks on voting rights.

Yet even if this claim is true, the danger lies farther ahead. Suppose another candidate with authoritarian tendencies is elected in the future and obtains a congressional majority. It is not hard to imagine that president using the Democrats' expansion of the Court as a precedent for adding a new wave of loyal justices. And if that were to happen, would democracy in America really look different from that of Venezuela, Turkey, or Hungary?

The public's growing distrust of the Court matters in our hotly partisan moment. The United States may not be able to withstand much more erosion of our foundational democratic institutions. The public already possesses staggeringly low levels of trust in other national institutions. Seventy-five percent of Americans disapprove of Congress.[67] Sixty percent have "not very much" trust or "none at all" in the mass media.[68] And since 2004, the sitting president has almost always held an approval rating below 50 percent, with the exception of a honeymoon period at the start of the Biden administration and three short periods under President Obama.

We cannot afford for the Supreme Court to suffer the same fate. If it does, it is unclear what norms—or institutions—will remain to convince the American people that our democracy is worth maintaining. The United States lucked out in 2020–21, when a handful of Republican election officials refused to buckle to immense pressure to alter their state election results. We may not be so lucky the next time.

2
The Partisanship Trap

If the core problem with today's Supreme Court is that it has lost the public's trust, then the solution seems straightforward: fix the root cause behind the public's declining confidence. Once we fix the root problem, after all, the Court should regain the public's faith and reclaim its role as a guardian of our democracy.

The logic is seductively simple. Yet the hard part is correctly identifying the root cause. Like a doctor who treats a dangerously ill patient, misdiagnosing the underlying problem might lead us to a course of treatment worse than the disease.

The most common diagnosis for the Supreme Court's public trust problem is political partisanship. We often hear complaints that the justices are little more than "politicians in robes."[1] As the *New York Times* put it in 2018, even before the bruising battle over Brett Kavanaugh's confirmation, "one reality is increasingly clear about the Supreme Court—it has become another polarized institution in the polarized capital of a polarized nation."[2]

At the heart of the partisanship diagnosis is the following charge. The best way to predict how today's Court is likely to come out on a high profile case is not to familiarize oneself with the legal arguments on both sides and assess their relative strength. Instead, the best predictor is simply to ask which outcome would be preferable to the political party that appointed a majority of the Court's justices. Neal

Devins, a leading scholar of politics and the Supreme Court, describes the problem this way: "It is clearly the most partisan court ever, where you can actually look at Republican and Democrat and use that as a proxy for voting and behavior on the Court."[3] Social science research supports this view: the justices' behavior is highly correlated with political ideology.[4]

The Court's partisanship is not only an esoteric concern among academics and the media. The people share it, too. A recent survey showed that 62 percent of Americans believe that Supreme Court justices are "too influenced by politics," compared to just 32 percent who don't.[5] This belief is markedly stable across nearly all demographic groups: sizable majorities of men, women, Democrats, independents, college-educated, and non-college-educated respondents all agree that the Court is too political. Even a significant number of *Republicans* (42 percent) share this view—a surprising finding given that politics delivered them a supermajority on the Court. So partisanship is clearly an important *part* of the Supreme Court's public trust problem.

On its own, however, partisanship is an incomplete explanation. How do we know? Because the Supreme Court and its individual justices have always been partisan throughout American history. Yet despite this partisanship, the Court has also frequently enjoyed periods of widespread public confidence. This chapter focuses on two such periods: the Court under the leadership of Chief Justice John Marshall, and the New Deal Supreme Court that existed after 1937. Taken together, these periods suggest that if partisanship by itself were enough to torpedo public trust, the Court we've come to know would have never gotten off the ground.

Picture this. It is presidential election season, and the United States is about to hold the most important election in recent history. At stake are two starkly different visions for the nation's future.

The incumbent is "hot-tempered" and "suspected of wanting to be king."[6] He is so agitated by his political opponents (and so thin-skinned) that he supports a law that would allow him to throw them in jail.

The challenger is a highly esteemed vice president, a prominent national figure, and a man who rose to success despite great personal heartbreak, including the tragically premature death of his beloved wife.[7]

The contest is filled with "mudslinging, backstabbing, and chicanery."[8] Religion plays a paramount role, as people of faith around the nation side with the incumbent. In the end, however, the vice president wins. He sweeps the national popular vote, though the outcome in the Electoral College is much closer. So close, in fact, that the vice president's victory depends in part on a decision to count disputed electoral votes from Georgia.[9]

On his first day in office, the now-former vice president calls for national unity, preaching in his inaugural address that "every difference of opinion is not a difference of principle."[10] He says this even though the ousted incumbent made a bald-faced effort to squeeze out a lasting partisan advantage in the final days of his presidency—including through a controversial Supreme Court appointment and a hotly criticized last-minute plan to stock the federal courts with loyal judges.

The year this happened was not 2020 but 1800. The incumbent was Federalist John Adams; his challenger, the vice president, was Democratic-Republican Thomas Jefferson. And a peaceful transition of power happened even though there were moments of real doubt—worries, in the words of historian Edward Larson, that the election of 1800 "might be the . . . republic's last."[11]

For present purposes, though, our focal point is John Adams's last-ditch effort to install partisan loyalists throughout the federal courts. Those efforts reveal how the judiciary—and especially the Supreme Court—has never really been above politics. From our nation's earliest moments, presidents have always appointed judges with the hope that they will advance the political aims of the president's party. And from the beginning, those judges have delivered.

Start with Adams's plan to pack the lower courts. As soon as the election returns were in, showing that the Federalists had lost control of the White House and both houses of Congress, party operatives schemed ways to retain some measure of control over the federal government. Their solution was to overtake the third branch, the only option remaining in light of their sweeping electoral defeat. On February 13, 1801, with just nineteen days left in his presidency, Adams signed the Judiciary Act of 1801.

Because of what it did, the law was soon nicknamed the Midnight Judges Act. It established six new circuit courts across the country and created sixteen judgeships to staff those courts. Adams scrambled to fill the new posts in a way that left little doubt as to the overriding qualification: a reliable commitment to Adams's particular brand of federalism. One nominee to the Sixth Circuit, William McClung, was nominated after Federalist senator Humphrey Marshall sent Adams a letter describing McClung as a "friend to the Government."[12] (It did not hurt that McClung was also the brother-in-law of John Marshall, Adams's secretary of state and the future chief justice.) Surveying the appointees "as a whole," historian Kathryn Turner noted that "the group of midnight judges reflected the . . . political positions of the men who had appointed them."[13]

Filling the circuit courts with partisans was just one part of the strategy. The greater prize was the Supreme Court. Here the Federalists made two fateful eleventh-hour gambits. One was to include in the Midnight Judges Act a provision declaring that "after the next vacancy that shall happen in the [Supreme Court], it shall consist of five justices only" rather than the six who had served on the Court since 1789.[14] By depriving Jefferson of the power to fill the next vacancy that would arise at the Court, the Federalists launched the first attempt in our nation's history to manipulate the size of the Supreme Court for partisan advantage. (The attempt failed when Democratic-Republicans in Congress repealed the Midnight Judges Act before any vacancy arose, keeping the size of the Court at six.)

Adams's second and by far more consequential gambit was to appoint a new chief justice of the Supreme Court. The one he'd inherited upon succeeding George Washington in 1797 was Oliver Ellsworth, a prominent Federalist leader who had played a significant role at the Constitutional Convention. Ellsworth was a former senator from Connecticut and a highly regarded lawyer. Remarkably, he had spent much of the later portion of his tenure as chief justice in France, helping the Adams administration negotiate trade policies with Napoleon. In December 1800, however—after his loss to Jefferson—Adams received a letter from Ellsworth announcing his resignation from the Court on account of poor health.[15]

If Adams had any hesitancy about appointing a Supreme Court justice in the waning days of his presidency, he did not show it. On January 20, 1801, he nominated his close friend, Secretary of State John Marshall, to the chief justiceship.[16] And if the United States Senate had in mind anything like the "no election year appointment" rule Mitch McConnell would cite 215 years later to deny a hearing to Merrick Garland, the Senate did not show it either: it confirmed Marshall on January 27, just five weeks before Jefferson was to take office. (In a further sign of the partisan nature of the appointment, Marshall served out the rest of Adams's term as secretary of state even after taking up his post as chief justice.)[17]

Jefferson was furious. Looking out at the new Federalist appointees on the nation's courts, he fumed that "the Federalists have retired into the judiciary as a stronghold . . . and from that battery all the works of republicanism are to be beaten down and erased."[18] Years later, he wrote to Abigail Adams that the "one act of Mr. Adams's life, and one only" that "ever gave me a moment's personal displeasure" was his "last appointment" of Jefferson's "most ardent political enemies"—meaning Marshall and the other Federalist judges.[19]

Jefferson had good cause for complaint. It was well known that Marshall would use every tool at his disposal as chief justice to oppose Jefferson and that this partisan objective was the overriding purpose of his selection. As historian R. Kent Newmyer observed in his biography of Marshall, "It was assumed by Adams when he appointed Marshall chief justice, and by Marshall when he accepted office, that the Supreme Court would play a significant role in checking the . . . victorious Democratic-Republican party."[20] Newmyer also described "Marshall's record of personal loyalty" to Adams and "the ideological compatibility between the two men" as major factors behind Marshall's appointment, noting that both men saw Jefferson's election as a "revolution" that "had to be stopped."[21] And "both men looked to the Supreme Court to get the job done."[22]

That is exactly what Marshall's Supreme Court proceeded to do. Across a range of high-profile legal disputes, Marshall consistently issued rulings favoring Federalist policy preferences. Does Congress have broad authority to enact federal legislation that may burden the states (as favored by Federalists), or is its authority much narrower (as Democratic-Republicans believed)? Marshall's answer: broad authority.[23] Who has the final say in disputes over the meaning of the Constitution and federal laws: the U.S. Supreme Court (Federalists) or state supreme courts (Democratic-Republicans)? The answer: the U.S. Supreme Court.[24] And of course, in *Marbury v. Madison,* the canonical decision that made all of the Marshall Court's pro-Federalist rulings possible, the Court unanimously upheld its own power of judicial review—the power to decide the meaning of the Constitution and federal law.

Thus, by the time Marshall became chief justice, barely a decade after the Constitution's ratification, the Supreme Court was already a hyperpartisan institution. Yet the evidence suggests that during Marshall's tenure, the Court was frequently quite popular. This conclusion admittedly involves some speculation. There are obviously no polls from the era, and any claim concerning the Court's popularity must acknowledge moments when the Court's public image was far from unassailable.[25] Yet the strongest case is as straightforward as this: it is difficult to imagine an unpopular institution achieving the surge in national prominence and power that the Supreme Court experienced between 1801 and 1835.

Begin with the state of the Court when Marshall was appointed. Harvard legal historian Michael Klarman argues that the Court of 1801 was "weak and its immediate prospects were bleak."[26] This very weakness, in fact, had led New York governor John Jay, Adams's first choice for chief justice before Marshall, to turn down the nomination. As Jay put it in a letter to Adams in January 1801, the Supreme Court was "so defective" that it would never "acquire the public confidence and respect which, as the last resort of the justice of the nation, it should possess."[27]

Yet over the next thirty years, the Supreme Court acquired precisely that degree of public confidence. (How it did so is an important question to which I'll return in the next chapter.) Writing in 1830, Alexis de Tocqueville made the remarkable suggestion that "the peace, the prosperity, and the very existence of the Union are vested in" the United States Supreme Court.[28] Nearly a century later, Princeton professor Edward Corwin argued that by the end of Marshall's tenure, the Court had become "one of the great political forces of the country," a point with which Michael Klarman has agreed.[29] By "early

1833," Klarman points out, "Congress had bestowed upon the federal judiciary its first significant jurisdictional expansion in years, and both Congress and the President were celebrating the Supreme Court as the ultimate arbiter of the Constitution's meaning."[30]

That Congress and the president would support the Court so fully is all the more remarkable given that Democratic president Andrew Jackson and the Democrat-controlled House of Representatives were staunch supporters of limited national government. As Klarman explains, Jackson had "repudiated Marshall['s] notions of national power" across a number of major cases.[31] What's more, the Federalists who appointed and confirmed Marshall never regained political control: Democratic-Republicans won the next *seven* presidential elections. The Court's ability to increase its national stature so dramatically in the face of these headwinds is evidence that it had managed to gain widespread public support despite its partisan, pro-Federalist leanings.

A more recent episode in American history further illustrates how partisanship and public trust can coexist in the Supreme Court.

In 1932, in the midst of a depression that would leave roughly one in four Americans jobless and millions of children malnourished, New York governor Franklin Delano Roosevelt swept into the White House on the promise of a "new deal for the American people."[32] Although six of the previous seven presidents had been Republicans, FDR, a Democrat, defeated incumbent Herbert Hoover by a national popular vote margin of more than 17 percent, capturing 472 of the then 531 total electoral votes. Democrats also seized control of the House and Senate. An even greater blowout followed in 1936, when FDR won reelection by more than 24 points, carrying every state but Maine and Vermont. Democrats also earned supermajorities in both houses of Congress. Everything, it seemed, was on FDR's side.

Everything, that is, except the Supreme Court. For decades before Roosevelt's election, the Court had executed a probusiness, antiregulatory agenda characterized by stiff opposition to state and federal economic regulation—precisely the kind of regulation Roosevelt promised as part of the New Deal. No single ruling has come to symbolize this economically conservative agenda more than the Court's decision in *Lochner v. New York* in 1905. (That entire era of the Court's history, in fact, is known to legal scholars as the *Lochner* era.)

Joseph Lochner was a Bavarian immigrant who owned and operated a bakery. When evidence emerged that one of his employees had worked more than sixty hours in a week, Lochner was prosecuted for violating a New York law regulating the maximum hours a bakery employee could work. He was fined $25, or roughly $800 in present-day dollars. Lochner appealed his conviction, arguing that New York's maximum hours limit violated the Constitution, and the Supreme Court agreed. New York's law, the Court wrote, interfered unreasonably with Lochner's "liberty of . . . free contract, by determining the hours of labor, in the occupation of a baker." The Court thus concluded that the law violated the Fourteenth Amendment's guarantee that no state shall deprive a person of liberty without "due process of law."[33]

Lochner itself struck down only a low-stakes regulation of a narrow sector of one state's labor market.[34] But the legal and economic principles that *Lochner* exemplified led the Court to issue far more consequential rulings, including the invalidation of minimum wage laws, bans on child labor, and legislation in aid of organized labor.[35] By 1932, the Court's frequent interference with economic regulations had made it a common target of criticism—including from FDR himself. Speaking on the campaign trail shortly before election day, FDR posed a rhetorical question: "Let's see who is responsible for [the] failure" of the national economy, he mused. "The Republican

Party" has been "in complete control of all branches of the federal government," including "for good measure [and] to make it complete, the Supreme Court."[36]

For a short time after FDR's victory, the Court seemed willing to bow to public opinion and backtrack from *Lochner*. In 1934, for example, it issued two decisions favorable to Democrat-supported economic regulations, one involving a Minnesota moratorium on mortgage foreclosures and a second concerning a New York milk price-fixing law.[37] But then it issued a string of high-profile rulings against the Roosevelt administration in 1935 and 1936, invalidating prominent New Deal programs such as the National Industrial Recovery Act and the Agricultural Adjustment Act.[38]

Much has been written about Roosevelt's response, in particular his failed effort to appoint six additional Supreme Court justices who would vote to uphold the New Deal.[39] I'll return to this court-packing saga in chapter 9, as it reveals some lessons for today's Court. For now, what is most fascinating is how FDR eventually secured his dominance over the Court: not by increasing its size but by filling vacancies in the usual course with politically loyal justices who were committed to upholding his New Deal programs.

Consider his decision to appoint Felix Frankfurter to the Court in 1938. An eminent Harvard law professor who had mounted the leading academic defense of the New Deal's constitutionality, Frankfurter was a longtime friend and political adviser to Roosevelt. As Professor Noah Feldman has written, Frankfurter was "thoroughly committed" to FDR.[40] The commitment was reciprocal. Early in 1937, the president had promised to nominate Frankfurter to the Court in exchange for his tacit support for the court-packing proposal. Frankfurter delivered on his end of the bargain, sending the president "lengthy and detailed notes" about the plan.[41] FDR followed through as well, eventually nominating Frankfurter to fill the seat of the late Benjamin Cardozo. In a telling sign of the expectations Roosevelt held for Frankfurter's service on the bench, FDR famously remarked that "Felix is the only man who could" sway the Court with respect to the constitutionality of the New Deal.[42]

Another of FDR's appointees, Robert Jackson, reflected similarly partisan calculations. Even more than Frankfurter, whose support for FDR's court-packing initiative had been behind the scenes, Jackson was a leading salesman for the proposal. While an assistant attorney general in Roosevelt's Department of Justice, Jackson had testified in favor of the plan before the Senate Judiciary Committee.[43] He would later write a four-hundred-page book defending the court-packing effort as a success—all while being promoted up the ranks of the Justice Department. By 1941, when FDR made Jackson his seventh appointment to the Supreme Court, it was clear not only that Jackson "shared [Roosevelt's] beliefs and views," but that, in Feldman's words, he was "the lawyer closest to Roosevelt."[44] When FDR boasted to a private gathering on the day Jackson was sworn in that "it may not be proper to announce it, but today the Supreme Court is full," he hardly needed to finish the thought.[45] Full of what? Loyal jurists who would uphold his signature programs.

As Professor Barry Friedman has argued, FDR's appointments were "plainly 'political'" because they were made with the express aim of changing the meaning of the Constitution "dramatically on the question of government control over the economy."[46] And his appointees delivered on this objective, repudiating *Lochner* and refusing to strike down a single federal or state economic regulation. The Court's new political orientation was evident to the American public. A poll from 1946 found more Americans who agreed than disagreed with the statement that "the Supreme Court decides many questions largely on the basis of politics."[47] Under one common measure of judicial ideology, the years 1941 to 1944 were one of the most partisan periods in the Court's history—a time of partisanship rivaled only by today's Court.[48]

And yet despite its overtly partisan nature, the weight of evidence suggests that the Court was quite popular. Because opinion polls at the time did not ask directly about the public's level of confidence in the Court, the case is necessarily circumstantial. Yet the existing polls imply that it generally enjoyed a favorable public image. In 1941, for example, Gallup asked whether the Court was "too liberal, about right, or not liberal enough." Only 21 percent of respondents, *combined,* answered "too liberal" (18 percent) or "not liberal enough" (3 percent)—a remarkably low level of disagreement.[49] For comparison, when Gallup asked the same question in 2021, a combined 57 percent of respondents answered that the Court had gone too far in one direction or the other, with 20 percent feeling the Court was too liberal and 37 percent saying it was too conservative. This level of discontent is now the norm; since Gallup began asking the question regularly, in 1991, more than 50 percent of survey respondents have answered "too liberal" or "too conservative" in every year but one.[50] That so few Americans felt that way in 1941 suggests the Court enjoyed a healthy degree of public trust.

A second source of evidence is the public's reaction to FDR's court-packing plan. Roosevelt's popularity was perhaps never greater than in 1937, fresh off an election in which he received more than 60 percent of the popular vote. (His opponent, Kansas governor Alf Landon, secured a grand total of 8 electoral votes.) Yet despite his popularity and considerable personal investment, his proposal to add justices to the Court—announced with much fanfare in February 1937—was famously defeated in Congress.

This outcome alone could be taken to imply some meaningful degree of public support for the Court as it existed. But an analysis by political scientist Gregory Caldeira provides a more nuanced explanation. For a four-week period in March 1937, shortly after Roosevelt announced his court-packing plan, a plurality of Americans actually supported it.[51] By June, however, public opinion had flipped decisively, with opponents of the plan outnumbering supporters by a 50 percent to 37 percent margin. The proposal never recovered its momentum.

What accounts for the dramatic turnaround in public support for the Supreme Court? Two words: partisan politics. Caldeira identifies two political developments that turned the tide in the court-packing debate. First, in April 1937 the Supreme Court surprised onlookers by voting in *NLRB v. Jones & Laughlin Steel* to uphold the National Labor Relations Act, a key statute guaranteeing workers the right to organize in unions and bargain collectively. Commentators have famously described Justice Owen Roberts's decision to bow to public pressure and support the law, after having voted the other way in a similar case the year before, as "the switch in time that saved nine."[52] Caldeira's findings suggest that this characterization has some truth to it: *Jones & Laughlin Steel* was by itself responsible for a 4 percentage-point dip in public support for court-packing.[53] The flipside of the public's reduced demand for court-packing, of course, was an increase in satisfaction with the Court itself. The *Nation* reflected this newfound support when it called the Court's decision in *Jones & Laughlin Steel* "nothing short of a miracle."[54]

The second event was in May 1937, when one of the "four horsemen" of the Supreme Court—archconservative William Van Devanter—announced his retirement. Roosevelt eventually replaced him with Hugo Black, who in addition to voting reliably to uphold New Deal programs would go on to become one of the Court's great liberal lions. According to Caldeira, Van Devanter's departure reduced public support for court-packing by another 5 percentage points.

These two distinctly political developments—Justice Owen Roberts's about-face and Van Devanter's retirement—were thus substantially responsible for the Court's recapturing of public support. After another major decision in 1937 upheld broad government power over the economy, the *St. Louis Post Dispatch* observed that "every day, sentiment supporting the Supreme Court is growing."[55] Indeed, it grew to the point that the Court was able to frustrate a popular president's determination to change its composition. Far from undermining the Court's popularity, bowing to political pressure helped save it.

The Court's apparent popularity during the Marshall and New Deal eras suggests an imperfect relationship between partisanship and public legitimacy. In both periods, presidents nominated justices with the clear expectation that they would cast politically favorable votes on pressing and divisive political issues—and the justices delivered. This is precisely the kind of partisan behavior many complain about from today's Supreme Court. Yet in both periods, the Court's partisanship did not cause it to lose public confidence. Judicial partisanship alone did not lead to rampant public distrust.

The strongest counterargument is that the Court's partisanship and public support coexisted during these periods only because the Court was partisan in the same direction as the public writ large. The New Deal period is the best evidence for this view. After all, it is certainly reasonable to think the partisan New Deal Court gained in popularity because the public was in favor of the very programs the Court had taken to defending. As Professor Barry Friedman has argued, "the public seemed to have demanded" a pro–New Deal attitude from the Court "and to have accepted it happily when it came."[56]

At some level, this argument is undoubtedly correct. Of course the side that is winning at the Supreme Court will approve of the

Court's work. And if that winning side is a large enough slice of the population, the Court will score well in public opinion polls.

But as I argued in chapter 1, the fundamental question about the Court's public legitimacy is whether it enjoys enough support to serve as a guardrail for vital democratic norms such as mutual toleration and forbearance. Answering that question requires us to focus not on what the winners think about the Court but what the *losers* think. After all, winners of monumental cases have no reason to assail the existing system when it is working to their advantage. It's the losers in these big cases who must have sufficient faith in the Court to continue playing by the rules.

This is where evidence emerges that the New Deal Court was doing something to preserve public confidence beyond simply handing one political victory after another to a popular Democratic Party. Had that been all the Court was up to, one would have expected to see considerable public backlash from Republicans who, after all, still maintained a sizable vote share. For example, Republican presidential candidate Wendell Willkie received 44.8 percent of the national popular vote in the election of 1940. Yet in 1941, at the height of the Supreme Court's deference to the New Deal, a scant 18 percent of Americans believed that the Court was too liberal.[57] The upshot is that even as they were losing in case after case at the Supreme Court, a significant number of anti–New Deal Republicans did not complain about the Court's ideological direction. I'll explain in the next chapter just how the Court managed this feat by embracing a particularly humble form of legal reasoning that earned the confidence of Democrats and Republicans alike.

There are additional reasons to doubt the claim that a partisan Court can earn the public's confidence only when its political leanings are overwhelmingly popular. For one thing, public support for the New Deal was less sweeping than is often assumed. In 1937, for instance, Gallup found that 54 percent of Americans believed that the government should repeat the New Deal's spending policies in the event of another depression.[58] That's a majority, but hardly overwhelming. Another poll suggested even less support for the New Deal, finding that six in ten Americans believed that the Roosevelt administration's spending on economic recovery efforts was "too great."[59] To the extent that the New Deal Court was riding a wave of public support for expansive economic recovery programs, this wave might not have carried it far.

The claim is also difficult to square with the lessons from the Marshall Court, which was partisan in the way Adams and his fellow Federalists had hoped: in the direction of expansive federal power. Yet this political leaning hardly claimed overwhelming public support. True, there were certain periods of nationalist pride, such as after America's victory in the War of 1812.[60] Yet as Professor Friedman has argued, the Marshall Court's "nationalistic course" also drew the "enmity of those whose loyalties leaned more to state than Union."[61] Nor was that enmity some trivial minority position. For the first twenty-eight years after Marshall's appointment by a Federalist president, Jefferson's Democratic-Republican Party occupied the White House.[62]

The key takeaway is that today's troubling levels of public distrust in the Supreme Court must have some additional explanation beyond raw partisanship. If partisanship alone were enough to erode the public's confidence in the Court, it would have never earned its prominent position in our national life.

This is not merely an academic exercise. Just as with a medical patient who shows dire symptoms, we care about the right diagnosis not out of some abstract interest in setting the record straight but because we want to find an effective treatment. Settling on the wrong explanation for the Court's legitimacy crisis can lead us astray in our search for solutions. And as recent debates over reforming the Supreme Court show, going astray has real costs. Blaming the Court's predicament on partisanship alone isn't just inaccurate; it's a trap—and a perilous one at that.

Before explaining why, it's important to acknowledge that many on the political left are understandably angry about the blatantly political process by which Republicans secured their current supermajority on the Court. From Senate Majority Leader Mitch McConnell's refusal to grant a hearing to Judge Merrick Garland to the controversy surrounding Justice Kavanaugh and to the hypocritical rush to confirm Justice Barrett, it is easy to see why progressives might think excessive political gamesmanship is the Court's fundamental problem. It is no wonder that so many progressives have rallied around the idea of bringing balance to the Court, whether by adding justices, imposing term limits, or even ignoring it entirely.

The problem is that these proposals to curtail partisanship at the Court will be perceived very differently by Republicans: not as partisan deescalation but as its opposite. And this assessment would be plainly accurate for some proposals, such as a pending bill in Congress that would grant President Biden the opportunity to appoint four additional justices, giving Democratic appointees a seven-to-six majority. After all, even if Senate Republicans had rejected Kavanaugh in favor of a different Trump appointee, and even if they had treated Judge Merrick Garland and then-Judge Amy Coney Barrett consistently (either confirming both or confirming neither), today's Court would still comprise a five-to-four Republican majority. So it is understandable that Republicans might label any effort to upset that majority a partisan power grab—and that they might retaliate in kind.

It is also unclear why Republicans should perceive other, seemingly less aggressive proposals, such as imposing eighteen-year term limits on the justices or requiring a supermajority of justices to strike down congressional laws, as good-faith efforts to find a stable equilibrium. At first glance, term limits seem particularly worthy of consideration, as they satisfy a basic test of neutrality: both Republican and Democratic appointees would be required to retire after eighteen years of service. Yet the devil is in the details. The most crucial detail is whether term limits would apply only to future appointees or to the current justices as well. If the former, it could take more than fifty years before term limits would alter the Court's partisan balance.[63] That's certainly better than nothing, but it doesn't address the Court's conservative lean today.

Some have accordingly suggested immediately adding new, term-limited justices at the rate of one every two years, while grandfathering in the Court's current members to serve out the remainder of their life terms.[64] That approach would give the Court as many as thirteen members within two presidential election cycles, as new justices are added while the existing ones remain. Republicans would quickly conjure a particular phrase to describe that result, though, and it isn't "term limits." It's a thinly veiled effort to pack the Court.

Recognizing this critique, some have proposed to keep the Court at nine by applying term limits to the *current* justices, too. Yet those proposals fare no better. Under such a law, the longest-serving justice (Clarence Thomas) would be required to retire first, followed in two years by the next most senior justice, and so on. Under that approach, Democrats could flip the Court within just four years (assuming that they win the White House again in 2024) because the first two retirements would be Republican appointees Clarence Thomas and John Roberts. Yet it is that very consequence that makes any such proposal so offensive to Republicans. Why should they view a rapid Democratic takeover of the Court as anything other than a partisan effort to steal their majority?

There is, however, a deeper problem to which progressive court reform proposals may be responding: the severely antidemocratic way in which the Constitution allocates Senate seats and electoral votes. On this view, the problem is less that Senate Republicans were hypocritical in confirming Justice Barrett so quickly in 2020 and more that the Senate and White House were even in Republican hands. Donald Trump was elected president in 2016 despite receiving nearly three million fewer votes than Hillary Clinton. The senators who voted to confirm Brett Kavanaugh represented a staggering thirty-eight million fewer Americans than the senators who opposed him.[65] On this account, today's Supreme Court is fundamentally undemocratic *because our Constitution is fundamentally undemocratic.*

It's a powerful point, and there are undoubtedly strong reasons to reconsider both the Electoral College and Senate apportionment—proposals that go beyond the scope of this book. But until those constitutional ground rules are changed, it is enough to observe that in a functional democracy, the victories our opponents achieve in conformity with the rules are entitled to respect. They aren't entitled to perpetuity, of course: Democrats can and should work within the political process to win elections and prevail the next time around. That is what democracy means. But frustration with the basic rules of our constitutional order cannot serve as an excuse for overthrowing long-standing norms—like the norm against partisan court-packing—to rob one's opponents of their political victories. If the foundational norms of our constitutional system could be so easily cast aside, why would either side continue playing by them?

In summary, it is sensible to blame the Supreme Court's current shortfall of public confidence on partisanship given the many overtly political battles now being waged over Supreme Court appointments and important constitutional issues. Yet the partisanship diagnosis is dangerously incomplete. It's dangerous because even the most neutrally motivated legislative proposals to deescalate partisanship pose a risk of backfiring. That is especially true given that each proposal would require eliminating the Senate filibuster—a move Republicans will assuredly perceive as a partisan power play. Over the long run, adding more justices is likely to increase partisanship at the Court, not reduce it.

This is not to say, though, that reforms to the Supreme Court should be categorically rejected. To assess whether a legislative proposal is worthwhile, we have to know what the alternatives are. If, for example, the alternative were a Court that had actively subverted the lawful results of a democratic election by siding with Donald Trump's baseless claims of fraud in the presidential contest of 2020, then packing the Court or stripping it of power would be the (far) lesser of two evils. The same might be said of a Court that is hostile to democracy in more subtle ways, such as by continually undermining laws aimed at protecting the right to vote. On the other hand, if the Court were to somehow find a way to voluntarily moderate its own rulings, then proposals to pack or otherwise transform it would lose much of their justification. Proposals to reform the Supreme Court, in short, can't be evaluated in a vacuum. They have to be measured up against other options for restoring the Court's institutional credibility.

Do any such options exist? If so, what might they be? To answer these questions, we need to delve more deeply into the underlying problem at the Court that we're trying to solve. If what ails today's Court isn't partisanship alone but some other root cause, then perhaps we can address that alternative cause. Perhaps, in other words, a better cure is within our reach—one that doesn't entail an ever-descending cycle of vicious partisanship. The key to finding this cure might not be political at all. It could simply be a matter of starting with the right diagnosis.

3
Overconfidence

It was 1:00 p.m. on September 4, 2013, and I should have been chained to my desk. The work of a Supreme Court law clerk had taken over my life. The justices were back in the building after their summer travels, and the term's first set of oral arguments was drawing near. A never-ending stream of memos was due, which meant a tidal wave of briefs to read. Several stacks of those briefs sat on my desk, still unopened. Despite my best efforts, the stacks seemed to grow higher each day. I had the distinct feeling that, before the year was over, they would tip over and crush me.

But I was not at my desk. Instead, I was staring at a pricey menu in a swanky Italian restaurant in downtown D.C., wondering just how boozy lunch was going to get. That's when Justice Antonin Scalia spoke, wine glass in hand, eyes beaming with excitement.

"Ooh, we just *have* to order the grilled octopus. You'll never think of octopus the same."

The Supreme Court of the United States is steeped in tradition. One tradition, in place since the 1890s, is that oral arguments do not begin at the Court until each of the nine justices has shaken hands with all the others. (This tradition, like so much else, was put on hold during the pandemic, when the Court heard oral arguments telephonically for more than a year.) Tradition governs where the justices sit on the bench, with the Chief Justice in the center and the associate justices in descending order of seniority around him. White quills are placed at each counsel's table during oral argument despite the long-ago advent of more convenient writing implements. (Elite Supreme Court advocates often collect these quills and display them prominently in their offices, in what may be the closest thing lawyers have to trophy hunting.) Tradition even dictates that the most junior justice (now Justice Ketanji Brown Jackson) must keep notes and answer the door at the justices' private conferences.

A lesser-known tradition is the annual cross-chambers lunch that each justice holds with each set of clerks from the eight other chambers. Under this tradition, the clerks are responsible for two things: delivering written invitations to the eight justices for whom they do not work and paying the bill. The justices name the venue. Their selections sometimes offer a surprising peek into their personalities. Justice Stephen Breyer, a known Francophile, always insisted on dining at the same French restaurant. Justice Sotomayor prefers a brown-bag lunch in her office because she believes that law clerks—many of whom carry sizable student loan debts—should not be buying her a fancy lunch. Justice Ginsburg did not go out to lunch but invited the clerks to her chambers for an elegant afternoon tea. And Justice Scalia often chose a downtown Italian restaurant with tuxedo-clad waitstaff and white table linens.

As we sat down for lunch, it was clear that, unlike Justice Scalia, my three co-clerks and I did not quite fit the scene. We were too young, too poor, and, frankly, too diverse (three of us are people of color). But if our discomfort was at all apparent, Scalia did not seem to notice. He was warm and welcoming, steering our conversation fluidly across a range of subjects from his passion for tennis to his childhood love of Dick Tracy. His laugh was infectious, and his interest in us—a quartet of liberal thirty-somethings who disagreed with most of his deeply held political beliefs—was as sincere as it was surprising.

As we finished ordering (salmon for me and steak for Scalia) and the waiter took our menus, the conversation hit a brief lull. Each of us sensed the intricate dance in progress. How to maintain decorum at lunch with a jurist who has worked so hard to change the law in ways incompatible with our values? For one of my co-clerks, a gay Black man from the South, the challenge was especially immense. Scalia had written an infamous opinion in 2003 defending the criminalization of gay sex, and he had just belittled a landmark federal voting rights law as a "racial entitlement" rather than an effort to remedy our nation's sordid history of racialized voter suppression.[1] Opinions like these were why, on the day before our lunch, my co-clerks and I debated whether it might be best to treat the lunch like a family Thanksgiving and refrain from bringing up divisive issues at all.

Scalia quickly took that option off the table. He broke the silence by launching directly into a slew of controversial topics. Much like the first time I'd met him—when he declared the juvenile death penalty "easy, easy, easy"—Scalia showed no doubts. As we waited for our appetizers, the justice made comments much like those he'd uttered in public many times before. At a widely attended conference in 2012, for example, he had said, "The death penalty? Give me a break. It's easy. Abortion? Absolutely easy. Nobody ever thought the Constitution prevented restrictions on abortion. Homosexual sodomy? Come on. For 200 years, it was criminal in every state."[2] He had also once publicly rejected the idea of affording greater legal protections to Guantanamo Bay detainees because he "had a son on that battlefield and they were shooting at my son and I'm not about to give this man who was captured in a war a full jury trial."[3]

Knowing that Scalia was as unlikely to change our minds on these politically charged issues as we were to change his, my co-clerks and I tried pivoting to other topics. Beyond a desire to avoid contentious issues, we were motivated by a genuine curiosity about a legendary mind. A baser part of me also relished the thrill of the argument—

seeing whether I could hold my own with this legal titan. I wanted, in other words, to persuade the justice to come around to my view on *something*, or at least make him acknowledge the difficulty of an issue he once thought easy.

Luckily, I had just worked on a memo on a topic I thought would do the trick: an arcane rule that the Court announced in a criminal sentencing case called *Braxton v. United States*.[4] To understand the issue, it's helpful to start with the basics of criminal sentencing in federal courts. When a person either pleads or is found guilty of violating federal criminal law, a federal judge is responsible for choosing an appropriate sentence. For a long time, judges exercised essentially unbounded discretion, which led to predictable disparities in sentencing, including along racial lines.[5] So in 1984, Congress created the United States Sentencing Commission and tasked it with creating a set of guidelines to make criminal sentencing more uniform.[6] The result was the United States Sentencing Guidelines, an exhaustive list of factors that largely constrain judges to a set range of punishments for every federal crime.

Although motivated in part by an admirable concern for sentencing fairness, the guidelines have led to a number of controversies. In hindsight, this was unavoidable. Each sentencing factor listed in the six-hundred-page guidelines—from how to calculate a defendant's criminal history to whether a defendant was a "leader" or mere "supervisor" of criminal activity and to what counts as "acceptance of responsibility" for an offense—is a ground for litigation. Criminal defendants have every reason to argue for more lenient interpretations, while the government often takes the opposite view. Unsurprisingly, then, the guidelines have generated many interpretive disagreements in the lower federal courts.

Ordinarily, one of the Supreme Court's primary duties is to resolve these kinds of conflicts. Yet in most years, the Court declines to resolve a single dispute over the guidelines. A recent example is a case called *Longoria v. United States,* which involved a conflict over the meaning of Section 3E1.1(b) of the guidelines. This section provides that a criminal defendant may receive a one-level sentencing reduction by pleading guilty to a crime, thereby "permitting the government and the court to allocate their resources efficiently." In *Longoria*, the Fifth Circuit Court of Appeals held that the government may deny this sentencing reduction to a defendant who enters a conditional guilty plea while also moving to suppress questionable evidence, on the ground that doing so requires the government to expend resources preparing for a suppression hearing.[7] The Second Circuit has taken the same view. Yet several other circuit courts have ruled that because a suppression hearing rarely takes much work, it "is not a valid basis for denying the reduction."[8]

The issue may seem obscure, but it matters: a one-level reduction can take years off a defendant's prison time. The division among lower federal courts meant that, despite being governed by the same law, some defendants would receive the reduction and others wouldn't, all because of where they happened to live. *Longoria* thus seemed like exactly the kind of case the Supreme Court should decide in order to restore uniformity to the law.

Yet all nine justices refused to hear it. The reason is *Braxton v. United States,* a little-known case from 1991 in which the Court declined to resolve another lower court conflict over a different section of the sentencing guidelines. Writing for the *Braxton* majority, Justice Scalia explained that the Court was "not the sole body that could eliminate such conflicts."[9] Congress had directed the United States Sentencing Commission to "periodically review and revise" the guidelines, a task that could involve amending them to clarify a disagreement among the lower courts. Importantly, in *Braxton,* the commission had initiated a proceeding to do exactly that. So rather than resolve the disagreement itself, the Court let the commission do it.

Since then, however, the Court has used *Braxton* as a reason not to intervene in cases where the commission has taken no steps to eliminate a lower court conflict. Indeed, the Court has refused to settle disagreements over the meaning of important guidelines provisions even where those disagreements have persisted for decades. *Longoria* itself is an example: lower courts have diverged on the availability of a sentencing reduction when defendants move to suppress evidence at least since 1997, with no response from the sentencing commission.[10] It is hard to know how many people have already been affected as a result.

This was the puzzle I sought to present to Scalia. In light of the sentencing commission's failure to intervene, should the Court be more active in resolving lower court conflicts that leave different defendants facing different criminal sentences, all due to geographic happenstance? Was the *Braxton* rule wrong, or perhaps wrongly applied?

Scalia nodded along as I laid out the question. When I finished, he paused for a beat before answering. "I *wrote* Braxton, you know." (I knew.) "So of course I don't think there's a problem with it."

The table fell silent as we waited for him to explain why.

Instead, he cut a piece of octopus and set it emphatically on my plate. "You've gotta try this," he urged. "It's the best thing on the menu." As I took a bite—it was, in fact, quite good—Scalia changed the subject. And that was it. There would be no spirited back and forth about the logical foundations of the *Braxton* rule. No weighing the pros and cons of a different approach. No acknowledgment of the issue's difficulty or complexity.

To some, Scalia's black-and-white approach to the law holds a refreshing appeal. It is only human to prefer simple, clear answers over difficult and complex ones.[11] People don't want to think that the process of settling our legal rules involves a messy tangle of ambiguous arguments that yield uncertain answers. By showing absolute confidence in his views, Scalia avoided this messiness.

Yet his certitude did not earn universal admiration, even among his ardent supporters. One manifestation of his approach was a categorical rule limiting his law clerks' bench memos to no more than two pages, no matter how complex or consequential the case.[12] It is difficult to overstate how remarkable this rule was. In every Supreme Court case, the briefs filed by the parties alone will typically span more than one hundred pages, so it is virtually impossible to do justice to both sides' best arguments in just two. And that is before even considering amicus curiae briefs, or briefs filed by other interested organizations and scholars weighing in on the case. Prominent cases can attract more than one hundred amicus briefs, each with thirty-plus pages of additional argument. Not all of those briefs are critical to deciding a case, to be sure. But two pages is too little space to convey any sense of the nuanced arguments in a given dispute. Scalia's clerks were thus frequently frustrated by what they felt was an arbitrary limit. Judge Jeffrey Sutton, once a Scalia clerk and now a judge on the Sixth Circuit Court of Appeals, said of his reaction upon learning of the two-page limit: "We were like, well, I hope single spaced and no margins, right?"[13]

Scalia's blunt dismissal of my question about *Braxton* did not deter me. I spent the rest of the meal trying to come up with a better topic for debate. I recognized that I would not be able to argue with him over the law; in truth, it had been presumptuous of me to think otherwise. So I settled on a very different riddle, one that my co-clerks and I had spent an earlier lunch hour spiritedly debating. It was a question that, despite its surface frivolity, was both deceptively complex and morally freighted.

When our waiter passed out dessert menus and the table fell silent, I sprung my trap. "I'm curious what you think, Justice Scalia."

I paused for effect when he looked up.

"Is fish meat?"

Daniel Kahneman defines overconfidence bias as "our excessive confidence in what we believe we know, and our apparent inability to acknowledge the full extent of our ignorance and uncertainty."[14] Professor Don Moore, one of the nation's foremost experts on the subject, says that one of the most telltale manifestations of overconfidence is being "excessively sure that [we] know the truth."[15]

Overconfidence is problematic because it leads us to make mistakes we would have avoided had we only possessed a healthier sense of self-doubt. Moore describes the process through which this often occurs. First, overconfidence "leads [us] to be too confident that [our initial] interpretation of the facts is the right one."[16] Then, having rushed to a self-assured judgment, we quickly write off those who disagree with us as either "evil or stupid."[17] And after ignoring compelling counterarguments that might have changed our minds, we stumble forward with our mistaken judgments. The consequence, Moore explains, is predictable: "Excessive faith in erroneous intuitive judgments [leads us] to make mistakes."[18]

Too often, these mistakes are enormously harmful. This is why Kahneman has called overconfidence the most damaging of all cognitive traps and why Moore calls it "the mother of all psychological biases."[19] Consider a few examples.

Captain Edward Smith was a decorated officer in the Royal Naval Reserve and a longtime commander for the White Star Line, a renowned British shipping company. At the time he captained the *Titanic* on its maiden voyage in 1912, Smith had been commanding large vessels for White Star for twenty-five years. Speaking to the press before the *Titanic* set sail from England, he proudly declared, "I have never been in an accident of any sort worth speaking about, . . . nor was I ever in any predicament that threatened to end in disaster of any sort." Turning to his ship, Smith added, "I cannot imagine any condition which would cause [it] to founder. Modern shipbuilding has gone beyond that."[20]

This overconfidence contributed substantially to the sinking of the *Titanic*—and to Smith's own death. A United States Senate Committee investigation into the incident found that even after receiving reports of potentially dangerous ice masses ahead, Smith refused to change course. "No general discussion took place among the officers; no conference was called to consider these warnings; no heed was given to them. The speed was not relaxed, the lookout was not increased." Instead, Smith's "indifference to danger when other and less pretentious vessels doubled their lookout or stopped their engines" was "one of the direct and contributing causes of this unnecessary tragedy." "Overconfidence," the committee concluded, had "dulled faculties usually so alert."[21]

Captain Smith was not alone in succumbing to overconfidence bias. Under British Board of Trade rules, the *Titanic* was required to carry enough lifeboats to hold all of its passengers and crew in case of emergency. The original design plans thus included forty-eight lifeboats, enough to carry the ship's 2,223 passengers and crew. But the chairman of the White Star Line, J. Bruce Ismay, overrode those plans, arguing that the *Titanic* could comply with British regulations with just twenty lifeboats because the ship was so unsinkable that it should be considered a lifeboat itself.[22] Ismay's overconfidence led to a tragic shortage of lifeboats when disaster struck—and to the avoidable deaths of more than 1,500 passengers and crew.

Other examples of the harms of overconfidence abound in fields as diverse as medicine, finance, and war. A medical study published in 2001 compared the diagnoses offered by intensive-care unit doctors for 126 patients who later died, against those same patients' autopsy results. The researchers also asked the doctors to describe their confidence in their initial diagnoses. Doctors who reported being "completely certain" of their diagnosis were wrong 40 percent of the time.[23]

In finance, researchers at Duke University gathered more than eleven thousand forecasts of the Standard & Poor's stock index from chief financial officers of large corporations. One would expect such corporate insiders, steeped in knowledge and experience with financial markets, to have at least *some* ability to predict the index's behavior. The actual results were stunning: the statistical relationship between the CFOs' forecasts and actual market returns was slightly negative. In other words, when the CFOs predicted that the market would go up, it was more likely to do the opposite.[24]

Overconfidence also plays a role in war and all of its brutality. Professor Dominic Johnson describes how overconfidence lies at the heart of what's known as the "War Puzzle."[25] Rational nation-states should never go to war with one another given that they can instead negotiate a nonviolent outcome reflecting their relative degree of power. "Since wars do happen," Johnson observes, "states [must] overestimate their relative power." Think of Lieutenant Colonel George Armstrong Custer's infamous rallying cry at the Battle of the Little Bighorn, just moments before his men, numbering less than three hundred, were slaughtered by several thousand Lakota and Cheyenne warriors: "Hurrah, boys, we've got them!" That is overconfidence bias in a nutshell.

Why does overconfidence wreak such havoc? Moore offers a convincing account. Overconfidence, he explains, is a "gateway bias" that "gives the other decision-making biases teeth."[26] These other biases include a host of common psychological traps that we fall into when we "navigate our complex physical, intellectual, social, and informational worlds." Whereas a healthy sense of humility would check these biases, overconfidence unleashes them. As Moore points out, if we were "appropriately humble about [our] judgment, we would be better able to protect [ourselves] from the [biases] to which everyone is prone."[27]

The *Titanic* incident offers a useful illustration. When Captain Smith refused to slow the ship despite multiple reports of ice masses in the water, overconfidence gave teeth to *availability bias,* or the tendency to misjudge the likelihood of a future event based on the ease with which past instances of the event come to mind. Recall Smith's comment that he had "never been in an accident of any sort worth speaking about," much less "any predicament that threatened to end in disaster." Because he lacked memories of any instance of his ship being damaged by ice, availability bias tricked him into the mistaken belief that the odds of the *Titanic* suffering such damage were far lower than they actually were. A captain less confident in his own abilities or the *Titanic*'s unsinkability might have slowed the ship out of an abundance of caution. Smith was not that captain.

Or consider a common form of medical misdiagnosis. In January 2019, a seven-year-old girl visited an urgent care center with a fever, fatigue, upper body aches, and a cough.[28] This is a common patient profile during the winter months when millions of Americans contract the flu. So because of *confirmation bias,* or the human tendency to process information in a way that supports our preconceptions, an overconfident physician swiftly concluded that this particular patient also had the flu and sent her home to rest without further testing. Alas, the girl actually had pneumonia, a lung infection that became deadly after it went untreated. A less confident doctor could have avoided this mistake. Less sure of an initial flu suspicion—and thus more likely to seek out information that would disprove that preconception—such a doctor might have ordered a chest X-ray that would have revealed the infection in the patient's lungs.

Overconfidence acts as a gateway to other dangerous decision-making biases in judging, too. Availability bias, for example, played a powerful role in Justice Lewis Powell's decision to change his vote in a case from 1986 called *Bowers v. Hardwick*. The case involved a Georgia prosecution of a gay couple for consensual sexual activity. Powell had initially voted at conference to invalidate the Georgia criminal ban.[29] But he later changed his mind, resulting in a five-to-four ruling in the state's favor. In explaining why he switched his vote, Powell told one of his law clerks, "I don't believe I've ever met a homosexual."[30] Much as Captain Smith's personal experiences tricked him into misjudging the odds of an accident, Justice Powell's inability to call to mind a single gay acquaintance led him to underestimate the significance of his vote in *Bowers*. (Powell had in fact worked with several gay law clerks, including the one to whom he had made that remark. The clerk reportedly replied, "Certainly you have, but you just don't know that they are.")

Cases like *Bowers* show how the job of a Supreme Court justice is significantly different from that of a ship captain, doctor, or Fortune 500 CFO. Justices routinely make decisions that are freighted with political and moral implications for the nation. Can states prosecute persons for intimate, consensual sexual activity? Is the death penalty "cruel and unusual" punishment? Is an unborn fetus a "person" for purposes of the Constitution's guarantee that no state shall "deprive any person of life" without due process of law? Questions such as these trigger deeply moral and political beliefs. And once these values are activated, overconfidence unleashes another very different—and very dangerous—kind of psychological bias.

Biologically speaking, the case is airtight. "Meat" refers to the flesh of an animal. Fish are animals. So when we eat their flesh, we are, by definition, eating meat.

But the biological perspective is not the only one. There is a sociocultural dimension as well. Many people view "fish" and "meat" as nonoverlapping categories, akin to "yogurt" and "cheese." Like yogurt and cheese, fish and meat share many similarities. But these do not make fish a subset of meat any more than yogurt is a subset of cheese. (Try serving someone a turkey and strawberry yogurt sandwich and see how they respond.) This is why grocery stores typically have separate seafood and meat counters. And it's why the salmon I ordered was not on the same section of the menu as Justice Scalia's steak.

The sociocultural dimension is complicated, however. A growing number of human beings are vegetarian, which is defined by contradistinction to the consumption of meat. And for moral and other reasons, many vegetarians consider fish a kind of meat and thus refrain from eating it. Yet some do eat it, pointing among other things to the somewhat lesser environmental impacts. These individuals often self-identify as "pescatarians," a sign that what they are doing diverges from standard vegetarianism.

Each of these nuances is why I eagerly awaited Scalia's response. Removed from the comfortable confines of legal logic, perhaps he would finally admit to some uncertainty—and even be open to persuasion.

Yet again, I was wrong.

"Of course fish isn't meat!" he boomed. "Why else do I—and millions of Catholics—eat fish on Fridays during Lent?"

"But from a scientific perspective," I responded, "Isn't meat just the flesh of an animal? And aren't fish animals?"

Scalia scoffed. "You're telling me the pope has been wrong for centuries?"

All judges who approach cases with great political and social consequences believe they do so with the aim of objectively identifying the correct legal outcome. Perhaps no comment illustrates this belief more than Chief Justice Roberts's oft-cited remark that the job of a

Supreme Court Justice is to "call balls and strikes, and not to pitch or bat."[31]

Overconfidence serves as a gateway to a powerful set of cognitive biases that thwart this idealized judicial vision. The term that best encompasses these biases is the concept of *motivated reasoning,* which Yale Law School professor Dan Kahan defines as "the tendency of people to unconsciously process information . . . to promote goals or interests extrinsic to the decisionmaking task at hand."[32]

What kind of goals or interests might motivate judicial reasoning? Theoretically, the answer is unlimited. As psychologist Ziva Kunda has argued, one's reasoning could be motivated by literally "any wish, desire, or preference" as to the "outcome of a given reasoning task."[33] In practice, though, decision makers find certain kinds of preferences and desires to be especially significant. Chief among them is the desire to advance or protect the interests of groups with which one identifies, a process known as *identity protective cognition.* Human beings have a powerful, innate need to affirm their membership in culturally salient reference groups and to advance policies and beliefs favored by those groups. As Kahan points out, arguments that "contradict the groups' shared commitments can jeopardize their individual members' well-being," thus creating "psychic pressure to resist" the arguments.

The concept of identity protective cognition helps explain Justice Scalia's reflexive response to the question whether fish is meat. Rather than dispassionately considering arguments rooted in biology and social practice, he jumped immediately to his group identity as a practicing Catholic. That identity led him to a clear answer that reflected his group's moral values and shared commitments: fish is not meat.

To be clear, Scalia was no outlier; the same identity-based bias affects us all. When I asked a friend who is a biologist by training, he responded quickly that fish is obviously meat given the term's biological definition. A vegetarian friend of mine reached the same conclusion but grounded it in the identity-protective fact that he does not eat fish. Each of these examples shows that when human beings form opinions, our minds often skip over the logical *what* and *why* questions and jump instead to questions that begin with *who*. Instead of asking, "What's the best evidence?" or "Why might the answer be this instead of that?" we ask, "Who would hold this answer, and are they members of an identity I share?"

Scientists and vegetarians are not especially salient identity groups at the Supreme Court today. Religious identities are. Six of the justices identify as Catholic. It is no coincidence that their views on matters with significant religious implications, from same-sex marriage to abortion, often track the views of the Roman Catholic Church.[34]

But another group identity is more prominent than religion in present-day society—and thus even more likely to bias the judgment of overconfident individuals: partisan affiliation. In today's hyperpolarized political environment, few dimensions of group membership generate more intense commitments, and greater social divisions, than one's affiliation with a given political party or philosophy. For example, when asked whether they agreed with the statement that members of the opposing party are "not just worse for politics—they are downright evil," 42 percent of both Republicans and Democrats responded, "yes."[35] The result is a strong tendency for our decision making to become distorted by a subconscious desire to pursue outcomes in keeping with our politics.

Political scientists call this *partisan motivated reasoning*. And it is a powerful force. In one recent experiment, Professors Toby Bolsen, James Druckman, and Fay Lomax Cook asked participants to identify their political affiliation before answering whether they would support a bill to increase vehicle fuel efficiency standards and research funding for renewable energy.[36] One group of participants was informed that the energy bill was "widely supported by Democratic representatives," while another was told that it was favored by Republicans. A control group was not told of any endorsement by either party. The researchers hypothesized that partisan motivated reasoning would be so powerful that the mere mention that one's own party (or one's opposing party) had endorsed the bill would sway participants' support for it.

Their findings were remarkable—if unsurprising. Participants were significantly more likely to support the energy bill when it was endorsed by their own party, compared to when it received no endorsement at all. They were also significantly less likely to support the bill if they thought it was endorsed by the opposing party, even though the substance of the bill itself had not changed. We are so primed to form opinions according to our partisan identities that the identity itself becomes integral to our decision making.

Partisan motivated reasoning isn't implicated in every kind of decision. A critical care doctor's chest pain diagnosis advances neither Republican nor Democratic preferences. A captain's choice to slow a ship aligns with no discernible political affiliation. But Supreme Court cases touching on LGBTQ rights, the death penalty, abortion, gun control, and immigration? These are issues ripe for infection by partisan motivated reasoning.

The justices' behavior bears this out. Start with their aggregate voting patterns in divisive cases where the winning side prevails with just five votes—a rough proxy for politically salient disputes. Republican-appointed justices routinely vote in favor of conservative outcomes, while their Democrat-appointed counterparts do the opposite. Here are the percentages of pro-conservative votes for three of the Court's Republican appointees through the year 2017: Alito—84.1 percent, Roberts—82.4 percent, and Thomas—80.1 percent. Here are the same percentages for three of the Court's recent Democratic appointees: Breyer—21.4 percent, Sotomayor—10.1 percent, and Kagan—18.1

percent. (Data on Justices Gorsuch, Kavanaugh, Barrett, and Jackson are not yet available.)

How do these percentages materialize? One possibility is that the justices are *consciously* and *intentionally* partisan: they decide how to vote in major cases simply by gauging their own personal political preferences. They then disguise their partisan desires by dressing up their decisions with the pretense of legal analysis.

Some justices currently on the Court may well behave in this manner. It's difficult to know without peering into their minds. But the intentional-partisan account runs into a significant body of contrary evidence: the justices vote with surprising frequency for outcomes they find politically unpalatable. Chief Justice Roberts and Justice Gorsuch, for example, are both social conservatives who shocked the right by voting to extend federal antidiscrimination protections to LGBTQ workers. Justice Sotomayor, the most liberal justice on the Court, wrote an opinion in 2021 ruling against an undocumented immigrant who had been found guilty of unlawful reentry based merely on a conviction for driving under the influence.[37] All six conservative justices voted to reject a slew of lawsuits seeking to overturn the presidential election of 2020. Conservative justices have voted on multiple occasions to uphold the Affordable Care Act despite its unpopularity within Republican circles.[38] Many equally prominent examples abound. If naked policy preferences were truly the justices' driving motivation, it's hard to explain how so many of these rulings against political self-interest could have happened.

The likelier alternative is that partisanship *subconsciously* influences the justices' behavior. On this view, when the justices come across a difficult case, they start by genuinely asking what the law requires. But they are *overconfident* in their ability to discover an answer in two different, yet equally important ways. First, the justices are too self-assured in their selection of the correct approach to legal interpretation: they believe that they've identified the "one right theory" of determining what the law requires when in truth there are multiple plausible candidates for the task. Second, the justices are also overly confident when it comes to applying their preferred interpretive theories to individual cases. For all the reasons just described, this overconfidence leaves them vulnerable to other cognitive traps—and partisan motivated reasoning is chief among them. The justices do not set out, in other words, with the explicit aim of subverting the law to their political objectives. But they are human beings like the rest of us, susceptible to the same psychological pitfalls.

An example of partisan motivated reasoning in action can help to illustrate this process. In a 2021 case called *Brnovich v. Democratic National Committee,* the Court's six conservative justices voted to uphold an Arizona law requiring that voters' ballots be discarded entirely if they are cast at the wrong polling location. Most other states have a more lenient policy of counting the portion of such ballots that are lawfully cast, for example on a statewide or nationwide office, while discarding the portion cast in a local election for which the voter was ineligible. In condoning Arizona's blanket policy of throwing out the entire ballot, the conservative justices took a very different view of statistical evidence from that of the liberal, dissenting justices.

The district court in the case had found that 1 percent of all Black, Latino, and Native American voters had their votes discarded under this policy, compared to 0.5 percent of white voters. Writing for the Court, Justice Alito interpreted this evidence as support for his view that Arizona's policy was permissible because the state's voting system "work[s] for 98% or more of voters to whom it applies." Yet Justice Kagan, looking at the exact same evidence, argued that "Hispanics, African Americans, and Native Americans were about twice as likely—or said another way, 100% more likely—to have their ballots discarded than whites," a powerful reason to strike the law down.

Mathematically speaking, both numerical claims are entirely correct. But they point to vastly different legal conclusions that straddle the political divide. Partisan motivated reasoning offers a convincing explanation for this divergence.

Motivated reasoning in Supreme Court opinions is not inevitable. Or at least it is no more inevitable than cognitive bias dooming every medical diagnosis or ocean voyage. Decision makers can avoid these pitfalls if they have a healthy enough sense of intellectual humility. Doctors, for example, can reduce the odds of misdiagnoses by increasing their "self-awareness so that they can recognize when additional information is needed or the wrong diagnostic path is taken."[39] Kahneman describes the benefits of a process known as a "premortem," where stakeholders are told to assume that the decision on which they've agreed winds up a disaster and asked to discuss how and where they went wrong.[40] Such an approach checks overconfidence by "unleashing the imagination of knowledgeable individuals" in a "much-needed direction." I will return to the topic of humility in the second half of the book.

For now, it is enough to observe that Supreme Court justices do not employ confidence-reducing approaches when deciding cases. If anything, the whole process leading to a final opinion serves to reinforce the justices' instinctual viewpoints, from an oral argument where the justices ask questions aimed at undermining the opposing side's position to a private conference where the justices merely recite their views rather than engage in open discussion and to an opinion-writing process in which the justices rarely collaborate with one another.[41] Justice Louis Brandeis captured the problem perfectly when he remarked, "The difficulty with this place is that if you're only fifty-five percent convinced of a proposition, you have to act and vote as if you were one hundred percent convinced."[42]

Our Supreme Court is thus profoundly vulnerable to overconfidence. The justices genuinely believe that they can use skillful lawyerly analysis to discover objectively correct answers to the difficult controversies that divide our society. It is this very confidence in their abilities, however, that permits other cognitive biases—partisan motivated reasoning in particular—to sway their judgment. And this is true even though these are Supreme Court justices we're talking about: brilliant lawyers whose best efforts to ascertain legal meaning should theoretically be better than anyone else's. In fact, the justices' extraordinary legal acumen is not a corrective to their overconfidence but a contributing cause of it.

"Whatever you do, do *not* try to bring your own baked goods. Someone tried that a few years ago . . . and let's just say it did not go well."

My co-clerks and I had just sat for a working lunch with Justice Ginsburg's clerks (known endearingly in the Sotomayor chambers as "the RBGs"). Item number one on the one-item agenda was how to prepare for our looming tea with their boss. The prohibition against self-baked goods was the first piece of advice we received.

The leader of the Court's liberal wing and the mastermind behind the legal movement to guarantee women equal protection of the law, Ginsburg was the closest thing we had to a living legend. We felt enormously lucky to have the opportunity to meet her. But we were also nervous. Her incredible life's work was beyond intimidating, and collectively we lacked the background to make small talk. None of us shared her interest in opera or her educational history at Columbia University and Harvard Law School. It also didn't help that she was famously particular, apparently including in her taste in pastries. For an afternoon tea, the stakes felt surprisingly high. We did not want to screw up our time with her.

When the time finally arrived for tea later that week, Justice Ginsburg's assistant showed us into her chambers and seated us at a table to the side of the justice's enormous, mahogany-colored desk. A heavy tan tablecloth covered the table. On it were five place settings and a tray with an assortment of five handcrafted pastries. The pastries were almost comically small, no more than a square inch in area.

After a few minutes, Ginsburg entered the room. We stood. She walked slowly, deliberately, to join us. She was strikingly tiny and frail, an impression in sharp contrast to the stories of her resilience. (After undergoing surgery for colorectal cancer in September 1999, for example, Ginsburg worked from her hospital bed and ultimately did not miss a single day on the bench.) She asked us to sit, and an assistant placed one of the treats—a beautiful tart—on the justice's plate.

Silence.

Finally, I could wait no longer. I asked the justice about a set of framed photos she had displayed on the wall. One photo especially caught my attention: a grainy image of Ginsburg riding on the back of an elephant, seated behind a portly, dark-haired individual; both of them are smiling and waving at the camera. "That's Nino and me in India at a judicial conference," Ginsburg responded with a smile. (Nino was Justice Scalia.) "I wanted to sit in the front, of course, but the driver told me it was a matter of weight distribution." We laughed.

Ginsburg cut a tiny corner off the tart with her fork and took a bite, chewing slowly. The rest of us followed suit. We waited to see if she would resume her story.

She did not.

After another lengthy silence, a co-clerk asked her how she came to be so interested in civil procedure, a legal field that encompasses the rules and practice of civil (that is, noncriminal) litigation. It is a dry topic, yet Ginsburg was renowned for her passion and expertise in it. She told us she had fallen in love with the subject while researching it in Switzerland after her law school graduation in the 1960s.

Again, silence.

I looked around the table, hoping one of my co-clerks would ask something. Nothing. We stirred uncomfortably in our seats.

After a seemingly eternal silence, Justice Ginsburg cleared her throat and spoke.

"Speaking of the opera," she said, and entered into a long soliloquy on the coming season at the Washington National Opera.

We looked at each other, barely able to contain our smiles.

Ginsburg's unprompted lecture on the finer points of opera took up the remaining half hour of our time. I understood none of it, but the justice's enthusiasm was contagious. I nodded in rapt attention throughout. After the tea ended and we left her chambers, my co-clerks and I breathed a heavy sigh of relief. It had been an exhilarating yet oddly nerve-wracking conversation, one we would always treasure. Meeting a real-life legend can be hard work.

After our tea ended, we briefed Ginsburg's clerks on the experience. Upon hearing how the justice broke our awkward silence with the forced phrase, "speaking of the opera," one of the RBGs likened her interactions with law clerks to a police officer who drives down the road in a prominently marked police cruiser. When other drivers slam on their brakes, the officer looks around and believes everyone always obeys the speed limit. Likewise, after years spent regaling recent law school graduates with stories of the opera and finding that they all seem genuinely enthusiastic, Ginsburg must have thought every person in their late twenties was an opera fan.

Our episode with Justice Ginsburg helps to explain why the justices' legal expertise heightens, rather than diminishes, their vulnerability to overconfidence bias. There is a term for what made countless groups of law clerks feign interest in the opera while sitting for tea with the justice: hero worship. And it applies to justices across the political spectrum. Whereas the "Notorious RBG" was idolized by the political left, for example, Justice Scalia earned similar reverence on the right.

Sometimes hero worship can be harmless enough. A miscalibrated view of opera's popularity among young people is more endearing than troubling. Yet the same dynamic also produced a deferential instinct in situations where law clerks (and sometimes even other justices) might have pushed back against a justice on the law. Their failure to do so can give a justice an illusion of infallibility. For Ginsburg, this was perhaps most clear in her beloved specialty of civil procedure.

One of the major legal debates in civil procedure concerns a rule known as "personal jurisdiction," a doctrine that requires a defendant to possess sufficient "contacts" with a given state before the defendant can be sued there. (The doctrine has its basis in the Due Process Clause because forcing defendants to defend themselves in some remote and inconvenient court may be so burdensome as to deprive them of due process of law). The topic may seem obscure, but a story can help to show its significance to ordinary Americans, often in the most tragic of times.

Thirteen-year-old Victor Meier was on a family vacation at the Atlantis resort in the Bahamas when disaster struck. Victor was swimming on Atlantis property when one of the resort's chartered motorboats struck him, causing massive injuries. He was airlifted to Miami for emergency medical treatment. He survived, but he was permanently disfigured.[43]

After consulting with a lawyer, Victor's family decided to sue Sun International Hotels, the Bahamian corporation that owned the Atlantis resort. Understandably, the Meiers sought monetary damages for Victor's tragic injuries and medical treatment.

But where to file the lawsuit? The Meier family lived in Utah, so it would have been most convenient for them to sue Sun International

Hotels there.[44] Under the legal doctrine of personal jurisdiction, however, such a suit would be dismissed. Because Sun International Hotels was a Bahamian business with no Utah operations, forcing it to defend a lawsuit there would deprive it of due process.

Another obvious place to sue the hotel was the Bahamas, where the accident occurred. Yet that was not ideal for the Meier family. It would be costly and complicated to hire Bahamian lawyers to litigate the suit there and a burden to travel to the Bahamas for a potential trial. In addition, a Bahamian jury might be more sympathetic to the hotel, given its importance in the local economy.

So the Meiers decided to sue in Florida, where Sun International Hotels maintained corporate subsidiaries that engaged in extensive advertising, marketing, and accounting. Those operations, the Meiers argued, provided the necessary degree of Florida contacts for Sun International Hotels to be fairly sued there. But Sun International Hotels responded that the only proper place for the Meiers to sue was in the Bahamas, such that the Florida suit should be dismissed.

Who was right? The question is especially significant in our increasingly globalized society, where similar disputes occur with growing frequency.

In 2014, in a major case called *Daimler v. Bauman,* Ginsburg answered the question decisively in favor of large corporate defendants like Sun International Hotels. A corporation, she wrote for an eight-justice majority, may only be sued where it is "at home," which essentially means its principal place of business and place of incorporation. For a business like Sun International Hotels, that means the Bahamas. (A separate rule of jurisdiction permits defendants also to be sued in forums where the defendants' contacts gave rise to the plaintiff's injury. That rule helps plaintiffs when their injuries occur in their home states. But it does not help plaintiffs in cases like Victor Meier's, whose injury happened elsewhere.) The effect of Ginsburg's opinion was to make it vastly more difficult for plaintiffs who are injured away from home to obtain civil justice from corporate defendants.

The Court's conservative justices often show a pro-corporation bent, so it was perhaps unsurprising that some of them would have voted in this way in *Daimler*. But how did Ginsburg come to join them—and persuade two of her fellow liberals (Justices Breyer and Kagan) to do the same?

Hero worship played a major role. The Court and legal academy had long revered Ginsburg's civil procedure acumen. Speaking in New York City just days after *Daimler* was decided, for example, Justice Kagan described Ginsburg as a "pathmarking scholar of civil procedure" before recommending that students and lawyers read her opinion in *Daimler* for a "refresher course" on personal jurisdiction.[45] Thus, rather than think through the legal question critically, the Court largely deferred to Ginsburg's initial intuition—with painful consequences for private plaintiffs. (Years later, with Ginsburg no longer on the Court, Justice Gorsuch would revisit the issue with fresh eyes and rightly criticize *Daimler* for "hauling" individuals to far-off jurisdictions in order to bring suit. "What's the majority's real worry anyways," Gorsuch asked—"that corporations might lose special protections?")[46]

A second dynamic also reinforces overconfidence bias among our Supreme Court justices: a legal culture that places too much emphasis on skill. When lawyers talk about the justices, they do so with admiration for the justices' legal acumen and brilliance. It is skill and intellect, in other words, that enabled someone to become a Supreme Court justice under the conventional narrative—not luck. Yet the truth of the matter is that luck played a substantial role in every justice's nomination, whether they served on a law school faculty with the appointing president (like Justice Kagan, who taught at the University of Chicago alongside then-Professor Barack Obama), or benefited from the Senate's stonewalling of an earlier qualified nominee (like Justice Gorsuch).

Misattributing the justices' success to brilliance rather than luck fosters overconfidence. As Daniel Kahneman puts it, "The unrecognized limits of professional skill help explain why experts are often overconfident."[47] To illustrate the point, Kahneman describes a study in which 284 renowned political and economic experts were asked to predict the probability that certain events within their expertise would occur in the near future, such as war or the emergence of a new global market. The results were unsettling: the experts "performed worse than . . . dart-throwing monkeys."[48]

Why were these experts so often mistaken? The reason has to do with the erroneous belief that their prior success resulted from skill rather than good fortune. "The person who acquires more knowledge," Kahneman cautions, often develops an "enhanced illusion of her skill and becomes unrealistically overconfident." This is especially true in professional cultures, like the law, where success is defined through the illusion of skill. My own career reflects this very point. Students sometimes react with awe when they learn that I clerked for Justice Sotomayor. Yet how I got the clerkship is hardly awe-inspiring. Each year, literally thousands of people graduate from law school with the qualifications and ability to serve as a Supreme Court clerk. The reason I got the job rather than someone else was not skill or talent but luck: I happened to take classes with professors and work for a court of appeals judge who made compelling recommendations on my behalf.

One final factor accounts for Supreme Court justices' vulnerability to overconfidence: selection bias. To become a federal judge (let alone a justice), a lawyer has to be extremely confident in his or her legal views. That, after all, is what an appointing president and confirming senator is looking for. A prospective judge who routinely admits ignorance on important legal topics or uncertainty about hard questions would never get an appointment. Speaking about a similar dynamic in the field of medicine, Kahneman observes that "experts who acknowledge the full extent of their ignorance may expect to be replaced by more confident competitors."[49] The very process of becoming a judge is thus biased toward overconfidence. And once one is on the bench, that overconfidence only builds. As Richard Posner, one of the nation's most famous federal judges, once admitted, judges "become more confident" over the years because "they have behind them an ever-longer train of decisions that they no longer doubt are sound."[50]

True expertise requires knowing the limits of one's knowledge. But because of hero worship, the illusion of legal skill, and selection bias, modern Supreme Court justices find these limits difficult to admit. That was certainly true of Justices Scalia and Ginsburg. But it's equally true of all recent justices, regardless of where they fall on the political spectrum. When it comes to interpreting the meaning of the Constitution and our laws, all of the justices have a strong incentive to proclaim themselves all-knowing.

America's first female Supreme Court justice was a trailblazer in more ways than one. After growing up on a cattle ranch along the Arizona–New Mexico border, Sandra Day O'Connor attended Stanford for both college and law school. She graduated third in her law school class (her one-time boyfriend and future colleague on the court, William Rehnquist, claimed the first spot).[51]

O'Connor's legal career got off to a fitful start. Despite her academic success, law firms refused to interview her because she was a woman. (Ruth Bader Ginsburg would experience similar discrimination after graduating at the top of her Columbia Law School class.) Undeterred, O'Connor went to work as a deputy district attorney before winning office as a Republican state senator—and eventually becoming Arizona's Senate majority leader. As a legislator, she was known for her centrism and bipartisan approach. Bob Stump, the Democratic minority leader when O'Connor was majority leader, said he couldn't "remember a damn thing we ever came to blows over."[52] At the end of each legislative session, O'Connor invited every senator—Republican and Democrat alike—to her house for homemade burritos.

Even after her appointment to the Supreme Court by President Ronald Reagan in 1981, O'Connor did not leave her centrist instincts behind. She would routinely avoid issuing all-or-nothing rules, preferring instead more moderate, seemingly negotiated outcomes—a minimalist, one-case-at-a-time approach.[53] This approach infuriated some, including fellow Republican appointee Antonin Scalia, who frequently criticized O'Connor's legal reasoning.[54]

At a time when political centrism is increasingly rare, especially among Republicans in national office, it is easy to pine for O'Connor's distinctive brand of moderate conservatism. No one, however, should mistake this moderation for judicial humility. For all her centrist instincts, O'Connor was unflinchingly certain of her views. She once told a public audience that after making a decision, "I do not look back and say 'Oh, what if I had done the other thing' or 'Oh, I should have done something else.'"[55]

The landmark affirmative action case *Grutter v. Bollinger* offers a poignant example of this certitude. The question was whether the Michigan Law School's policy of considering an applicant's race as one among many factors in its admissions process violated the Fourteenth Amendment guarantee of equal protection of the law. (The Supreme Court is poised to reconsider this question in 2023 in a major case, *Students for Fair Admissions v. President and Fellows of Harvard College.*) In answering "no," the Court in *Grutter* permitted affirmative action in higher education to remain the subject of democratic debate, favored in some states but not others. Yet O'Connor's self-confidence was on full display at the end of her majority opinion: "We expect that 25 years from now, the use of racial preferences will no longer be necessary."[56] O'Connor cited no social science research, no brief, no evidence of any kind to support this assertion. When it came to marking the outer boundaries of constitutional law, her gut judgment was authority enough. As *New York Times* writer Jeffrey Rosen concluded in 2001 in a scathing feature, "O'Connor's jurisprudence has [been] a kind of judicial imperiousness: she views the court in general, and herself in particular, as the proper forum to decide every political and constitutional question in the land."[57]

Then there was the pillow. After interviewing her for his *New York Times* article, Rosen realized that he'd left a book in her chambers. When he went back in to find it, he saw a hand-stitched pillow on the chair where O'Connor had been sitting. On it was embroidered: "Maybe In Error But Never In Doubt."

Perhaps the pillow was in jest—though no one I've asked about it believes that. More likely the motto reflected O'Connor's hard-earned approach to judging in a profession that rarely admits doubt. Even so, it is difficult to know what is more remarkable: that O'Connor would be so aware of the errors her overconfidence concealed or that she would celebrate this as a sign of strength rather than something deeply broken in our legal culture. And it is difficult to think of a line that more powerfully captures the Court's overconfident approach to the monumental social controversies that come before it. It may get the answers wrong in any number of immense, society-altering conflicts. But when it errs, it will do so in spectacularly confident fashion.

Justice O'Connor's self-assured approach brings to mind the similar attitude held by Justice Scalia. Although the two did not always agree, they shared an unbending determination to avoid expressing uncertainty. (After Rosen's article came out, however, O'Connor did instruct her judicial assistant to hide the pillow whenever reporters visited chambers.)[58] O'Connor also tried to instill this approach among her colleagues. On Justice Sotomayor's first day at the Court, in 2009, O'Connor paid her a visit in chambers. "The worst thing you can do," she told Sotomayor, "is be indecisive. Make a decision, *right or wrong*. If you're known as indecisive you'll never belong fully."[59]

In some respects, O'Connor's advice was completely understandable—especially given her status as the first female justice ever to serve. On a Court where one's colleagues are supremely confident in their own legal conclusions, agonizing over the complexity of hard cases might do a new justice little good. And without exception, confidence is precisely the attitude the justices display.

Consider Clarence Thomas who, together with Justice Alito, serves as the anchor for the Court's current conservative wing. Thomas's views on the Constitution are so extreme—and so self-assured—that they sometimes proved too much for even Justice Scalia. Like Scalia, Thomas is a self-professed originalist who believes that the Constitution should be interpreted in accordance with its original public meaning at the time of its enactment. Unlike Scalia, however, Thomas has been willing to follow original meaning to its logical extreme, no matter the implications for American society.

Take the question of Congress's power to enact laws under the Constitution's Commerce Clause. A string of New Deal Court decisions construed this power broadly, permitting Congress to regulate any activity with a substantial effect on interstate commerce. It is this power that enabled Congress to forbid racial discrimination at lunch counters (since the sale of goods and services has a substantial effect on interstate commerce), set a minimum wage (since the payment of wages has a similar effect), and prohibit child labor, among other actions. Yet Thomas would cast this entire body of Commerce Clause doctrine aside—and with it, virtually all federal antidiscrimination and employment law.[60]

Thomas also holds a radical view of the First Amendment Establishment Clause. The Court has long held that the clause forbids the federal government to establish a religion. It has also held that the Fourteenth Amendment extends the same prohibition to the *states*: state governments, like the federal government, must maintain a strict separation between their own affairs and those of houses of worship.[61] Thomas disagrees. In his view, the Establishment Clause was actually "intended to protect *state* establishments of religion."[62] On that reading, states are perfectly free, under federal constitutional law, to enshrine an official state religion. Mississippi could proclaim itself the Baptist State, Rhode Island could anoint itself the Catholic State, and Vermont could call itself the Atheist State. The states could spend public dollars to advantage their preferred faiths, perhaps even requiring that they be taught in schools. And the United States Constitution would have nothing to say about it.

Only one who possesses truly extraordinary confidence in their legal conclusions could advance these views without regard for the upheaval they would cause. That is Justice Thomas. Scalia, who called himself a "faint-hearted originalist," once contrasted himself to Thomas this way: "I am an originalist. I am a textualist. I am not a nut."[63]

Overconfidence also prevails among the Court's liberals. Consider Justice Ginsburg's decision not to retire from the Supreme Court during the presidency of Barack Obama. To be sure, Ginsburg was still an intellectual force to be reckoned with—a fact I witnessed firsthand during my clerkship in 2013–14, when she was already eighty years old. But surely she understood the possibility that a Republican presidential victory in 2016 might leave the nomination of her successor in the hands of someone devoted to undoing her judicial legacy. That she chose to stay on the bench despite these enormous stakes for society is the product of excessive confidence—whether in her ability to predict the outcome of the election in 2016 or in her longevity.

Progressives can admire her considerable lifetime achievements while also lamenting how her refusal to retire has put many of those same achievements in jeopardy.

Or consider Justice Elena Kagan, who referred to herself during her confirmation hearings as a "famously excellent teacher." Her self-assuredness while serving as the solicitor general (the federal government's top lawyer in the Supreme Court) is legendary. Despite not having practiced law in two decades before taking the position and having never written a Supreme Court brief, she became renowned for taking a "hyperactive red pen" to the first drafts submitted by fellow lawyers in the Solicitor General's office, many of whom had argued dozens of cases at the Court. On her first day as solicitor general, staff lawyers handed her their final draft of the government's brief in a little-known case concerning a federal banking regulation. When she emerged with her edits hours later, her staff was stunned at the bloodbath of red ink. As author Jeffrey Toobin recounts, when "Kagan's handiwork was passed around the office, the nearly universal reaction was 'What the *fuck?*'"[64]

Stories of the justices' overconfidence paint a worrisome picture. They are backed up by empirical data.

One measure of the Court's increasing confidence is the frequency of decisions in which the Court invalidates a federal law. This metric is admittedly crude on a case-to-case basis, since federal legislation has changed over time and not all invalidations are the same. But over a long-enough time horizon, trends become meaningful. A Court that regularly upholds laws enacted by the people's chosen representatives is less likely to be overconfident than a Court that regularly strikes such laws down.

What do the data reveal? In the 207 years following the Constitution's ratification, from 1788 to 1994, the Supreme Court invalidated just 135 provisions of federal law—roughly 0.6 per term.[65] Between

1995 and 2018, however, the Court invalidated 75 federal laws, just over 3.1 times per term.[66]

This fivefold growth in judicial intervention—a reasonable proxy for what some call "judicial activism"—is all the more notable given that the Court hears far fewer cases each year than it used to. Whereas today's Court decides roughly 60 cases per term, it decided 235 cases in 1930.[67] Today's Supreme Court resolves fewer disputes than at any point in recent history, yet it overrides Congress more than ever before.

Another data point comes at the problem from a different angle: the stridency of language used in the Court's own opinions. Using a computer analysis of roughly 2,500 opinions issued by the Court between 1791 and 2008, researchers Keith Carlson, Michael Livermore, and Daniel Rockmore set out to determine whether the Court's decisions reflect a trend toward more "negative" than "positive" words. Examples of negative words included such terms as "flawed" and "unfounded"; positive words included such terms as "sincerely" and "convincing."[68] They found a "highly significant" correlation between time and the use of negative words in opinions—evidence that these opinions have grown harsher over time. (Reporting on the study for the *New York Times,* Adam Liptak observed that the opinions had gotten "grumpier.")[69]

As the authors of the study recognize, increased grumpiness on the Court could result from a multitude of factors, including the growing number of dissenting opinions or general changes in language usage over time. Yet to the extent that overconfidence can be discerned in one's language, the increasingly bitter tone of Court opinions suggests that the justices are becoming more strident in their views. Whereas counterarguments in years past may have generated respectful responses from the justices, they are increasingly likely nowadays to trigger negative words, or flat condemnation. This is another sign of overconfidence in action.

• • •

By giving teeth to the justices' partisan biases, overconfidence harms our society in at least two important ways.

First, overconfident judges write opinions full of overconfident language, and those expressions of certitude are not harmless embellishments. They exacerbate partisanship among the public that consumes the Court's decisions, deepening the polarization that threatens the Court's legitimacy and our democracy.

Recall *Brnovich v. Democratic National Committee,* the landmark case in 2021 that upheld a pair of Arizona voting restrictions and weakened the Voting Rights Act. The legal question in the case was actually surprisingly tricky. The relevant text of the act prohibits states from enacting voting procedures that "result in" abridgment of the right to vote on account of race. Arizona's restrictions did exactly that. Yet the act also makes clear that its drafters intended it to curb efforts by states to dilute the power of minority voters by, for example, using racially gerrymandered legislative districts.[70] This more specific concern is not obviously implicated by rules like Arizona's facially neutral rule against out-of-precinct voting.

Yet far from treating the issue as a difficult one on which reasonable people could differ, both the majority and dissenting opinions expressed their views in remarkably arrogant language. Alito, writing for the majority, argued that the Court's opinion "follows directly from" what the Voting Rights Act "commands," whereas the dissenting opinion "strains mightily to obscure" its "radical project" of "rewrit[ing] the text" of the law. Kagan dissented in language just as heated. The majority opinion, she wrote, "inhabits a law-free zone" and is founded on a "list of mostly made-up factors, at odds with the [Voting Rights Act] itself."[71]

It is understandable that Alito and Kagan would use such unforgiving language in such a high-profile conflict. Supreme Court justices are lawyers, and lawyers like to argue. They especially like to win, even at the price of ugliness. But vicious arguments in dueling Supreme Court opinions are bare for all the public to see, and they carry an enormous cost. Rather than persuading those who hold opposing views to change their minds (or at least to credit the other side's good faith), overconfident language drives a wedge between us.

Suppose you support the more protective interpretation of the Voting Rights Act. When Justice Alito issues an opinion that describes your view as a "radical project" and accuses you of "rewriting" the law, are you more or less likely to believe that the majority has engaged in a good-faith effort to decide the case? And if you believe in the narrower interpretation of the act, is Justice Kagan's scathing complaint that your opinion "inhabits a law-free zone" likely to engender a sense of reasonable disagreement?

Of course not. In both cases, the justices' overconfident language encourages the reader to believe that the opposing side is being willfully deceptive, dumb, or perhaps both. Sensing duplicity in our opponents, we dig into our positions still further. It is no surprise that studies of motivated reasoning have found that pronouncements of certitude, like those common at the Court, deepen conflicts between groups.[72] Far from helping unite a badly divided American public, overconfident Supreme Court opinions drive us further apart.

Even worse, overconfidence bias leads to judicial mistakes with incredibly harmful consequences. When faced with monumental cases that affect our society, a humble Court might worry about what happens if it gets a legal question wrong. Such a court might take steps to soften the blow of its rulings.

An overconfident Court ignores the possibility of error and marches headlong into fateful mistakes. One shudders at Chief Justice Roger Taney's misguided belief that the Court's *Dred Scott* ruling—which confidently asserted that slaves were "property" under the Due Process Clause and could never become U.S. citizens—would somehow end the national conflict over slavery and avert a civil war.

For a more recent example, consider the Court's decision in *Shelby County v. Holder*. In a five-to-four decision along partisan lines, the Court invalidated a crucial provision of the Voting Rights Act even though the law passed by a vote of ninety-eight to zero. The unanimous, bipartisan support for the law among our nation's elected officials, reached after numerous hearings and extensive deliberation, meant nothing to the Court. In an incredible display of overconfidence, Justice Scalia even insinuated that widespread support among elected officials from both parties was a reason the Court should strike the law down. "You know," Scalia injected during oral argument, "the Israeli Supreme Court, the Sanhedrin, used to have a rule that if the death penalty was pronounced unanimously, it was invalid because there must be something wrong there."[73] (The Talmud explains that the real reason for this rule was not to confer additional power upon the Sanhedrin, but to force the body to engage in meaningful deliberation—a humility-forcing measure quite the opposite of Scalia's approach.)[74]

The greatest trick the Supreme Court ever pulled is convincing the American people that it knows all the answers. It's a trick that has done our society immense harm, which continues to this day. Overconfidence is how the Court pulled it off.

We've seen now how overconfidence bias serves as a gateway to other psychological traps at the Court, most notably partisan motivated reasoning. This puts us in a position to return to the Court as it operated in two earlier periods in our history: during the chief justiceship of John Marshall and in the aftermath of the New Deal.

I argued in chapter 2 that the Court was trusted and popular during both eras, even though it was blatantly partisan. How did it manage this? In both periods, the Court was humble—or, at least, substantially more humble than the Court today. Without the amplifying effects of overconfidence, partisanship did not threaten its legitimacy.

Let's start with the Court under Chief Justice Marshall. Just as Federalist president John Adams had hoped, the Marshall Court displayed a strong partisan instinct in supporting a powerful national government, both by broadly construing congressional power and by asserting final judicial authority over state courts. It did so even while the national political climate favored Jeffersonian Republicans and their states' rights agenda. One might expect the Court to have lost popularity as a result. Instead, it grew markedly in stature, cementing its role as a coequal branch of government.

How did the Supreme Court maintain its legitimacy despite partisan leanings that went against the popular majority? In fairness, one piece of the explanation is luck. The Court's public image would have surely suffered, for example, had states rights' advocates been able to put up a unified resistance. As Harvard professor Michael Klarman points out, the Court issued rulings "distinctly unpopular in a majority of the states in the Union" between 1809 and 1824. Yet these states failed to "coordinate their opposition to the Court," viewing their defeats as one-off wrongs rather than cause for a common front.[75] The Court's public stature also benefited from the failure of a Republican effort to impeach Associate Justice Samuel Chase in 1805. (The effort failed only after six Republican senators defected and voted to acquit Chase in order to settle an unrelated squabble with Republican Speaker of the House John Randolph.) Finally, the Court benefited from South Carolina's ill-conceived effort to nullify a federal tariff in late 1832. Before the nullification attempt, President Andrew Jackson was on the verge of leaving unenforced an important Supreme Court decision concerning a federal treaty with the Cherokee tribe—an act that would have surely tarnished the Court's public image. Nullification shifted the political environment, forcing Jackson to align himself with the

Court and declare it the final arbiter of the Constitution, in order to preserve the federal government's revenue.[76]

Luck thus played a meaningful role in the Marshall Court's national popularity. But another factor was critical as well: Marshall's brilliant humility. He consistently expanded the authority of the national government through opinions that humbly recognized the limits of the Court's own power. He would often announce a broad, federalist constitutional principle in an opinion that actually sided with the Court's political opponents on the narrow dispute at hand. The classic example is *Marbury v. Madison,* which involved a controversy over one of President Adams's midnight judges. In the waning moments of his presidency, Adams had appointed William Marbury to be a justice of the peace in the District of Columbia. But Adams left office before officials could formally deliver Marbury his commission. When Jefferson took office, he refused to do so. Marbury sued, demanding his commission.

Marshall's opinion for the Court in *Marbury v. Madison* is famous for announcing the principle of judicial review: "It is emphatically the duty of the [Supreme Court] to say what the law is."[77] Without this monumental power, today's Court would hold a tiny fraction of its influence. Yet what's less known about *Marbury* is that the ruling ultimately sided with the Jefferson administration on the specific controversy at issue, declaring that the Court lacked the power to grant Marbury's requested relief. It was humility, in other words, that led Marshall to recognize how Jefferson would have never followed an order to deliver Marbury's midnight commission—and to rule in Jefferson's favor. And it was tactical brilliance for Marshall to do so in an opinion that staked out broad judicial power in the far more significant war over the Court's place in interpreting the Constitution. When Jefferson ultimately agreed with the Court's authority on the narrow issue of Marbury's commission, he also implicitly accepted the far larger claim of judicial review.

Marshall took a similar approach in another major case called *Cohens v. Virginia*.[78] The battle in the *Cohens* case was over Virginia's power to prosecute a pair of brothers who had sold lottery tickets in violation of Virginia law. In their defense, the Cohen brothers pointed to a federal statute authorizing them to sell the tickets, which they claimed overrode Virginia's contrary law under the Supremacy Clause. The Virginia Supreme Court ruled against the Cohens, who then sought relief from the U.S. Supreme Court.

Virginia argued that the Supreme Court did not have the power to decide the case because state sovereignty insulated Virginia judicial rulings from Supreme Court review. If this argument was accepted, state courts would be free to issue constitutional interpretations that directly conflicted with rulings issued by the U.S. Supreme Court, and that Court would be powerless to do anything about it. Yet again, Marshall humbly conceded the narrow case at hand to his political opponents, ruling in *Cohens* that Virginia could indeed prosecute the brothers because the federal statute was never meant to apply in Virginia in the first place. But in the process, Marshall resolved the larger question in favor of broad federal power, declaring that the Supreme Court can review state court interpretations of federal law. Yet again, the Marshall Court was able to enshrine broad federalist principles without seeming to foist them on its political enemies.

The New Deal Supreme Court employed a different kind of humility to preserve its public legitimacy. Recall that for decades in the late nineteenth and early twentieth centuries, a conservative majority on the Court had imposed its laissez-faire economic philosophy on the American people despite an uncertain constitutional warrant. The *Lochner* case, discussed in chapter 2, is a prime example. When elected officials in New York set a sixty-hour maximum work week to protect the health of bakers, the Court overrode their judgment on the ground that the law interfered with the "liberty" of bakers and their employers to enter into contracts.

The Fourteenth Amendment does guarantee us "liberty," and the term plausibly encompasses the freedom to enter into employment contracts. But this doesn't fully answer the constitutional question. The Fourteenth Amendment goes on to state that government may deprive us of our liberty interests so long as it provides "due process of law." Did New York's maximum hours regulation satisfy or transgress *that* vague limit? Legal scholars have filled bookshelves debating the issue.[79] For now it is enough to observe that the question has no easy answer.

How then should the Court decide such cases? *Lochner* itself exemplified the mindset of an overconfident Court. Writing for a five-member majority, Justice Rufus Peckham began by recognizing the general power of states to enact laws to protect the "safety, health, morals, and general welfare of the public."[80] So far so good. Yet when it came to deciding whether a given state law fit within that power, Peckham continued, "[T]hat question must be answered by the Court." On that front, the majority was exceptionally self-assured—and just as ungenerous to the judgment of New York's elected lawmakers.

New York's first argument was that its maximum hours regulation should be upheld because it was a reasonable *labor law*—that is, it was an effort to grant bakery employees a measure of bargaining power over the conditions of their employment. The majority's arrogant answer? "There is no reasonable ground for interfering with the [liberty of contract], by determining [bakers' maximum] hours of labor." Indeed, the Court found the labor protection defense so "simple" that it could be "dismissed in a few words."[81]

New York's second argument was that the law was a reasonable *public health law* aimed at protecting bakers from the health effects of working under difficult conditions. As Justice John Marshall Harlan pointed out in his dissent, there was evidence that "the constant inhaling of flour dust causes inflammation of the lungs," and that "the average [life expectancy] of a baker is below that of other workmen; they seldom live over their fiftieth year." Yet again, the Court disagreed with remarkable certitude: "There is, in our judgment, no reasonable foundation for holding this to be . . . appropriate as a health law to safeguard [bakers]." The law's public health justification, like the labor law justification, was dismissed out of hand.[82]

When it eventually overruled *Lochner* and the hyperconfident attitude it embodied, the New Deal Court took a more modest approach. Rather than boldly pronouncing its belief that elected officials lacked "reasonable" grounds for thinking a particular law might protect members of the public, the Court owned up to its uncertainty. And after acknowledging the limits of its knowledge, the Court deferred to the judgment of those same democratically accountable lawmakers.

The case of *West Coast Hotel v. Parrish* exemplified this new, intellectually honest approach.[83] The dispute arose when the West Coast Hotel refused to pay its employee, Elsie Parrish, the minimum wage required under Washington state law. The hotel argued that the minimum wage requirement transgressed the same "liberty of contract" recognized in *Lochner*. There was good reason to think that the hotel would prevail: the Court had struck down a D.C. minimum wage law just fourteen years earlier on that precise basis. But in *West Coast Hotel,* Justice Owen Roberts changed his vote. This change was critical not just because it allowed states to enact minimum wage laws but because it represented the arrival of a far humbler approach to judicial review.

Writing for the Court, Chief Justice Charles Evans Hughes started by recognizing the genuine difficulty of the legal question. On one hand, he noted, the Court had invalidated a similar D.C. minimum wage law in an opinion characterized by great "earnestness and vigor." Yet the Washington legislature offered strong opposing arguments. What to do? Unlike the *Lochner* Court, which simply injected its *own* preferences under the guise of constitutional law, the Court in

West Coast Hotel trusted the views of *others*. "Even if the wisdom of the policy be regarded as debatable and its effects uncertain," the Court wrote, "still the Legislature is entitled to its judgment."[84]

More than anything else, it is this humble approach—deferring to the legislature and thus presuming the constitutionality of a challenged law—that defined the New Deal Court. The Court used it not only to decide challenges to state economic regulations but also in cases involving congressional power. It thus deferred to Congress's judgment to enact federal labor law, the Social Security Act, and countless other New Deal programs. In one landmark case upholding a federal milk regulation, the Court echoed the humble sentiments pronounced in *West Coast Hotel*. "The existence of facts supporting [Congress's] judgment is to be presumed," the Court wrote. And because legislative decisions are "for Congress" to make, "the [contrary] finding of a court" cannot be "substituted for it."[85]

These outcomes were popular, to be sure, as they matched the public's demand for greater economic regulation after the Great Depression. But just as vital was the Court's new style of reasoning. No longer would it cavalierly override the judgment of elected officials like a superlegislature. Instead, it would recognize the limits of its knowledge, leaving debates over the law in the hands of the people and their elected officials. Unlike the Court's *Lochner* era decisions to strike down state and federal economic regulations, which left the people essentially powerless to enact minimum wage and other important laws, the New Deal Court's deferential approach left losers with more meaningful options. The businesses that lost these major economic cases still had the power to take their arguments back to elected officials and push for regulatory compromises. Often that is exactly what happened, as for instance when Congress modified federal labor law in response to industry concerns.[86]

Reflecting on this revolution in the Court's approach to judicial review, historian Robert McCloskey described the New Deal Court as "overwhelmed by considerations of judicial modesty."[87] One of that Court's giants, Justice Robert Jackson, went so far as to admit that "we are not final because we are infallible, . . . we are infallible only because we are final."[88] Such open recognition of the justices' imperfect judgment went a long way toward bolstering the New Deal Court's credibility.

History, however, did not end in the 1940s. The passage of time brought new challenges, although they stemmed from old problems. The Court's more deferential posture could not—and would not—last.

4

The Times They Were a Changin'

For a time it appeared that the New Deal Court had reached a lasting constitutional settlement. Gone were the days of the *Lochner* era in which the Court imposed its own social policy preferences under the pretense of law. After 1937, a more restrained approach would govern: the Court would defer to the judgment of elected lawmakers and leave contests over economic and social policy to the democratic process. Aware of the limits of judicial expertise, the Court would stay in its own lane.

This was a paradigm shift in American constitutional law. In the six years before Justice Owen Roberts changed his vote in *West Coast Hotel,* for example, the Court invalidated all or part of a federal law in 29 cases—or 4.8 per year. In the six years after that decision, it struck down *zero*.[1]

The New Deal and the national economic mobilization occasioned by World War II eventually ended the Great Depression. Yet the America that emerged in its wake was far from well. Nowhere was this truer than in the South. For decades, white majorities had ignored the post–Civil War Reconstruction amendments and subjected Black Americans to violence, vote denial, segregation, and other forms of invidious discrimination. As debates over economic regulation subsided, debates over America's legacy of racial injustice grew sharper. Those debates proved deeply problematic for the Court's new philosophy of deference to elected officials.

Sometimes, lawmakers and the majorities who elect them do terrible things.

Texas has a long history of racially motivated voter suppression. After the Fifteenth Amendment was ratified, in 1870, to forbid the denial of the right to vote on account of race, a Black pastor named George Brooks began registering Black voters in Millican, Texas.[2] Local whites reacted with anger, and the Ku Klux Klan mobilized against Brooks and his parishioners. It's unclear how the shooting started, but the result was a massacre. Twenty-five Black citizens were murdered.[3] Not a single white person was hurt.[4]

Violence was just the beginning. Racist Texas officials gerrymandered district maps and closed down polling precincts to dilute and obstruct Black voters' participation. They enacted poll taxes and literacy tests aimed to block Black citizens from casting ballots. And to prevent Black voters from holding any influence over the state's dominant political party, lawmakers granted the Democratic Party itself the power to determine who could vote in primary elections. To no one's surprise, the Texas Democratic Party quickly declared that only party members could vote in its primaries—and that only "*white citizens* of the State of Texas [were] eligible [for] membership."[5]

The National Association for the Advancement of Colored People (NAACP) filed suit to challenge Texas's all-white primary. In every way but one, the case was straightforward. The Fourteenth Amendment guaranteed Black citizens "equal protection of the laws," and the Fifteenth expressly prohibited denial of the right to vote "on account of race." Forbidding Black voters to participate in primary elections ran afoul of both. The harder question was who was doing the forbidding. Both constitutional amendments apply on their face only to states: "No *State,*" they say, shall deny equal protection or the right to vote on account of race. So Texas argued that its all-white primary system was permissible because the Democratic Party, not the state, was the one engaging in racial discrimination. This was the surprisingly difficult legal question that the Supreme Court confronted in 1944 in the case of *Smith v. Allwright.*

Parties to landmark Supreme Court cases don't usually fall off the face of the earth, but Lloyd Gaines did. Then twenty-eight, Gaines was staying at the Alpha Phi Alpha fraternity house in Chicago in the spring of 1939 when he told a door attendant he was leaving to buy postage stamps. That was the last time anyone saw him.[6]

Family members were initially untroubled by his disappearance. In 1940, Gaines's older brother told a reporter that "he always kept kind of to himself, so we figured he knew what he was doing and whatever he did was his own business." Gaines had always been bright and independent: he finished first in his high school class before earning a degree from Lincoln University, an all-Black liberal arts school in Jefferson City, Missouri. But as the months went on with no sign of contact, worries of foul play grew. Rumors circulated that Gaines had been kidnapped by white supremacists, murdered, and buried in an unknown place. Others speculated that he had moved to Mexico City. Decades later, when the NAACP demanded that the Federal Bureau of Investigation (FBI) finally investigate his disappearance, Gaines's great-niece lamented in a newspaper interview, "When you think of those old photos of lynchings and burned bodies, who wouldn't want to think that he lived a full life in Mexico?"[7]

At a time when Black Americans were routinely in danger of being kidnapped and attacked, Lloyd Gaines would have been a conspicuous target. That's because he was the named plaintiff in the headline-grabbing Supreme Court case of *Gaines v. Canada.*

The dispute arose when Gaines applied for admission to the University of Missouri Law School. Everyone, including university officials, agreed that he deserved to be admitted based on his academic credentials. Yet the university rejected Gaines because he was Black.

Under the legal doctrine of separate but equal, state law required the university's board of curators to establish an all-Black law school at Lincoln University, where Gaines had gone to college. Yet no such school had been created, in large part because the law vested the board with discretion to establish the school whenever "necessary and practicable." There was no sign the board would ever find those conditions satisfied. So Missouri offered to pay Gaines's tuition if he would leave the state to attend law school somewhere else.

With the backing of the NAACP and powerhouse lawyer Thurgood Marshall, Gaines sued. Missouri, the NAACP argued, should either admit Gaines to its flagship law school at the University of Missouri or establish an equal law school for Black students at Lincoln University. Missouri responded that its willingness to pay for Gaines's out-of-state tuition satisfied the requirement of separate but equal. The case reached the Supreme Court in 1938. Gaines disappeared the next year.

Dr. Charles Buxton had just become the chair of the Yale School of Medicine's Department of Obstetrics and Gynecology when he made an unwelcome discovery. Buxton had previously maintained an active practice in New York, where he prescribed married women contraception for reasons of health and family planning. He expected his practice to continue after he moved to Connecticut. Certainly the need existed: one couple sought a prescription for contraception after three prior pregnancies ended due to multiple congenital abnormalities; another requested contraception to save the life of a woman whose first pregnancy had resulted in partial paralysis.[8] Connecticut law, however, made a criminal of "any person who assists" another in the use of "any drug, medicinal article or instrument for the purpose of preventing conception."[9] Buxton faced up to a year in prison for assisting these patients.

Buxton sued. Joined by the director of the Connecticut chapter of Planned Parenthood, Estelle Griswold, Buxton and his lawyers argued that Connecticut's law violated a constitutional right belonging to his patients. But *which* right? There is, of course, no "contraception clause" in the Constitution. And the Court had recently overruled *Lochner*'s expansive interpretation of the "liberty" protected under the Due Process Clause. This was the legal puzzle before the Court in the landmark case of *Griswold v. Connecticut.*

Texas's invidious discrimination against Black voters, Missouri's separate and unequal educational facilities, and Connecticut's severe intrusion on private, medical decisions all demanded a new paradigm from the Supreme Court. In these cases and many others, what the justices needed was a judicial approach fit for declaring the challenged state laws incompatible with the one-and-only meaning of the Constitution. What the justices had inherited from the New Deal settlement, however, was an approach singularly unfit for the task. The New Deal judicial philosophy called on the Court to defer to the very elected officials whose odious judgment now needed overturning. Racist public officials were particularly keen to capitalize on the Court's deferential approach. One group of lawmakers sought to defend a policy of racial segregation on the legal ground that "every possible presumption" ought to be made "in favor of the validity of a statute"—precisely the theory of deference employed in *West Coast Hotel.*[10]

This tension represents the fundamental challenge that faced the Supreme Court in the post–New Deal era. On the one hand, the Civil Rights movement underscored the pressing need for the Court to intervene against racist majorities. On the other hand, the Court could not declare the challenged laws inconsistent with the Constitution while remaining true to the principle of legislative deference. McCloskey sums up the puzzle this way: "In the years after 1937 . . . the case for judicial modesty was not easy to refute. But neither was it easy to dismiss the argument that civil rights are the essence of democratic government."[11]

The Court ultimately decided it was necessary to intervene. At first it did so haltingly, invalidating laws on a case-by-case basis without suggesting a unifying judicial philosophy. In *Smith v. Allwright,* for example, it recognized that political parties are typically private organizations whose membership rolls are "no concern of a state." It had unanimously upheld Texas's all-white primary on just that basis less than a decade earlier.[12] Yet the Court reversed course in *Smith,* ruling eight to one that where political party membership is a qualification for "voting in a primary . . . the state makes the action of the party the action of the state."[13] In *Gaines v. Canada,* the Court accepted the repulsive premise that "separate but equal" facilities could satisfy the Fourteenth Amendment Equal Protection Clause. Yet it found Missouri's offer to ship Lloyd Gaines to an out-of-state law school impermissible because it was *unequal.* Forcing him to "go outside the State to obtain [a legal education] is a denial of equality of legal right," the Court explained, "and the provision for the payment of tuition fees in another State does not remove the discrimination."[14]

The Court's newfound willingness to second-guess the judgment of elected officials did not go unnoticed. The most outspoken critic among the justices was Felix Frankfurter, FDR's old confidant and the leading proponent of the New Deal Court's judicial restraint. In dissent after dissent, Frankfurter chastised his colleagues for their hypocrisy. The Court is "not free to act as though we were a superlegislature," Frankfurter declared. "Judicial self-restraint is equally necessary *whenever* an exercise of political or legislative power is challenged," regardless of whether it involves economic regulations or civil rights. And in the cases where it did strike down laws, Frankfurter continued, the Court had not put forward any consistent basis for doing so: "Such undefined destructive power was not conferred on this Court by the Constitution."[15]

For a Court that prided itself on the quality and consistency of its reasoning, this was a charge that stung. The justices (and legal academy) eventually responded by articulating what U.S. Court of Appeals judge J. Harvie Wilkinson III has decried as "cosmic constitutional theories . . . that purport to unlock the mysteries of our founding document much as . . . Einstein attempted to explain the universe."[16] A full recounting of each of these theories and their variants would occupy multiple books. So here I will touch on four of them.

The first two theories, penumbra theory and political process theory, had some early success but then fell into disuse. The other two, originalism and living constitutionalism, have achieved lasting prominence. Both theories give the Court a tool for declaring legislative acts inconsistent with the Constitution's one-and-only meaning. That is the good news. But it's also the bad news. For both theories have also contributed significantly to the emergence of our overconfident Court.

The Court's early forays at justifying a more interventionist approach did not go smoothly. One constitutional theory was advanced by Justice William Douglas in *Griswold v. Connecticut,* the case that invalidated criminal bans on contraception. Douglas began his opinion by recognizing the crux of the problem. How could the Court deem the freedom to use contraception a "liberty" protected against state regulation under the Fourteenth Amendment after it had repudiated *Lochner* for doing the exact same thing with respect to the freedom of contract?

Douglas's answer was not to return to *Lochner* as "our guide." Instead, the Court would discover the Constitution's meaning by looking elsewhere. Where, exactly? To the Constitution's "penumbras"—or the outer margins of constitutional rights formed by "emanations" from specific constitutional guarantees. On this approach, it was inconsequential that the right to contraception could not be located in the Constitution in so many words. The First Amendment right to free speech, Douglas argued, implies a penumbral right of free association, which in turn implies another penumbral zone of personal privacy. The Third Amendment right against the quartering of soldiers in one's home "is another face of that privacy." The Fourth Amendment's right to be free from unreasonable searches and the Fifth Amendment protection from self-incrimination also have shadowy areas from which emanate a general sense of privacy. If you add up all of these penumbras and shadowy areas, Douglas concluded, they create a general "zone of privacy" that encompasses the right to use contraception.[17]

Douglas's penumbral approach drew immediate fire from virtually all quarters. "I like my privacy as well as the next one," Douglas's colleague Justice Black wrote in dissent, but "I get nowhere in this case by talk about . . . emanation from one or more constitutional provisions."[18] A *Michigan Law Review* article criticized Douglas's penumbral theory as "ambiguous and uncertain in its use of the specifics of the Bill of Rights."[19] Yale Law School dean Harry Wellington was more direct: "penumbras" and "zones of privacy" were an "unfortunate invention."[20] The invention did not last. In the years after *Griswold,* Douglas's penumbral theory of constitutional interpretation fell by the wayside.

A second grand theory took a different approach. Rather than relying on contested interpretations of the Constitution's substantive provisions (whether rooted in penumbras or elsewhere), Professor John Hart Ely argued that the Court should focus on the process through which laws are enacted. On that view, the Court should typically do what the New Deal Court promised: defer to legislatures. "In a representative democracy," Ely wrote, "value determinations are to be made by our elected representatives." Yet he also recognized that sometimes our representative democracy is "systematically malfunctioning," to the point that the political process is "undeserving of trust." In those cases—where the *process* of democratic lawmaking is broken—the Court should flip its presumption of constitutionality and intervene aggressively. Ely had in mind two particular kinds of process malfunctions: when those who hold power choke off access to the channels of political change (such as through restrictions on voting and free speech) and when laws are rooted in prejudice against minority groups.[21]

There is much to commend Ely's process approach. Among other things, it offers a powerful justification for vigorously protecting free speech, voting rights, and the right of Black Americans to be free from discrimination. (It fares less well with Connecticut's ban on contraception.)

Yet political process theory also incited strong critiques from across the political spectrum. Judge Robert Bork, a renowned conservative, complained that the theory lacked any textual basis in the Constitution.[22] Progressive scholars like Laurence Tribe and Bruce Ackerman raised different problems. Looking at the Constitution's most important guarantees—including the First Amendment rights to free speech and religious freedom and the Thirteenth Amendment's prohibition against slavery—Tribe wondered how Ely could claim "that the Constitution is or should be predominantly concerned with process and not substance."[23] Ackerman argued that in trying to apply process theory, judges would necessarily make just the kind of substantive judgments the theory disclaimed. How, after all, are judges to decide which groups suffer sufficient "prejudice" to warrant special protections from the Court without a particular, substantive view of society and its ills?[24] In the hands of a liberal Court, political process theory might identify racial minorities as the victims of societal prejudice who deserve judicial protection. A conservative Court, however, might view white Christians as the target of social opprobrium.[25] In the 1980s, these critiques took hold at the Court. It has not relied on process theory since.

A third theory showed more staying power. Originalism is an umbrella term covering multiple theories that share two key precepts. First, the meaning of constitutional provisions is fixed at the time of enactment. Second, this fixed meaning constrains the permissible choice set for judges.[26] Not all originalists agree on which original meaning is fixed in time; some point to the meaning intended by the Constitution's framers, while others—presently the dominant group among originalists—believe that the relevant meaning is the one understood by the public. Either way, originalists believe the Supreme Court must decide cases in keeping with the relevant original meaning, however it is determined.

A number of justices have claimed to be originalists. Justice Scalia was easily the most famous, though the theory's earliest proponent on the Court was actually the (mostly) liberal Hugo Black.[27] Black's originalism was on full display in his dissenting opinion in *Griswold.* "I realize," Black wrote, "that many good and able men have eloquently spoken and written . . . about the duty of this Court to keep the Constitution in tune with the times. . . . I must with all deference reject that philosophy." The founders, he continued, "knew the need for change and provided for it" via the Article V amendment process. "That method of change was good for our Fathers, and being somewhat old fashioned, I must add it is good enough for me."[28]

Today, there are three self-professed originalists at the Court: Clarence Thomas, Neil Gorsuch, and Amy Coney Barrett. A fourth, Justice Brett Kavanaugh, described himself as an originalist during his confirmation hearings but has yet to show the same methodological commitment as the other three.

These justices subscribe to originalism for significant reasons. For one thing, it has a theoretically attractive claim to democratic legitimacy. By holding up the original public understanding of the Constitution's text as the ultimate arbiter of constitutional meaning, the Court ensures that the will of the people who ratified the Constitution governs, not the will of unelected judges. This ability to restrain judges was, in fact, its chief calling card.[29] As Black once argued, any other approach "would make of this Court's members a day-to-day constitutional convention."[30]

Originalism also avoids the conceptual difficulty of permitting the Constitution's meaning to change over time. Consider a clause like Article IV, Section 4, which provides that upon request by any state, the federal government must "protect" the state "against domestic Violence." Although we don't use the term "domestic violence" this way anymore, in its original understanding this clause encompassed local uprisings like Shays's Rebellion, a revolt in 1786 by farmers who were upset over Massachusetts' aggressive efforts to collect taxes. Yet if shifts in language can change the Constitution's meaning over time, does the clause now commit Congress to assist states in the elimination of violence among intimate partners? If you are inclined to answer "no," that is a sign that originalism possesses some intuitive force.

The theory's immense power at the Court was demonstrated by the case of *District of Columbia v. Heller* in 2008. Dick Heller was a special police officer who was licensed to carry a gun while at work. When he applied for a license to keep a handgun at home as well, D.C. officials refused. Heller sued, arguing that D.C.'s ban against home handgun possession violated the Second Amendment. The full amendment provides that "a well-regulated militia, being necessary to the security of a free state, the right of the people to keep and bear arms, shall not be infringed." In 1939, in a case called *United States v. Miller,* the Court had interpreted this amendment narrowly, to create a right to own firearms only with some "reasonable relationship to the preservation or efficiency of a well regulated militia."[31] But after an exhaustive dive into historical evidence, including the law in the states from the founding through the nineteenth century, five (conservative) justices voted in *Heller* to overrule *Miller*. Four (liberal) justices dissented, mustering equally exhaustive historical evidence to support *Miller*'s military-purpose interpretation of the amendment. Just like that, many public safety laws aimed at reducing gun violence were no longer enforceable.

Like originalism, living constitutionalism refers to a broad family of theories. The common strand of those theories is visible in the views of Justice William Brennan, who served on the Court from 1956 to 1990. In a speech given at Georgetown University in 1985, Brennan described his preferred approach to interpreting the Constitution. "Justices read the Constitution," Brennan observed, "in the only way we can: as Twentieth Century Americans. The ultimate question is what do the words of the text mean in our time."[32]

University of Chicago law professor David Strauss offers a leading description of one way the justices put living constitutionalism into practice. The document's text "does not always govern," Strauss explains; living constitutionalism allows the justices even to announce rules that are "inconsistent with the text."[33] This happens through a process of continuous judicial interpretation and gradual change known in legal circles as the "common law." Under it, the justices decide each controversy before them by relying in part on the Constitution's text but also significantly on precedent, or the rules announced in prior Supreme Court opinions. The Court is thus constrained by all that has come before, but that constraint is not absolute. In cases implicating novel problems, where precedent is unclear, the Court is free to rule in whatever way is "more fair or . . . more in keeping with good social policy."[34] In this way, Strauss suggests, the Court uses "common law processes . . . to adapt the Constitution to new circumstances."[35]

Living constitutionalism's virtues are apparent. Because the Constitution often speaks in vague and abstract terms (what, anyways, are the "liberties" that states may not deprive absent "due process of law"?), judges will invariably need to discern more specific rules from those majestic generalities. And when they do so, perhaps it is only sensible that they should keep our Constitution meaningful in modern times. The world we live in today is vastly different from the world our founders inhabited; a constitution that ignored that reality would quickly lose its credibility. This is what Benjamin Cardozo meant when he famously argued that the Constitution states "not rules for the passing hour, but principles for an expanding future."[36]

Living constitutionalism is also consistent with canonical cases in our national story. No acceptable theory of constitutional interpretation could suggest, for example, that *Brown v. Board of Education* was incorrectly decided. Living constitutionalism does not suffer from that problem. To living constitutionalists, it does not matter that at the time the Fourteenth Amendment was enacted, twenty-four of thirty-seven states in the union either permitted or required segregated public schools.[37] Maybe the Equal Protection Clause, as originally understood in 1868, didn't forbid racial segregation, but to the living constitutionalist that is no problem: it does so today.[38]

The Court has continued to update the Constitution in other contexts, too, though not always with the same consensus as in *Brown*.

One controversial recent example arose from the horrific case of Patrick Kennedy. Kennedy's stepdaughter, L. H., was eight years old when Kennedy called the police to report that she had been raped. When police arrived, they found injuries to L. H. too gruesome to describe—one forensic expert described them as "the most severe" he had ever seen in his career. Kennedy and L. H. maintained that she was attacked by "two neighborhood boys" who had then fled. Investigators quickly uncovered, though, that Kennedy himself had committed the crime.[39]

Louisiana prosecuted Kennedy, and a jury unanimously determined that he should be sentenced to death. In 2008, in the case of *Kennedy v. Louisiana,* the Court overturned this sentence, holding on a five-to-four vote that "a death sentence for one who raped but did not kill a child . . . is unconstitutional."[40] The Court's reasoning exemplified living constitutionalism. The problem with Kennedy's death sentence, the Court explained, was not that the original understanding of the Eighth Amendment's prohibition against "cruel and unusual punishment" barred it. (Indeed, in the eighteenth century, execution was "the standard penalty for all serious crimes.")[41] The Court held instead that the Eighth Amendment's meaning should be determined in accordance with "evolving standards of decency."[42] And because five justices believed that those evolving standards were inconsistent with executing Kennedy, the Court remanded his case for the state to impose a different sentence.

Both originalism and living constitutionalism set out to give the justices a legal theory powerful enough to override the judgment of elected lawmakers. People of every political affiliation can easily find examples of cases in which they approve of the Court's having done this. Conservatives may be enthusiastic about decisions like *Heller;* liberals may be equally enthusiastic about *Obergefell v. Hodges,* which overturned many states' prohibitions against same-sex marriage. And all Americans should celebrate rulings like *Brown* and the civil rights victories that followed.

But no matter where you fall on the political spectrum, it is important to recognize that these favorable judicial outcomes also come with costs. Grand theories like originalism and living constitutionalism empower the justices to announce singular answers to enormously difficult questions of law. The result is a legal culture in which the justices rarely own up to uncertainty or admit when both sides in a dispute have credible arguments. Instead, the justices act as though any complexity or ambiguity can be resolved with the right lawyerly tool, whether law office history (as for originalism) or judicial efforts to apply precedent in accordance with society's evolving values (as for living constitutionalism).

In setting the justices down this path, both interpretive theories have imbued the Court with great confidence. Far from the New Deal era's humility, today's justices are emboldened by high theory to believe they have the capacity to discover singular constitutional meanings—and solutions to society's deepest disagreements. But since the legal questions they confront seldom lend themselves to simple answers, partisan motivated reasoning seeps inevitably into the justices' analysis. After applying their favored interpretive theories, what the justices too often discover is their own preferences.

For living constitutionalists, this danger is plain to see. Convinced they have both the capacity and the duty to update the Constitution to respond to modern problems, living constitutionalists face subconscious pressure to focus on the problems that lie closest to their own political orientations. For originalists, the danger lies further beneath the surface. If the original meaning of disputed constitutional provisions were always clear, the theory might deliver on its promise of democratic legitimacy and constraint. The problem is that the text and historical evidence are often deeply uncertain. Many leading originalist academics, to their credit, now freely admit this.[43] Yet the originalist justices themselves do not acknowledge this indeterminacy. Instead, they've forged ahead as though original meaning always yields obvious answers. Given the conflicting and ambiguous nature of historical evidence, the originalist justice's interpretation (like that of a living constitutionalist) is invariably influenced by partisan reasoning. *Heller* is a perfect example: both the majority and dissenting justices used originalist reasoning to reach opposing conclusions on a straight party-line vote.

Justices Brennan and Scalia were thus both correct about *something:* their critiques of the opposing theory. Originalism, Brennan argued, is "little more than arrogance cloaked as humility." As he explained, "It is arrogant to pretend that from our vantage we can gauge accurately the intent of the Framers on application of principle to specific, contemporary questions. All too often, sources of potential enlightenment such as records of the ratification debates provide sparse or ambiguous evidence."[44]

Yet living constitutionalism is guilty of the same vice. The living constitutionalist justice, Scalia once panned, "goes home for dinner and tells his wife what a wonderful day he had." He tells her "that it turns out 'the Constitution means exactly what I think it ought to mean!'" Touché.[45]

This, then, is the fundamental puzzle facing today's Supreme Court. Armed with their favorite grand constitutional theories, today's justices approach difficult legal questions with a dangerous degree of overconfidence in their ability to uncover correct answers. That, in turn, has intensified partisanship at the Court and widened stark divisions among the American people. The Court may continue down this path. But it is a path rife with danger.

At the same time, we cannot return to the New Deal Court's philosophy of judicial restraint. History is filled with stories of legislators—encouraged by the majorities who choose them—passing laws that inflict terrible suffering. A blindly deferential Court would abandon its crucial role in preventing these harms.

So what is the Court to do?

PART TWO
The Solution

• • •

If overconfidence lies at the root of the Supreme Court's legitimacy crisis, the first step to a solution must begin with overconfidence's natural antidote: humility.

Daniel Kahneman conveys the essence of humility in a simple observation. "True experts," Kahneman writes, "know the limits of their knowledge."[1] In the context of judging, humility is the ability to recognize—and admit—that in some of the major cases that divide our society, no amount of skillful legal analysis can uncover a clear answer. Judge Learned Hand, one of America's most renowned jurists, came close to capturing this virtue when he remarked that "the spirit of liberty is the spirit which is not too sure that it is right."[2]

A healthy degree of judicial self-doubt is a necessary start, but it can go only so far. A Supreme Court justice's defining responsibility is to decide cases no matter how hard they may be. Admitting the limits of one's knowledge does not satisfy that responsibility; it complicates it. What a humble Court needs is an approach that not only acknowledges the difficulty of many modern-day disputes but also resolves them—all despite the absence of any singular "right" answer under conventional interpretive theories.

This seems like a lot to ask. Fortunately, we can find helpful guidance without straining our imaginations. Human beings confront significant decisions all the time without a clear sense of which way to go. In these situations, the most useful approach is often to begin with a humble yet powerful admission: "I don't know." By acknowledging the limits of our knowledge, we open the door to decision-making approaches that are far wiser than lurching ahead blindly, ignorant of the risks of error.

The second half of this book describes how the Supreme Court has proceeded in precisely this manner in a surprising number of cases. Although it has not done so consistently—especially in a number of recent blockbuster rulings—the Court has admitted the genuine difficulty raised by the legal questions in several key decisions. Moreover, it has resolved many of these cases in a promising way: by ruling against the side with the best options for avoiding the harms of an adverse decision. By ensuring that the losing side has the ability to protect its interests in other ways, the Court minimizes the harm of what, given the difficulty of the case, it knows could be an erroneous ruling. I call this the *least harm principle* of judicial decision making.

As the American people grapple with a modern-day Court that has lost their trust, the least harm principle offers the justices a plausible path forward. In 1937, the New Deal Supreme Court redeemed its public image by embracing judicial restraint. Today's justices cannot do the same; history, and the Civil Rights movement in particular, shows the dangers of unflinching deference to elected officials and the majorities who choose them. The least harm principle offers a compelling alternative—one that the Court has used with some recent success. Key conservative justices such as John Roberts, Neil Gorsuch, and Brett Kavanaugh have written or joined major opinions relying on the least harm principle's core logic, even if not by name. They haven't done so enough; that much is clear from the Court's record-low levels of public trust. The Court's best chance to earn back that trust—and to continue serving as a guardrail for our democracy—is to embrace the principle more openly and consistently.

5

What We Do When We Don't Know

The human brain accounts for just 2 percent of the average adult's body weight, but it requires 20 percent of our oxygen.

Without it, bad things happen. When the brain's supply of oxygen is interrupted for just thirty seconds, a person loses consciousness. After three to four minutes, brain cells start dying. The death of those cells is catastrophic, as the brain struggles to send vital messages to every part of the body. At six minutes, the brain begins to suffer permanent damage.[1] In most people, complete brain death occurs after ten minutes. After being deprived of oxygen for just one cycle of the snooze button, all brain activity is irretrievably lost.[2]

On January 11, 1983, twenty-five-year-old Nancy Cruzan was driving home from her night shift at a Missouri cheese factory when she lost control of her car. The vehicle flipped violently off the road, hurling Nancy thirty-five feet to land facedown in a ditch. By the time paramedics arrived and began trying to resuscitate her, her brain had been without oxygen for twelve to fourteen minutes.[3]

Nancy spent the next three weeks in a coma. When she appeared miraculously to regain some consciousness, doctors implanted a permanent feeding and hydration tube in her stomach. But efforts at rehabilitation proved unsuccessful.

Nancy's family eventually moved her to Missouri's Mount Vernon State Hospital, where her condition entered a holding pattern. Doctors explained that she was "oblivious to her environment, except for reflexive responses to sound and perhaps painful stimuli." Her loss of brain cells was "irreversible, permanent, progressive, and ongoing." Her body was locked in a fetal position, the result of "irreversible muscular and tendon damage to all extremities." And although her breathing and heart activity were normal, she was unable to swallow food or water. Nancy was thus dependent on her feeding tube for nutrition. In short, she existed in what is known as a persistent vegetative state, a condition close to brain death in which a person exhibits minor motor reflexes but shows no signs of cognitive function.[4]

Nancy spent the next four years in this state. When it became clear that Nancy had no chance of regaining brain function, her parents, Joyce and Joe Cruzan, faced a wrenching decision. Nancy had executed no living will or other formal document to express her end-of-life wishes. She had, however, discussed the subject with a roommate a year before her accident. If she "couldn't be normal" and "do things for myself," she had suggested, she wouldn't "want to live."[5] Based on that conversation, and as the people who were closest to her and knew her best, Nancy's parents asked the hospital to terminate her artificial nutrition.

Hospital staff were horrified. "You just can't do that!" exclaimed the head nurse in Nancy's unit. The hospital's chief administrator, Don Lamkins, was equally upset. "Starve someone to death, we don't do that," he said. "That's beyond our ability to think."[6] The hospital informed the Cruzans that they would not withdraw Nancy's feeding tube without a court order.

So in 1987, Joyce and Joe Cruzan went to a county courthouse to ask for one. They had no way of knowing that it would take three more years —and a trip to the United States Supreme Court—to get their answer.

What should the Supreme Court do when answers to the difficult moral and legal questions before it are unknowable? Nancy Cruzan's case offers a powerful example. Given that her life hung in the balance, her case possessed grave moral stakes. The legal question at the heart of the dispute also lacked anything close to a clear answer.

Yet against all odds, the Supreme Court ultimately resolved Nancy's case in a way that would satisfy everyone—from Nancy's parents and proponents of the right to die, to the State and those who support its interest in preserving human life. How the Court managed to do so is a story that contains the seeds of a humble and promising approach to the hard cases that divide us.

Start with the moral stakes. The Court faced a question of profound significance: In the absence of clear instructions from Nancy herself, should Joyce and Joe Cruzan be allowed to terminate their daughter's life-sustaining treatment, ending her life? Or should the state's competing interest in the preservation of human life prevail?

It is impossible to overstate the interests on both sides. On one side was the tragic plight of Nancy Cruzan and her parents. By refusing her parents' request and forcibly feeding Nancy through an implanted tube without her consent, the state was arguably infringing on a liberty interest and personal choice of the utmost significance. Nancy's supporters called it the "right to die with dignity."

Yet interests of great weight were on the other side of the case, too. The State of Missouri has a genuine and important desire to preserve and protect the lives of its people. Few state objectives are more foundational. This interest is even more important in cases where, as with Nancy, the patient's end-of-life wishes are uncertain. Given the frequency with which legal guardians abuse incapacitated persons—consider the story of April Parks, who acquired guardianship over hundreds of vulnerable Nevada residents, only to kick them out of their homes and steal millions of dollars—Missouri had a substantial interest in continuing life-sustaining treatment absent a clear indication of the patient's intent.[7]

The right to die with dignity and the state's interest in protecting human life. These were the momentous—and incommensurable—stakes confronting the Supreme Court in *Cruzan v. Missouri*. There is no objective way to compare the two, no way to weigh them against each other on a common scale of justice. One could certainly advance arguments as to why the individual's right to die with dignity ought to be considered more (or less) important than the state's interest in protecting human life. But any such argument would ultimately rest on a deeply contested moral judgment. When asked which interest is paramount, the most honest objective answer is, "I don't know."

Cases like this are standard fare at the Supreme Court. Each year, the justices must resolve numerous conflicts where both sides advance interests of deep moral and societal significance. Recall *Kennedy v. Louisiana,* the case about the constitutionality of the death penalty for child rapist Patrick Kennedy. Some Americans—40 percent, according to a 2020 Gallup poll—believe it is wrong for the state to put *any* criminal to death.[8] Yet others, faced with the gruesome facts of Kennedy's crime, could quite reasonably find moral justice in his execution.

Or consider one of the many religious freedom disputes that implicate LGBTQ rights. In a case in 2021 called *Fulton v. City of Philadelphia,* city officials stopped referring children to a Catholic foster care agency after learning that it had a policy of refusing to certify same-sex couples as foster parents. The agency explained that it was happy to refer any such couple to one of dozens of other agencies that would serve them but that actively placing a child with such a couple would violate its core religious tenets. This case, too, implicated sincerely held interests of the highest order on both sides: a city's desire to protect LGBTQ persons from discrimination and a church's wish to follow its sincerely held religious beliefs.

What all of these cases have in common is that the two sides have conflicting reasonable claims to the moral high ground. Modern disputes at the Supreme Court, in other words, are often nothing like those of the Civil Rights Era. The cases of that period, such as *Brown v. Board of Education,* were amenable to single, unambiguously correct moral responses (although the underlying *legal* questions were often substantially more complicated). As a matter of moral judgment, *of course* government-sanctioned segregation of Black school children is inherently stigmatizing and abhorrent, and the desire of white parents to avoid having their children interact with children of color is of inferior significance by many orders of magnitude. No reasonable jurist or person could conclude otherwise. But that is not true for cases like Nancy Cruzan's. What the Court needs to decide a case like hers is a humbler approach, one that acknowledges—rather than papers over—the important interests on both sides.[9]

The Supreme Court does not only confront cases that are morally difficult. It also faces cases that are legally difficult. Here, too, *Cruzan* is a perfect example.

When Joyce and Joe Cruzan sought the court order that hospital employees demanded in order to terminate Nancy's treatment, their first stop was the Jasper County Circuit Court in rural southwest Missouri. A judge named Charles E. Teel Jr. was assigned to the case. Elected to the bench in 1980, Teel was a prominent community leader and a member of St. Philip's Episcopal Church.[10]

Judge Teel approached the case with care. After listening to exhaustive testimony concerning Nancy's condition, he agreed with medical experts that Nancy's brain loss was permanent and irreversible and that she would never recover cognitive function. He also concluded that while Nancy could live with a feeding and hydration tube for another thirty years, removing the tube would result in her death. Finally, he heard testimony from Athena Comer, Nancy's onetime roommate. Although Nancy had not executed a living will, Comer testified that

Nancy had once told her that if she were ever sick or injured, she would not wish to continue living unless she could do so "halfway normally."[11] On the basis of this evidence, Judge Teel deemed it more likely than not that Nancy would have wanted her feeding tube withdrawn. He ordered state hospital employees to comply with her parents' request.

The state appealed to the Missouri Supreme Court, which reversed Judge Teel's ruling. The Court did not disagree with any of the judge's factual findings. Its argument sounded instead in the legal register. In order to "cause the death of an incompetent" under one's guardianship, the Court held, a legal guardian must offer more than a minimal indication of the patient's likely wishes. Instead, the guardian must present "clear and convincing evidence." Because Nancy's single conversation with her roommate a year before her accident fell short of this high standard, the Missouri Supreme Court ruled in the state's favor. "In the face of uncertainty of Nancy's wishes," it explained, "the State's interest in preserving human life outweighs any rights invoked on Nancy's behalf to terminate treatment."[12]

Joyce and Joe Cruzan petitioned to the Supreme Court of the United States. With legal assistance from the American Civil Liberties Union, the Cruzans framed the question at the heart of their case in very specific terms. The Missouri Supreme Court's demand for "clear and convincing evidence" of Nancy's end-of-life wishes, they argued, violated the Fourteenth Amendment guarantee that "no state shall deprive any person" of "liberty" without "due process of law." This guarantee applied to Nancy's circumstance, the Cruzans contended, because the term *liberty* had long been interpreted to encompass a "constitutionally protected liberty interest in refusing unwanted medical treatment."[13] Nancy's wish to refuse artificial nutrition was just such a liberty, even if expressed by less than clear and convincing evidence. By ignoring Nancy's likely wishes, the Cruzans argued, Missouri was violating their daughter's constitutional right.

If the Cruzans were correct, the violation was a substantial one. By the time the Supreme Court heard oral argument in December 1989, Nancy had been lying in a Missouri hospital bed for nearly seven years, forcibly connected to a feeding tube against what her parents believed to be her own wishes.

Did Missouri violate Nancy Cruzan's constitutional rights when it refused to remove her feeding tube? I am a professor of constitutional law. I've studied and taught this case for years. Here's the truthful response: I don't know. Like so many high-profile disputes that make it to the Court, the legal question at the heart of the *Cruzan* case does not lend itself to a simple answer.

What it does have are strong arguments on both sides. Start with the legal argument in Nancy's favor. The text of the Fourteenth Amendment guarantees individuals a right to "liberty" that the state may not take away. In its most uncontroversial form, this term means freedom from unwanted physical restraint.[14] Imprisonment is the canonical example. But less absolute restraints also qualify. The Fourteenth Amendment right to liberty would be equally implicated if the government were to shackle your legs and wrists but let you live in your home.

Now tweak the intrusion a bit more: suppose the government surgically implants a permanent tube into your stomach and pumps in unwanted artificial nutrition. Doing so would deprive you of a particular form of liberty: your freedom to not have a tube forcibly lodged in your gut. This, of course, is what Joyce and Joe Cruzan argued Missouri was doing to their daughter. So the textual case for Nancy's position is quite strong.

But the argument on the other side is strong, too. The Fourteenth Amendment protects us from deprivations of our liberty "without due process of law." This means government *can* take away our liberty interests so long as it provides "due process." A great many judges and scholars have interpreted this to suggest only that the government must provide us certain procedures before taking away our liberty—such as the enactment of a valid law and a hearing before a neutral decision maker.[15] Missouri did that. It applied a general requirement that legal guardians must provide clear and convincing evidence of a patient's intent to withdraw treatment, and it afforded Joyce and Joe Cruzan a chance to satisfy this standard in a neutral hearing in its courts. Nancy Cruzan was also permitted under state law to express her end-of-life intentions in a living will or some other similar instrument. Sadly, at the age of just twenty-five when her accident occurred, she had not done so. What more process could the Cruzans have asked for?

This argument, however, invokes another response. When the Fourteenth Amendment prohibits governmental deprivations of "liberty" without "due process," the word "due" must also serve a function. It connotes a tight relationship between the kind of process the state must provide and the importance of the liberty at stake. For less important "liberties" (say, my freedom to purchase a forty-eight-ounce soda from McDonald's), scant process seems "due" before the government can deprive me of my right. If the legislature enacts a law banning super-sized sodas and then gives me a hearing at which I can assert my innocence before imposing a fine ("It was only water, your honor!"), that's all the process the Constitution affords me.

Now suppose the government enacts a law ordering all firstborn children to be taken from their parents and sent to a distant labor camp. This law implicates a liberty interest of a far higher order. So how much process is *due* before the state can begin removing children for this dystopian purpose? The answer must be more process than in the soda example: surely the government could not simply enact its law and then give me a hearing where I can contest my child's first-born status. Indeed, if the amount of "process" to which one is "due" is a function of the significance of the liberty interest the government seeks to infringe, then in theory some liberty interests—such as taking away one's child for forced labor—may be so great that *no amount* of process would suffice. And perhaps the same is true of an individual's interest in rejecting the insertion of a state-compelled feeding tube.

But also . . . arguably not. It's hard to ground our answer to the question in something outside our own moral intuitions. We can stare at the operative words in the Constitution's text—"deprive," "liberty," and "due process of law"—for ages, but they will not yield a decisive answer to how much evidence Missouri may demand before permitting legal guardians to terminate life-sustaining treatment for a patient in a persistent vegetative state.

This is ostensibly why the Court and scholars developed grand theories of constitutional law like originalism and living constitutionalism. When the legal effect of our founding document is not apparent on its face, these theories purport to give the Court the tools it needs to discover a clear answer. Yet the *Cruzan* case shows how these theories can be just as unilluminating as the Constitution itself.

Take originalism. The idea that eighteenth- and nineteenth-century Americans shared some clear consensus about the general contours of the "liberty" protected under the Due Process Clause—to say nothing of the more specific question whether that term encompassed the right to refuse a feeding tube—is fanciful. For starters, the medical technology was undeveloped. Surgically implanted feeding tubes were not used until the mid- to late nineteenth century and even then were largely unsuccessful.[16] There's also little reason to think the founding or Civil War–era public would have understood the vague Due Process right to "liberty" to signify anything about a state's demand for a particular quantum of evidence before removing a forced feeding tube that same public had no concept of in the first place. And even if ordinary eighteenth- and nineteenth-century persons *did* understand "liberty" to convey some position on an evidentiary standard, it's hardly likely they'd have agreed on what that standard was. In a nation inhabited by millions of people, each holding his or her own ideas about the meaning of abstract rights, how is a judge to know centuries later which is most consistent with the Constitution's original understanding?

But if the Due Process Clause's original meaning (and the original expectations of the founders or the general public) are woefully indeterminate, it is every bit as unrealistic to expect living constitutionalism to give us a clear answer. After all, if the theory's goal is to apply the Constitution's fundamental principles and precedent in accordance with evolving societal values, those values will frequently prove elusive. Whether a state should be allowed to require clear and convincing evidence before a patient can remove a feeding tube is a contested question. People of good faith occupy both sides of the debate. Thirty-one percent of Americans believe categorically that doctors should "always do everything possible to save the life of a patient in all circumstances," including a patient in a persistent vegetative state. Sixty-six percent believe there are at least "some circumstances" in which a patient should be allowed to die.[17] Yet even this seeming consensus is nowhere near specific enough to resolve the *Cruzan* dispute. Missouri itself agreed with the 66 percent who believe there are at least some circumstances in which a patient in a persistent vegetative state should be allowed to die. Under Missouri law, such a patient could have their feeding tube removed so long as "clear and convincing evidence" existed of that desire. The state's reason for this heightened showing was surely legitimate: its legislators wanted to avoid the wrongful termination of care in cases where a patient's legal guardians may possess some ulterior motive—for instance, if they stand to inherit from the patient's estate.

The real question for the living constitutionalist is if these conflicting and evolving societal views cast definitive light on the existence of a constitutional right to have one's feeding tube withdrawn even when one has made that desire known in a less than clear and convincing manner. That's an impossibly difficult question. And it shows why the honest answer to the legal conflict in *Cruzan* can be summed up in three words: "I don't know."

What should the Supreme Court do in the face of such legal uncertainty? Its typical response has been to issue decisive opinions that boldly pretend no legal difficulty exists. *Maybe in error, but never in doubt.*

Yet the Court has not been overconfident in every case. Sometimes it has acted with greater humility, recognizing the serious interests and legal arguments on both sides of a dispute. In doing so, it has opened the door to a more promising judicial approach. The Court's opinion in *Cruzan* offers a powerful example. In a fraught controversy, it found a way forward that acknowledged both sides' deeply held views—and that left both sides reason to respect the Court's ultimate decision.

"The question," Chief Justice Rehnquist wrote for the majority, is "whether the United States Constitution prohibits Missouri from choosing the rule of decision which it did": the requirement that Joyce and Joe Cruzan produce "clear and convincing evidence" of Nancy's wish to terminate treatment.[18] The Court's answer, unlike those the Court has given in so many other high-profile disputes, displayed admirable awareness of the case's moral and legal difficulty.

The Court began by frankly recognizing the significant moral stakes. "All agree," it observed, that this "is a perplexing question with unusually strong moral and ethical overtones." The Court went on that "in deciding a question of such magnitude and importance, it is the better part of wisdom not to attempt, by any general statement, to cover every possible phase of the subject."[19]

The Court then turned to the parties' legal arguments, explaining why they, too, were far from easy. With respect to the Cruzans' claim that Nancy had a constitutionally protected "liberty" interest in refusing unwanted medical treatment, it largely agreed. Such an interest, it recognized, "may be inferred from our prior decisions," including a case from 1905 recognizing the liberty interest in rejecting an unwanted vaccine.[20]

Yet a key complication distinguished Nancy's case from those earlier rulings: because of her medical condition, Nancy was unable to express her desire to refuse treatment. Such refusal could only be expressed by a surrogate on Nancy's behalf. Given that fact, the state had chosen to establish a "procedural safeguard to assure that the action of the surrogate conforms as best it may to the wishes expressed by the patient while competent." That safeguard was the state's requirement of clear and convincing evidence.[21]

Why did the state impose this safeguard? Here, too, the Court credited the parties' good-faith arguments. "Missouri relies on its interest in the protection and preservation of human life," it announced, "and there can be no gainsaying this interest." The Court also recognized Missouri's more specific interest in "guarding against potential abuses" in end-of-life decisions. The Court took pains to recognize that Nancy's surrogates, Joyce and Joe Cruzan, were "loving and caring parents." But it observed that "not all incompetent patients will have loved ones available to serve as surrogate decisionmakers." Moreover, it continued, "even where family members are present, there will, of course, be some unfortunate situations in which family members will not act to protect a patient."[22]

The Court was thus left with an inescapably difficult moral and legal puzzle. Nancy possessed a liberty interest in refusing unwanted treatment, yet the state possessed an interest in protecting patients against abusive or incorrect end-of-life decisions. Was the clear and convincing evidence standard a permissible way to navigate this tension?

The Court's ultimate answer was "yes," making the State of Missouri the nominal winner of the case. But what matters most is how it got to this outcome. Rather than try to locate the answer in the sparse text of the Due Process Clause, uncertain original public understandings, or conflicted evolving societal values, the Court asked a simple question: If it got this case wrong—a distinct possibility, given its legal difficulty—which side would be better able to protect itself from the resulting harm?

The Court started by assessing what would happen if it were to mistakenly allow Missouri to continue Nancy's artificial nutrition. "An erroneous decision not to terminate [Nancy's treatment] results in a maintenance of the *status quo,*" the Court explained. Such a "wrong decision" could "eventually be corrected or [have] its impact mitigated" in several ways. For instance, the Cruzans could discover "new evidence regarding [Nancy's] intent," thereby satisfying the clear and convincing evidence standard. Alternatively, public pressure could prevail upon the state legislature to enact "changes in the law," such as by lowering the required evidentiary showing or encouraging persons to specify their end-of-life wishes in advance. Other possibilities included "advancements in medical science" and "the unexpected death of the patient," either of which would also mitigate the harm of the Court's adverse ruling.[23]

The Court then contrasted those possibilities against what might happen if it issued "an erroneous decision to withdraw life-sustaining treatment." Such a mistake, it explained, would not be "susceptible of correction." Because death is "final and irrevocable," there would be no way to undo the harm that would result if it turned out the Court got the case wrong.[24]

So the Court ruled in the state's favor. Not because the justices thought the Constitution's text, history, or evolving values required it. Instead, they owned up humbly to the possibility that they might decide the case incorrectly and that such an error would inflict significant harm on the losing side. In light of this distressing fact, the Court did the most sensible thing it could. It chose the outcome in which the losing side would retain the greatest ability to avoid its harms. Unable to find a single, "right" answer to a dreadfully difficult question, the Court tried to do the least harm possible.

This approach, I want to argue, is both intuitive and good. It's also surprisingly common. In many situations, people faced with big decisions amid deep uncertainty have wisely chosen the option that will produce the least harm. Sometimes those choices have dire impacts for a few affected persons; at other times they have global consequences. In all events, though, an approach to uncertainty that aims to minimize harm can be far better than forging ahead in a fog of overconfidence.

For parents of young children, few things are scarier than watching a child struggle to breathe. Respiratory distress is accordingly one of the leading causes of pediatric emergency room visits. In some cases, the cause is straightforward and a proper treatment can be readily identified. A doctor armed with little more than a stethoscope can often detect pneumonia and prescribe antibiotics. A child with a history of asthma can be treated with an inhaler. The children aren't necessarily out of danger; they may need continuous monitoring. Yet the crucial questions facing the emergency room physician—the source of respiratory distress and how to treat it—are clear enough.

Sadly, this isn't always the case. Consider this tricky yet common clinical situation described in a medical textbook: "A four-year-old girl is brought to the Emergency Department following the acute onset of cough and increased work of breathing while at a friend's birthday party. What is your diagnosis? How would you evaluate and manage this patient?"[25]

The textbook mentions two primary possibilities. The first is "foreign body aspiration," the accidental inhalation of food or some other object into one's airway. The second is anaphylaxis triggered by a food allergy. Both conditions can be life threatening, and both are consistent with the primary symptom—difficulty breathing. Yet neither is always susceptible to easy diagnosis. Other symptoms that may indicate a particular diagnosis, such as a skin rash for a food allergy, are not always present. If the child has no reported history of food allergies and no one saw the child inhale an object, the result can be a difficult medical puzzle.

What should the emergency room physician do in the face of this uncertainty? One option would be to continue clinical assessments in the hope of uncovering the correct diagnosis. The doctor could order a chest X-ray to detect a foreign body and schedule skin and blood tests to identify a food allergy (assuming the physician knows all of the ingredients the child recently consumed).

But doing so carries risks. A child suffering from anaphylaxis can die in fifteen minutes. A child whose airway is completely obstructed could die quickly as well, though such patients usually present with different symptoms, such as a complete inability to speak and a bluish skin tone. Even a child with a partial obstruction could face severe complications, however, including pneumonia or a lung abscess.

Given all of this, the physician's choice is simple. Even though the actual cause of the child's breathing difficulty remains unclear, the doctor should proceed as though the child has food allergy anaphylaxis.

Why? Because that choice would produce the least harm if it turned out to be wrong. At the point when it becomes clear the problem is not anaphylaxis, the alternative explanation remains readily resolvable. The same cannot be said for an incorrect diagnosis of foreign body aspiration.

Start with an incorrect anaphylaxis diagnosis. The proper treatment for food allergy anaphylaxis is to inject the patient with epinephrine. This treatment is stunningly effective: the drug quickly suppresses the release of the chemical responsible for allergic reactions. Millions of Americans have EpiPen autoinjectors for this reason. Epinephrine also has virtually no adverse side effects. In our clinical case, then, one of two things will happen after our patient receives her injection: either her condition will quickly improve (in which case anaphylaxis was the proper diagnosis) or it won't (in which case a foreign body is to blame). Crucially, if her condition doesn't improve, the hospital can still conduct a chest X-ray to detect a foreign body. The mistake isn't costless—a four-year-old child will have gotten a painful shot and will still have a blocked airway in need of treatment. But that treatment can still proceed in the usual way.

Now consider a mistaken foreign body diagnosis. The usual approach is to perform a chest X-ray, which will often provide visual confirmation of an inhaled object. If the blockage is only partial, the child can sometimes cough it out. If the obstruction is more complete, the standard procedure is to remove it surgically under general anesthesia. But if the foreign body diagnosis is incorrect and the child is actually suffering from food allergy anaphylaxis, she could stop breathing before even making it to the X-ray table.

Such a mistake, it goes without saying, cannot be corrected. So faced with our uncertain case of a child in respiratory distress, the doctor should proceed in the way that, if wrong, will produce the least harm. Food allergy safety advocates have a catchphrase for just this approach: "Epi first, epi fast."

I know this from experience. Five years ago, when my one-year-old son was struggling to breathe, a pediatric physician quickly urged my wife to inject him with an EpiPen. It saved his life.

In the financial crisis of 2008, Americans collectively lost about $10.2 trillion in home equity and shareholder value.[26] To put the number in perspective, in the previous year America's gross domestic product was roughly $14.5 trillion. In a matter of weeks, the mortgage crisis and stock market crash of 2008 wiped out two-thirds of that amount.

It might have been worse. On September 15, 2008, Lehman Brothers, then the fourth-largest investment bank in the United States, filed for bankruptcy after suffering crushing losses in the subprime mortgage market. A similar fate loomed for other prominent banks.[27] Five days after Lehman's demise, Federal Reserve chairman Ben Bernanke and Secretary of the Treasury Hank Paulson proposed to bail out the banking industry with a $700 billion federal fund that would purchase the banks' distressed mortgage-related assets.

The proposal was immediately controversial. Because the crisis was unprecedented in both its scope and origins in the subprime mortgage market, no one could say whether bailing out large investment banks was truly necessary to save the American economy. And critics forcefully complained that, by creating the expectation that the banks' poor choices would always be backstopped by federal taxpayers, the bailout plan would reward foolish risk-taking, ensuring a future economic crisis that would be even worse.[28]

The public was divided. As with many difficult issues, the nature of that divide depended on how the question was framed. A Bloomberg/Los Angeles Times survey asked whether "the government should use taxpayers' dollars to rescue ailing private financial firms whose collapse could have adverse effects on the economy and market." Fifty-five percent of respondents opposed the bailout, compared to 31 percent in support.[29] Yet Pew Research found the opposite. When told, "the government is potentially investing billions to try and keep financial institutions and markets secure," 57 percent thought this was a good idea.[30]

Congress ultimately agreed with Bernanke and Paulson, enacting the bank bailout into law on October 3, 2008. Within months, the federal government purchased nearly a quarter of a trillion dollars in troubled assets. By June 2009, the Great Recession was over and the nation entered a painfully slow recovery.

Were federal officials correct to bail out the banks? Even in hindsight, there is no way to know. We cannot go back in time to see how events would have unfolded without a bailout: perhaps the markets would have stabilized on their own, perhaps not.

At the time, key economic officials recognized that erring in either direction would risk major problems. Failure to act could, in the worst scenario, lead to the collapse of the worldwide banking system and a dangerous economic downturn. Bailing out the banks would create perverse incentives for improvident risk-taking and, in its own worse case, lead to future economic depressions whose consequences would be impossible to predict.

Clearly, though, the former choice would trigger harms that are harder to avoid than the latter. Even if the economy avoided a complete disaster, history teaches that collapsed economies are exceedingly difficult to revive. Loss of wealth leads to a vicious cycle of reduced spending, reduced demand for goods and services, and firms cutting back on production and laying off workers—all of which trigger still greater wealth loss, more reductions in consumer demand, and more job losses. By contrast, an incorrect decision to bail out the banks would lead to serious harms that could still be prevented by reining in reckless financial institutions through more robust regulation. Congress, in fact, enacted the Dodd-Frank Act in 2010 with that exact aim in mind. In the face of intractable uncertainty, officials wisely chose the option that, if in error, would produce the most easily correctible harms. President Bush summarized this approach succinctly to the American people: "The risk of doing nothing far outweighs the risk of the package."[31]

An emergency room doctor quickly injecting a child with epinephrine; federal officials intervening to support a distressed economy; and the Supreme Court upholding Missouri's decision to continue treating Nancy Cruzan do not, on their face, have much in common.

But these scenarios share two fundamental characteristics. First, no matter how decision makers proceed, their choice holds potentially enormous consequences. A child may stop breathing; an economy could collapse; a comatose patient might be kept alive—or die—against her wishes. Second, irreducible uncertainty prevents the decision makers from identifying the "right" choice. The doctor doesn't know why the child is in respiratory distress; federal officials can't know whether the economy will crash without a bailout; and the Supreme Court can't say for certain whether the Constitution promises Nancy Cruzan a right to die in the absence of her clearly expressed wishes.

In each instance, the ultimate decision makers bypassed the usual mode of medical, economic, and legal analysis. Instead of forging ahead with a best guess about the true source of the child's symptoms, the likely future of the global economy, or the constitutional status of the right to die, they acted with a very different aim: to minimize the harm of an erroneous decision. In each case, the decision makers chose the option that, if in error, would inflict harms that could still be corrected.

Surprisingly, doctors, economists, and lawyers do not have a single, common term to capture this sensible approach to hard decisions. The lack of a common label may partly explain why the approach is not widely discussed in legal circles. It is time to give this idea a name: let's call this approach to difficult decisions the *least harm principle*. In hard cases, where traditional legal tools do not yield a clear answer, the Supreme Court should do the least harm possible. And it should do so in a very specific way: by ruling against the side with the best options for protecting its interests after defeat.

In the *Cruzan* case, a tragic dispute with no easy answers and many impassioned feelings, the Court's decision to do the least harm led to the closest thing possible to a satisfactory ending.

Missouri governor John Ashcroft said after the ruling, "I am grateful that the U.S. Supreme Court reaffirmed Missouri's objection to the removal of life sustaining food and water from an individual who has made no clear expression of her wishes."[32] Members of the right-to-life movement, many of whom had taken a strong interest in the case, also approved. The president of the American Life League, Judy Brown, stated that she was "pleased the U.S. Supreme Court has defended the right of Nancy Cruzan to live out her natural life without the threat of legally sanctioned starvation."[33]

On the other side, the initial reaction was understandably different. Upon hearing the news, Nancy's father cried.[34] One supporter of the right to die complained to *USA Today* that the Court's decision would "create a nightmare in which oversight or ignorance can leave people, unconscious, trapped between life and death."[35] Another lambasted the Court's decision to "deny family members the right to make decisions" for patients in a persistent vegetative state as "cruel."[36]

Less than six months after the ruling, however, Jasper County probate judge Charles Teel issued a new order instructing doctors at the state hospital to remove Nancy Cruzan's feeding tube. Her parents and family gathered around her bedside to say good-bye. And early on the morning of December 26, 1990, she died with no signs of pain or distress.[37] In a turn of events that was unimaginable just a half-year earlier, the Cruzan family's long struggle had finally ended.

How did this peaceful ending come to pass? The answer reveals the wisdom of the Court's choice to rely on the least harm principle.

Recall the basis of the Court's decision. Missouri did not prevail because the Court found the "right to die" wholly unprotected by the Constitution. Given the document's ambiguity and the lack of a clear answer in history or evolving societal standards, the Court rightly refrained from making any such categorical statement. The Court instead held that Missouri should prevail because Joyce and Joe Cruzan possessed the better options for avoiding the harms of an incorrect ruling. One option in particular caught the attention of the Cruzans and their attorney, Bill Colby.

"An erroneous decision not to terminate [life support]," Chief Justice Rehnquist had written for the *Cruzan* majority, leaves open "the potential that a wrong decision will eventually be corrected or its impact mitigated." The Court then listed several ways this might occur, including "advancements in medical science," "changes in the law," the "unexpected death of the patient," and the "discovery of new evidence regarding the patient's intent."[38] Upon reading the last of these possibilities, Colby would later describe his reaction: "*Eight words.* After all we'd been through, the thousands of pages written, could the case really have come down to just eight words?"[39]

By identifying these other ways for the losing side to protect its vital interests, the Court did more than explain the reasons for its ultimate decision. It created a playbook for how the Cruzans could still secure their daughter's wishes despite their legal defeat.

In the fall of 1977, some five years before Nancy's car accident, a woman named Debi Aaron began working at the Stapleton School in Joplin, Missouri. The school served students with the most severe disabilities, many of whom had been victims of severe abuse. One child, a three-year-old girl named Melissa, was a particularly heartrending case. Unable to eat enough food orally to survive, Melissa's home caregivers had fed her through an artificial feeding tube. When she arrived at the school she was eighteen inches long and weighed just twenty pounds. Melissa was also both deaf and blind. Debi later recalled how, during her entire six months of day-to-day interaction with Melissa, she never once believed she'd been able to communicate with her.[40]

Because the job was so demanding, the state provided funds for two classroom aides to assist Debi in her work. Both aides quit after the fall 1977 semester, leaving Debi to hire two new aides in January 1978. One was named Marianne Smith; the other was Nancy Hayes. The three women worked together closely for six months before Hayes left the job.

Neither Debi nor Marianne saw or thought of Hayes again, until eleven years later, when they saw her picture on CNN during a segment about the *Cruzan* case. Nancy Hayes, it turns out, had been married when Debi and Marianne worked with her at the Stapleton School. Hayes was her husband's name. After getting a divorce, Nancy went back to her maiden name: Cruzan. All at once, memories of their work together came rushing back to both women.

Two months after the Supreme Court's ruling, Joyce and Joe Cruzan asked Judge Teel for a hearing in which they could produce new evidence of their daughter's end-of-life wishes. Because the Supreme Court had indicated in eight words of its opinion that the Cruzans could do exactly that, Judge Teel agreed.

Marianne Smith testified first. She told Judge Teel how she came to work with Nancy and Debi at the Stapleton School in 1978. She explained how difficult the job was, including how the three women had to care for Melissa, the tiny three-year-old who could neither see nor hear. Much of their time with Melissa, Marianne explained, was spent trying to teach her to eat orally with a syringe-like device called an InfaFeeder. It was not an easy task, as Melissa would reflexively stick out her tongue, spilling the food everywhere.

Then Marianne recounted a conversation she and Debi had with Nancy in March 1978. "We were sitting on small children's chairs at the table," Marianne recalled, "and Nancy was holding Melissa" patiently feeding the child and cleaning her when the food would come back out. That's when Nancy remarked how sad it was that Melissa "didn't even know she was alive" and that "she would have lived out her whole life and not even known the beauty of life." Nancy described Melissa as "a vegetable" and said "she'd never want to be force-fed like that."[41]

Debi, in her testimony, recalled the same story. Both women stated unequivocally that they did not believe Nancy would have wanted to continue artificial nutrition in her current circumstances. And both women explained that they hadn't come forward earlier because until they saw her picture on TV, they didn't know the Nancy Cruzan in the news was the Nancy Hayes they'd once worked with.

With this additional testimony, Judge Teel ruled that the Cruzans had satisfied the state's "clear and convincing evidence" standard. He authorized the removal of Nancy's nutrition and hydration tube. Neither the state nor hospital employees objected. Nearly eight years after Nancy's car flipped off an icy Missouri road, the tragedy was finally over.

The discovery of additional evidence brought closure to Nancy's individual case. Thanks to advancing medical technology, however, thousands of Americans enter a persistent vegetative state each year.[42] Newly discovered evidence won't be available in all of their cases. So how were proponents of the right to die to ensure that these persons would be able to effectuate their end-of-life wishes, too?

Yet again, the Court's use of least harm reasoning proved prescient. One of the options by which the right-to-die proponents could avoid their harms, the Court explained, was by bringing about "changes in the law." Just months after *Cruzan* was decided, advocates persuaded Congress to enact the Patient Self-Determination Act. That law required hospitals to provide patients information about living wills, or advance directives in which people can specify what treatment they want (if any) if they become incapacitated, and who should make decisions for them. By increasing the number of persons who provide such clearly written instructions, the law reduced the frequency of future tragedies like Nancy's. In just the first month after *Cruzan* was decided, the Society for the Right to Die received *300,000 requests* for advance directive forms.

In the end, then, the Cruzans and supporters of the right to die lost at the Supreme Court. Yet they did so in the best of ways. Not because the Court overconfidently declared that the Constitution guarantees no such thing as a right to die with dignity. Rather, they lost because the Court found numerous other options by which they could avoid their harms. Those options worked, producing a peaceful resolution to a dispute that seemed all but impossible at the outset. This is just the kind of reasoning—and outcome—that the Supreme Court needs to dial down the temperature in the hot-button disputes that engulf our nation.

Promisingly, the Court followed the least harm principle in a number of important cases in 2020, earning the public's confidence in the process. The next chapter describes that surprising development. Unfortunately, this development was short-lived. As chapter 8 explains, the Court has departed from the principle in its more recent decisions, to the great detriment of its public standing. Which approach it will take in the major cases that lie ahead is thus a crucial question facing the Court—and the American people.

6
The Least Harm Principle

The images and events that defined June 2020 are unforgettable. TV news channels were filled with gut-wrenching footage of intubated patients dying alone in their hospital beds; Minnesota police officer Derek Chauvin senselessly kneeling on George Floyd's neck until he died; angry protesters marching to demand racial justice; and the beginnings of a presidential election that promised to be the ugliest anyone could remember. Never in modern history had America been so divided.

Meanwhile, the Supreme Court of the United States was in the final weeks of a term in which disaster seemed all but unavoidable. For the first time in a century, the Court had postponed oral arguments in response to worsening public health conditions.[1] But the real crisis was the slate of monumentally divisive issues before it. When oral arguments resumed by telephone in May 2020, for example, the Court confronted a pair of disputes with the potential to influence that year's presidential election. In both cases, Democratic officials sought troves of private financial records belonging to President Trump, including elusive tax returns that the president's opponents had sought to make public since before he took office. Whatever position the Court took seemed sure to draw fury from the losing side, be they his supporters or his opponents.

Several other explosive cases were pending as well, each with similar damned-if-you-do, damned-if-you-don't consequences. One case concerned the legality of the Trump administration's choice to terminate a program known as DACA, or Deferred Action for Childhood Arrivals. Under that program, roughly seven hundred thousand "Dreamers," undocumented immigrants who'd been brought to the United States as young children, were granted forbearance from deportation and authorization to work. In deciding the case, the Supreme Court would either put all seven hundred thousand of these people at risk of immediate removal to countries where many had no memory of ever living or uphold the program to the dismay of the hardline conservatives set on restricting immigration.

A similar choice confronted the Court with respect to Title VII, a major federal law that prohibits employers from discriminating against employees "on the basis of sex." Several workers sued their employers arguing that they'd been victims of discrimination based on their sexual orientation or transgender status. Does Title VII protect these characteristics? The Court's answer would undoubtedly inflame one side of the culture wars. Other contentious cases included disputes over a Montana private school voucher program that excluded religious schools, a Louisiana abortion regulation, and whether much of eastern Oklahoma remained an Indian reservation.

But instead of dividing the nation still further and eroding what little remained of the public's confidence in it, the Court found a way to do the opposite. On July 9, 2020, it recessed after issuing its rulings on presidential subpoenas, DACA, LGBTQ rights, school vouchers, abortion, and tribal rights. Four weeks later, Gallup released its annual Supreme Court public opinion survey. The results were stunning. The Court's popularity had soared to its highest level in recent memory, with virtually uniform support among Republicans (60 percent) and Democrats (56 percent).[2]

How on earth did the Court manage this feat?

• • •

Commentators trying to account for the Court's surprising popularity coalesced around two explanations. One was that the Court had successfully mimicked popular opinion in its rulings; the other was that it had traded off strategically between conservative and progressive outcomes. Neither explanation holds up.

Let's start with the argument that the Court's major decisions in 2020 simply mirrored public opinion. If true, this would suggest that the Court can bolster its public approval merely by following opinion polls. But it didn't. In perhaps the most significant case of the year, the Court allowed President Trump to block Congress's effort to subpoena—and ultimately make public—his private financial dealings. Yet more than 60 percent of Americans disagreed with this ruling.[3] In other big cases, such as a dispute over abortion, a case concerning contraception coverage, and a battle over the president's power to fire the director of the Consumer Financial Protection Bureau, the public was closely divided. In these cases, there was no clear public preference for the Court to follow.

The second explanation is that the Court increased its public confidence in 2020 because it deliberately traded off between progressive and conservative victories. On this view, what mattered was not the outcome of any single case (indeed, each case could have been decided just as well by coin flips) but that liberals and conservatives each got some wins. This, too, is unpersuasive: an extensive body of literature shows that the reasons judges give matter to the public. For example, in their pioneering book, *The Social Psychology of Procedural Justice,* law professors Allan Lind and Tom Tyler provided compelling evidence that people's willingness to accept the legitimacy of adverse judicial rulings turns on the degree to which courts give fair consideration to their arguments. It is not only outcomes that matter but the *reasons* for those outcomes, too.

The importance of judicial reasoning points to a third possibility. Perhaps the Court earned the public's trust precisely because of the reasoning it used. I'll argue in this chapter that many of the Court's high-profile decisions in 2020 applied the same least harm principle that the Court used successfully in *Cruzan*. Rather than arrogantly asserting that the Constitution produces a single, clear winner and loser across these hard cases, the Court ruled in a way that assured the losing groups would be able to avoid their harms after defeat. To be sure, most members of the public did not read these opinions closely. But leading advocacy organizations, political elites, and media commentators did, and they communicated their reactions and the meaningful options that the Court left available to their respective audiences. By ensuring that losing groups retained these productive responses, the Court was seen to deliver measured decisions that enhanced its legitimacy.

For more than forty years, every American president has released his federal tax returns for public inspection. The origin of this precedent was President Richard Nixon's response to the Watergate scandal. Eager to reestablish his public credibility, White House officials encouraged the president to address a group of more than four hundred reporters in a question-and-answer session from, of all places, Walt Disney World. When one of the reporters asked about his personal finances and whether he'd received improper benefits from public office, Nixon looked into the camera and declared, "I welcome this kind of examination, because people have got to know whether or not their President is a crook. Well, I am not a crook."[4] He released his tax returns the following week, and every president since has done the same.

Every president, that is, until Donald Trump. In May 2014, before he declared his candidacy, Trump showed little reluctance over his tax returns. "If I decide to run for office, I'll produce my tax returns, absolutely," he affirmed. But after encountering unexpected success in the primary, candidate Trump began to backtrack. "We'll get them out at some point, probably," he said without visible enthusiasm in February 2016.[5]

By the summer, with the Republican nomination in hand, the Trump campaign began arguing that some of his returns were being audited by the Internal Revenue Service and therefore couldn't be released. Of course, as the IRS itself noted in a public statement, nothing in the law prohibits the public release of a tax return that is under audit. Even worse, Trump had given no evidence that his returns were even being audited at all.

Trump's refusal to disclose his tax returns did not cost him the election, but speculation over their contents continued after he took office. In January 2017, a Pew Research Center Poll showed that 60 percent of Americans believed the president had a "responsibility" to release his returns. Many of their concerns had to do with Trump's trustworthiness and ability to lead; others concerned the possibility that Trump had broken the law.[6]

First, the public was understandably curious whether Trump, who claimed to be a "self-made billionaire," was as wealthy as he claimed. For a candidate whose appeal rested in large part on his supposed business success and deal-making ability, this was no idle issue: if Trump had been in dire financial straits all along, presumably the public might have doubted his acumen.

Second, Trump had long described himself as a generous philanthropist, but serious doubts existed about those claims. Disclosure of his tax returns would have revealed whether he'd been as charitable as he let on.

Third, the president's refusal to place his business holdings in a blind trust raised legitimate concerns. Earlier presidents, from Jimmy Carter to both Bushes, had done exactly that in order to avoid any appearance of financial conflicts of interest. Yet Trump insisted on vesting control over his branded properties in his children, leaving himself able to mobilize the federal government's resources for his own financial benefit.

Fourth, and perhaps most troubling, was the specter of Russia. Before taking office, Trump and his family had routinely bragged about their financial connections with Russia. Trump's son Eric, for instance, once told a reporter that "we don't rely on American banks" to fund Trump developments because "we have all the funding we need out of Russia."[7] Foreign investment in an individual's businesses might not normally raise many eyebrows, but when the individual is the president of the United States, such investment may create untoward financial pressure to put a foreign nation's interests above our own. And when a special counsel investigation led by a former FBI director identified "numerous links between individuals with ties to the Russian government and individuals associated with the Trump Campaign," that prospect became quite concerning.[8] Was the president in debt to the Russian government, and did that explain why Russian actors so aggressively boosted Trump's candidacy and undermined his opponent, Hillary Clinton? Had Russia's leaders supported Trump in the hope of being able to influence U.S. policy? Public disclosure of his tax returns would have shed light on these crucial questions.

Finally, some thought the president might have broken the law in his tax filings. Rumors circulated that he had misstated the value of his properties in order to secure tax breaks.[9] His financial records were the key to finding out whether these rumors were true. At a minimum, disclosure might trigger substantial back taxes and penalties payable to the IRS. (Indeed, Richard Nixon's decision to disclose his tax returns in 1973 eventually revealed improprieties for which the IRS imposed—and Nixon eventually paid—a $460,000 bill.)[10]

For all of these reasons, the public remained interested in Trump's financial records after he entered the Oval Office. In theory, Congress could have used its oversight authority to demand those records on the president's first day in office. But at that time, Republicans controlled both houses of Congress and had no intention of investigating a president of their own party.

That changed when Democrats won the House of Representatives in the 2018 midterm election. Democrat-controlled committees in Congress quickly issued subpoenas to President Trump's personal accounting firm, Mazars USA, seeking a combination of his personal and business financial records. Although Trump's tax returns were among the requested documents, the subpoenas extended much further, including a host of financial documents from his children, their immediate family members, and numerous affiliated business entities. According to the congressional committees, lawmakers needed this information to evaluate legislative proposals on topics ranging from money laundering to ethics in government. New York State prosecutors followed suit, issuing virtually identical subpoenas to the same accounting firm for the distinct purpose of investigating whether individuals affiliated with the Trump businesses had violated state law.

The president, however, refused to comply. Blasting efforts to investigate his financial records as a "hideous witch hunt," he sued to block both the congressional and New York State subpoenas.[11] In both cases, lower court judges ruled against him, recognizing the broad, historically grounded power of Congress and state prosecutors to issue subpoenas. But the president believed he would have the last word. The final decision would be made by the Supreme Court of the United States and its (then) five-to-four conservative majority—including two justices he had personally appointed.

Trump turned out to be half-right. In a surprising twist, the Court ruled in his favor with respect to the subpoenas issued by Congress but not those issued by New York prosecutors.

On the surface, this divided outcome may seem hard to comprehend. The two sets of subpoenas were essentially identical. How could one be permissible and the other not? But it turns out a powerful—and persuasive—rationale explains the divergence: the least harm principle. In the New York case, President Trump had several good alternatives for avoiding the harm of an adverse ruling; the State of New York did not. In the case involving congressional subpoenas, the opposite was true: Congress had better options for avoiding harm than did the President.

Start with the New York case, *Trump v. Vance*. (The respondent, Cyrus Vance, was the New York district attorney whose office was responsible for the subpoena.) The district attorney sought ten years of detailed financial records from Trump's accounting firm for the purpose of investigating what Vance's office described as "business transactions" that "may have violated state law."[12]

The real impetus for the subpoena was more salacious. In bombshell testimony before Congress in February 2019, the president's one-time lawyer and "fixer" Michael Cohen had testified that Trump had personally directed him to pay pornographic actress Stormy Daniels $130,000 in exchange for her silence about an affair she'd had with Trump, so as to bury the story during the presidential election cycle in 2016. Vance's office wanted to find out whether the Trump Organization had claimed this hush-money payment as a legal expense for tax purposes—a false business record and thus a crime under New York law.[13]

The president had other ideas and sued to block the subpoenas in federal court. His lawyers argued that because he was the president, the Constitution gave him "immunity from state criminal process." The Supreme Court disagreed, seven to two, allowing the subpoenas to proceed. Critically, however, the Court did not act as though this outcome was clearly dictated by some grand constitutional theory. Instead, it humbly recognized the difficulty of the legal question and the important interests and reasonable arguments on both sides.

Writing for the majority, Chief Justice Roberts began his opinion by reviewing historical instances in which presidents had been required to comply with subpoenas related to criminal proceedings in *federal* court. From Thomas Jefferson to Richard Nixon, a lengthy precedent existed for the rule that when the federal government seeks to investigate criminal wrongdoing, it can seek evidence from "every man"—the president included. But Roberts recognized that *Vance* was different: "Here we are confronted for the first time with a subpoena issued to the President by a local grand jury operating under supervision of a *state* court."[14] That fact made the *Vance* case more difficult. The federal government is a single entity whose criminal investigations will only rarely implicate a president's records. But opening the door to subpoenas from all fifty states might risk greater impairment of a president's ability to fulfill his duties in office.

Roberts could have attempted to discern some answer in the Constitution's original meaning. But nothing in Article II, which governs the executive branch, describes the scope of presidential immunity, if any, from state criminal process. He thus declined to ground the Court's decision in a self-assured application of originalism.[15] Instead, he even-handedly considered the harm that would be inflicted on each side if the Court ruled in either direction and then ruled against the side with the best options for avoiding it.

Roberts recognized three kinds of harms the president might suffer if states were permitted to serve him with subpoenas: diversion from his official duties, the stigma of being targeted by a subpoena, and harassment by politically motivated states. On the other side of the case, he described the harm to New York from a ruling in the president's favor: the state would be unable to "acquire all information that might possibly bear on its investigation" into violations of state law. Both of these sets of harms were significant, and Roberts did not pretend as though the Court could objectively declare one more important than the other.[16]

Instead, the Court determined which side would have greater ability to protect itself should it lose the case. The president had several options. First, Roberts wisely explained that "longstanding rules of grand jury secrecy aim to prevent the very stigma the President anticipates." Any information in the president's private records, in other words, was protected from public disclosure because New York law made it a felony for anyone connected with a grand jury proceeding to reveal the information. With respect to diversion and harassment, the president had multiple alternatives. A subpoena issued in "bad faith" or for the purpose of harassment could be blocked under New York law. In addition, federal courts retained the power to "quash or modify the subpoena" if evidence emerged that complying with it "would significantly interfere with [the President's] efforts to carry out" his public duties. For all these reasons, Roberts concluded that a ruling against the president would not leave him with "no real protection."[17]

The harmful consequences of a ruling against New York, meanwhile, would be far more difficult to avoid. "Fair and effective law enforcement," Roberts wrote, requires "comprehensive access to evidence." Blocking the subpoena would undermine that objective and potentially allow legal violations to go undiscovered—and thus unpunished. The Court considered the alternative of preserving the subpoenaed evidence for review until after the president's term expired. But even that option would hamper law enforcement by depriving the state of "investigative leads that the evidence might yield" and "allowing memories to fade and documents to disappear." Not only would this lost evidence "frustrate" the state's effort to indict wrongdoers "for whom applicable statutes of limitation might lapse," but it would also "prejudice the innocent by depriving the grand jury of *exculpatory* evidence" that might prove their innocence. Unlike the president, in other words, New York would have no meaningful way to protect its interests in criminal justice if it lost the case. So the Supreme Court ruled for New York.[18]

Based solely on the top-line result, one might have expected Trump to issue a blistering response after his loss in *Vance*. His actual response underscores the least harm principle's ability to lower the stakes of defeat. "The Supreme Court sends case back to Lower Court, arguments to continue," Trump tweeted in surprisingly mellow fashion, referring to the alternative legal arguments Roberts had identified in the Court's opinion.[19] By leaving other options available to the embattled president, the Court had avoided an outcome that would tarnish its public legitimacy.

On the very same day it decided *Trump v. Vance,* the Court also issued its opinion in the case involving subpoenas issued by Congress. (This case was entitled *Trump v. Mazars* because the president had sued his accounting firm to prevent it from complying with the subpoenas; Mazars eventually took no position in the case and congressional Democrats intervened to defend the subpoenas.) Just as in *Vance,* the lower federal courts ruled against the president in *Mazars,* permitting the subpoenas to proceed. The president hoped that the conservative Supreme Court would save him.

That, it turned out, is exactly what the Court did. For our purposes, the key question is how it did so. Once again, Chief Justice Roberts wrote the majority opinion. Just as in *Vance,* he did not overconfidently declare that there was a single, correct answer to a legal dispute that was in truth quite difficult. Instead, he recognized the significant harms each side would suffer in defeat and asked which side would have the greater options for avoiding them. Here, however, this approach cut in a different direction from the decision in *Vance*. Congress, not the president, had better options for protecting its important interests.

To see how, it is helpful to start by explaining why Congress has the power to issue subpoenas in the first place. The Constitution does not expressly grant Congress the subpoena power; Article I instead empowers Congress to enact legislation on certain specified subjects (such as the regulation of interstate commerce or to tax and spend for the general welfare). Article I also grants Congress the authority to "make all laws which shall be necessary and proper for carrying into execution" its lawmaking powers.[20] The subpoena power fits within this authority because subpoenas enable Congress to get the information it needs to pass effective laws. As the Supreme Court has put it, "Without information, Congress would be shooting in the dark, unable to legislate wisely or effectively."[21]

The crucial question in *Mazars* thus did not concern the existence but rather the *scope* of Congress's subpoena power. When are congressional subpoenas of presidential records permitted? The lower courts ruled that Congress may subpoena the president's personal records so long as they "relate to a valid legislative purpose." In doing so, they rejected President Trump's position that his records should not be subpoenaed by Congress unless they are "demonstrably critical" to some legislation.

In the Supreme Court's view, however, neither of these positions was appropriate, because each exposed the opposing side to substantial harm. For its part, Congress's preferred test would leave the president vulnerable to a remarkable degree of intrusion by a coequal branch of government. "Any personal paper possessed by a President," Roberts pointed out, "could potentially 'relate to' a conceivable subject of legislation, for Congress has broad legislative powers that touch a vast number of subjects." He continued: "The President's financial records could relate to economic reform, medical records to health reform, school transcripts to education reform, and so on." Roberts thus seemed to be asking a striking question: Do we really want to subject all future presidents to this degree of personal intrusion by a Congress that might be acting from political motivations?[22]

But the Court found the test proposed by President Trump's lawyers just as unpersuasive. Such a severe limit on Congress's ability to gain access to presidential records, Roberts wrote, would "risk seriously impeding Congress in carrying out its responsibilities," which include "legislative inquiries [into] the President in appropriate cases."[23] How, in other words, is Congress to pass laws governing a subject like presidential ethics reform if it cannot get detailed information concerning the ethical conflicts presidents actually face?

What the Court needed was thus a test for evaluating presidential subpoenas that fit somewhere between the parties' proposed approaches. Sadly, the Constitution offered no answer; as noted, it doesn't even mention congressional subpoenas. Nor could an answer be found in history or evolving societal values. So the Court took the same approach it had taken in *Vance:* it sought to ensure that the losing side retained strong options for avoiding the harm of an adverse decision.

More specifically, the Court held that congressional subpoenas seeking information belonging to the president should be evaluated for three specific considerations. First, "Congress may not rely on the President's information if other sources could reasonably provide Congress the information it needs in light of its particular legislative objective." This is one obvious way Congress may be able to avoid harm if its subpoena is blocked: if a different person's records would serve as an equally effective "case study" for money laundering or other legislation being considered, Congress could get the information it needs by subpoenaing that person instead of the president.

Second, the Court held that subpoenas should be "no broader than reasonably necessary to support Congress's legislative objective." This factor also aims to uncover an alternative strategy for Congress to protect its interests if a subpoena to the president is blocked: Congress can simply issue a narrower subpoena. It might be reasonable, in other words, to seek *some* information from the president's accounting firm to consider certain ethics reform laws. But seeking ten years of financial information from the president, all of his children, and their immediate family members might have gone too far, at least without some particularized showing of need.

Finally, the Court explained that Congress must show that it is actually pursuing a valid legislative purpose. If it is not interested in enacting new laws concerning money laundering or ethics but is instead using those topics as an excuse to harass the president, there is no harm to Congress's legitimate lawmaking powers in denying the subpoena.

After announcing these factors, the Court vacated the lower court rulings that had enabled Congress's subpoenas to proceed and ordered those courts to apply the new multifactor test. The immediate consequence was that President Trump's records would no longer be disclosed to Congress before the presidential election of 2020—a clear victory for his campaign.[24] But by leaving Congress with options for responding to its defeat, whether through narrower subpoenas or those more closely tied to actual legislative proposals, *Mazars* did not cause an uproar among congressional Democrats, either.[25]

By following the least harm principle, *Mazars* and *Vance* produced bipartisan outcomes that both sides could live with. All four liberal justices joined the conservatives in voting for the president in *Mazars,* and three conservatives (including Justices Gorsuch and Kavanaugh, Trump's own appointees) joined the liberals in ruling against the president in *Vance*. The Court thus dialed down the temperature of two blockbuster disputes that could have inflamed America's partisan divide.

Other major rulings from the 2019–20 term followed the same principle. Although each case involved a difficult issue that stoked intense political opinions, the Court consistently articulated how the losing side had other ways to protect itself. Armed with these clear options for responding to their defeats, none of the losing litigants had reason to assail the Court's credibility.

The DACA case, *Department of Homeland Security v. Regents of the University of California,* is a good example. In 2012, the Department of Homeland Security (DHS) under President Barack Obama announced a new immigration policy called Deferred Action for Childhood Arrivals, or DACA. Under DACA, undocumented immigrants who had been brought to the United States as children were eligible to apply for a two-year "forbearance of removal" during which they could not be deported. Once approved for this forbearance period, DACA recipients—known as Dreamers—also received eligibility for work authorization and other federal benefits.

Many conservatives opposed DACA. As a presidential candidate, Donald Trump promised to "immediately terminate" DACA if elected. His administration did so in September 2017. In a short memo, Acting Secretary of Homeland Security Elaine Duke wrote that the "DACA program should be terminated" because Attorney General Jeff Sessions had concluded that it was "likely" unlawful in light of an earlier Court of Appeals ruling that rejected the provision of federal benefits and work authorization to a different group of immigrants—the parents of Dreamers. Duke's memo declared that DHS would stop accepting new DACA applications and cease entertaining renewals after six months.[26]

DACA's revocation threatened human suffering of dramatic proportions. Many of the seven hundred thousand Dreamers had been brought to the United States as infants or toddlers and had never returned to the countries where their parents once lived. Santos Toledo, for example, was just two years old when he arrived in the United States. His parents had temporary visas but then they never left. Santos worked full-time jobs to put himself through community college before eventually attending UC–Berkeley and then Harvard Law School. Deporting a person like Santos from the United States—where he had lived, attended school, worked, paid taxes, and followed the law since age two—to return him to a country where he retained no connections would have caused him extreme hardship.

Numerous plaintiffs sued to block Secretary Duke's decision from going into effect. By the time it reached the Supreme Court, the case involved several complicated legal issues. Some lower courts had held that the Trump administration's decision to rescind DACA violated the Equal Protection Clause because it reflected discriminatory animus against Latinos. The administration argued that DACA was itself an unlawful policy that DHS had no choice but to terminate. But the Supreme Court ultimately ruled in favor of the Dreamers on a different ground altogether—one rooted in the least harm principle.

The problem with the Trump administration's choice to terminate DACA, the Court explained, was that it "failed to consider" important aspects of the policy choice before it, in particular the possibility that DHS could eliminate the benefits afforded to DACA recipients without eliminating forbearance from removal.[27] That approach would have fixed the legal problems Attorney General Sessions had identified in DACA while retaining its core feature—protection from deportation. But Secretary Duke never considered this option. That failure, the Court held, violated a federal statutory requirement that agencies must "engage in reasoned decisionmaking."[28]

Crucially, however, this failure was one of process, not substance. The Court did not hold that the Trump administration could *never* rescind DACA, only that it had to offer a sufficiently well-reasoned explanation for doing so. "DHS has considerable flexibility in carrying out" this task, the Court declared. Put another way, the administration had a readily available response to its defeat in court: it could write a new memo reviewing all of the aspects of the policy choice that Secretary Duke's first memo ignored, and once again conclude that it must terminate the entire program.[29]

By ruling against the Trump administration on this basis, the Court left open the possibility that the losing side could redress its harms. (In the end, Trump lost the election of 2020 and left office before DHS could produce a new memo permanently rescinding DACA.) A ruling in the opposite direction, against the Dreamers, would have generated harms that were far more difficult to avoid. Hundreds of thousands of law-abiding Dreamers could no longer have worked or paid taxes lawfully in the United States. And many would have faced the threat of deportation to countries where they had no memory of living.

A similar concern for the losing side's options helps explain *Bostock v. Clayton County*, another landmark ruling issued in 2020. The question in that case was whether Title VII of the Civil Rights Act of 1964, which prohibits employers from discriminating against an employee based on certain protected characteristics, includes discrimination based on sexual orientation and transgender status.

The legal question is strikingly difficult. On the one hand, Title VII's plain text bars discrimination based on five specific traits: "race, color, religion, sex, [and] national origin."[30] A group of employers who had been sued for sexual orientation and transgender discrimination argued that neither characteristic is enumerated on the list. The statute does list "sex" as a protected trait, but the employers pointed out—correctly, as a matter of historical fact—that neither the public nor the lawmakers who voted to enact the Civil Rights Act in 1964 would have understood sex to encompass sexual orientation or transgender status.

Yet there is an equally strong argument on the other side. When an employer discriminates against an employee because of their sexual orientation or transgender status, that discrimination is inherently because of the employee's sex. Pamela Karlan, the lawyer who argued the case on behalf of LGTBQ rights in the Supreme Court, gave the following example in oral argument. "[If] two employees come in, both of whom tell you they married their partner Bill last weekend, [and] you fire the male employee and you give the female employee a couple of days off so she can celebrate the joyous event, that's discrimination because of sex."[31] The logic is identical for transgender discrimination: to fire a transgender male employee because they were born biologically a female but not a cisgender male employee who was born biologically a male is necessarily to act because of the employee's sex.

In an opinion written by Justice Neil Gorsuch (and joined by Chief Justice Roberts plus the four liberals), the Court held that Karlan had the better reading of Title VII. Significantly, however, the opinion did not stop there. Gorsuch also explained why this ruling would leave the losing side with meaningful options for avoiding its harms.

In particular, the Court recognized the concern that its LGBTQ-protective reading of Title VII could forbid some religious employers to discriminate against LGBTQ persons, thus forcing them to "violate their religious convictions."[32] But such employers, Gorsuch explained, would retain three powerful legal arguments for exceptions from the law. First, Title VII has a statutory carve-out exempting religious organizations from certain aspects of the law. Second, the Free Exercise Clause could afford such employers additional exemptions. And third, a federal statute known as the Religious Freedom Restoration Act would grant religiously motivated employers even greater protections. Although none of the employers in the *Bostock* case raised any of these arguments in the Supreme Court, Gorsuch wrote that such arguments would "merit careful consideration" in future cases.[33]

In other words, the Court explained yet again how its ruling would leave the losing side options for minimizing its harm.

Progressives counted both the DACA and LGBTQ rights rulings as victories, but they did not run the table on major decisions in 2020. One important example is *Espinoza v. Montana Department of Revenue*. The case concerned a Montana private school voucher program, a policy long favored by conservative supporters of school choice. The program provided private school tuition scholarships to low-income families and families who have children with disabilities. Montana's constitution, however, forbids the state to provide aid to any "sectarian school" that is "controlled in whole or in part by any church, sect, or denomination."[34] The Montana Department of Revenue, observing this provision, enacted a rule prohibiting families from using the private school voucher at religious schools.

Several families sued. Each family wished to enroll a child in the Stillwater Christian School, a religious private school barred from participation in the state's voucher program by the Montana Department of Revenue's rule. The families argued that by forbidding them to use the voucher at a religious school, the state was discriminating based on religion, in violation of the First Amendment Free Exercise Clause.

The Supreme Court agreed in an opinion that again identified how the losing side retained options for minimizing its harms. "A State need not subsidize private education," the Court declared. "But once a State decides to do so, it cannot disqualify some private schools solely because they are religious."[35] Put another way, if Montana voters were worried about state subsidies of private religious schools, they could eliminate the state's voucher program altogether. That response is not far-fetched. Montana reenacted its constitutional amendment forbidding aid to religious schools in 1972, suggesting considerable support for that prohibition in somewhat recent times. And school voucher programs are hardly a political inevitability: just sixteen states have enacted them.[36] Indeed, three of Montana's four neighboring states, Wyoming, Idaho, and North Dakota, do not offer any form of school voucher. Montana may have lost the case, in other words, but it retained a plausible option to offset its defeat. By abolishing its voucher program, the state would simply join a widely accepted position across the nation.

Cases like *Espinoza, Bostock, DHS v. Regents of California, Mazars,* and *Vance* show why respect for the Supreme Court rose in 2020. Both progressives and conservatives won notable victories, so both groups had reason to celebrate. But just as critically, in the cases in which each side suffered defeat, the Court itself charted a path forward. President Trump had other legal avenues to challenge any subpoenas he felt were issued only to harass him; his administration could still revoke DACA with a fuller explanation; and religious employers could seek exemptions from Title VII's protections for LGBTQ workers. Democrats in Congress could issue narrower subpoenas more clearly tailored to legislation, and Montana progressives could work to limit or eliminate Montana's voucher program. With such meaningful post-defeat options, neither side felt the need to assail the Court's credibility.

All of this helps to explain how, after decades in which the Court's approval rating remained doggedly underwater, some 58 percent of Americans across the political divide reported a favorable view of the Court in the summer of 2020. By doing the least harm possible, the Court made major headway in bolstering its credibility.

This consistent use of the least harm principle in the final weeks of the 2019–20 term raises the tantalizing prospect of a humbler and less harmful Supreme Court. This approach seems novel, for it marks a dramatic departure from the kind of hyperconfident rulings produced under originalism and living constitutionalism. But the least harm principle has surprisingly deep roots. *Cruzan* is not the only high-profile decision from earlier periods in which the Court relied on least harm reasoning. A quick description of two other celebrated opinions employing this principle shows that it is an approach the Court has used before in other difficult cases, and to great effect.

"I was wondering if someone would ask that."

These were the first words Alexander Butterfield spoke in response to a crucial question from Senate Watergate investigators on July 13, 1973. They are among the most important words ever uttered in the political scandal that led to Richard Nixon's resignation from office—words exceeded in significance only by what Butterfield said next: "There is tape in the Oval Office."[37]

In 1972, during Nixon's campaign for reelection against Democrat George McGovern, certain Nixon aides approved a plan to conduct illegal surveillance of Democratic National Committee (DNC) headquarters in the Watergate office building in Washington, D.C. Five individuals affiliated with the Nixon campaign would burglarize the DNC's offices, photograph sensitive campaign documents, and install listening devices on telephones, allowing the president's campaign to spy on its political opponents throughout the election cycle.

There was just one problem: the burglars weren't very competent. After a security guard found tape covering the latches on doors leading to the Watergate parking garage, he called the police, who soon came to investigate. The burglars had stationed a "spotter" named Alfred Baldwin in a hotel room across the street to alert them if the police arrived. But Baldwin was too busy watching a sci-fi horror movie, *Attack of the Puppet People,* and failed to give the signal. The burglars were apprehended, leading to a scandal that rocked the nation.

There was no question that somebody—or a bunch of people—broke the law by directing and participating in the Watergate break-in. The crucial question was whether President Nixon had known about the plan and participated in efforts to obstruct the FBI from investigating it. As Tennessee senator Howard Baker Jr. famously asked, "What did the president know, and when did he know it?"

This is where Butterfield came in. As a longtime deputy assistant to President Nixon, he had been responsible for installing a covert taping system in the oval office at Nixon's direction. The system involved nine microphones hidden in Nixon's desk as well as in wall lamps and an adjoining meeting room. "Everything was taped as long as the President was in attendance," Butterfield explained, including, as it turned out, a series of conversations in which Nixon ordered payment of bribes to purchase the silence of the individuals who participated in the burglary. Not only had Nixon known of the Watergate break-in, but he had actively directed efforts to cover it up.

None of this would have come out had Butterfield not revealed the existence of the White House taping system. But another event was crucial in the tapes' eventual release to the public: the Supreme Court's unanimous ruling in *United States v. Nixon*. For faced with a request for the tapes from prosecutors seeking evidence to use against the burglars, Nixon initially refused to comply. The tapes, he argued, were protected by "executive privilege," or a constitutional rule of secrecy Nixon argued that he should enjoy in virtue of being president.

In considering this argument in *United States v. Nixon,* the Court did not purport to find a decisive answer in original meaning, evolving precedents, or any other theory for unearthing some singular meaning of our Constitution. Instead, it asked which side—federal prosecutors or the president—would be better able to avoid the harms of an adverse ruling.

The Court began by identifying the harm that would be inflicted by a ruling in the president's favor: "Allowance of the privilege to withhold evidence that is demonstrably relevant in a criminal trial would . . . gravely impair the basic function of the courts." And it immediately recognized that this harm would be hard to correct. "Without access to specific facts" contained in the tape recordings, the prosecution of all persons involved in the Watergate burglary "may be totally frustrated." Put another way, compelling Nixon to disclose the tapes was the only way to avoid letting guilty persons walk free.[38]

By contrast, the Court reasoned, a ruling against Nixon would lead to harms that, though equally weighty, were more susceptible to correction. Nixon had argued that executive privilege was essential because without it, his advisers might "temper the candor of their remarks" out of fear that their comments could one day be disclosed to the public. That concern, the Court admitted, was real and important: "[T]he need for confidentiality . . . is too obvious to call for further treatment." But presidents have other ways to avoid that harm. Most significantly, the district court judge who received the tape recordings could review the material privately and redact all sensitive conversations, including those "which are either not relevant or not admissible" to the criminal investigation.[39] Such a "scrupulous" procedure would ensure that sensitive conversations with White House advisers were kept secret, avoiding the harm Nixon feared. So the Court ruled against him. Sixteen days later, Nixon was out of office.

Another widely known and immensely consequential ruling that drew on least harm arguments is *Plyler v. Doe,* a case in 1982 about the right of undocumented immigrant children to attend public schools. It arose out of a Texas law that provided a certain allotment of funding to local school districts for each child they enrolled but none for children who were undocumented immigrants. The law also permitted school districts to deny enrollment to any child who was undocumented.

When the Tyler Independent School District adopted a policy requiring undocumented children in the district—and only undocumented children—to pay a "full tuition fee" to attend public school, a group of families filed a class action lawsuit challenging both the district policy and the state law.

Attempts to target undocumented children continue to captivate hardline immigration hawks to this day. In 2011, for example, Alabama enacted a law requiring public schools to verify their students' immigration status, a law that would have inevitably deterred undocumented children from attending school.[40] It was later invalidated as a violation of the rule announced in *Plyler v. Doe*—powerful testimony to the case's importance.

For our purposes, the significant fact about *Plyler* is that the Court did not declare Texas's law unconstitutional because it violated the original meaning or some updated understanding of the Equal Protection Clause. Instead, the Court considered the harm that a ruling in either direction would impose, and it ruled against the side with the best options for protecting itself after defeat.

Justice Brennan's majority opinion started with the obvious harms undocumented children would suffer from an adverse ruling, including increased risks of illiteracy, crime, and reliance on welfare. The Court then explained why the injured children lacked the power to avoid these harms: unlike their parents, who "have the ability to . . . remove themselves from the state's jurisdiction," the "children who are plaintiffs in these cases can affect neither their parents' conduct nor their own status."[41] Children, in other words, have little ability to educate or protect themselves once kicked out of public school.

Texas, meanwhile, had stronger options for protecting its interests if its law were struck down. The Court recognized the state's legitimate interest in providing a "high quality public education" to all children within its borders. But it could secure that interest without driving out its undocumented children. As the Supreme Court described the evidence developed at trial, "the record in no way supports the claim that exclusion of undocumented children is likely to improve the overall quality of education in the State."[42] Because the state could minimize any harm more easily than undocumented children could, the Court ruled in favor of the children. Shortly after the decision was announced, Texas lawmakers enacted a new law substantially increasing school expenditures and pegging state aid to actual daily student attendance—including undocumented children.[43]

The cases described above reveal a remarkable fact. The Supreme Court has quietly stumbled onto a workable approach for deciding hard cases that divide us. Rather than employ grand interpretive theories like originalism and living constitutionalism, the Court has often ruled with an eye toward producing the least amount of harm. It has done so by ruling against the side with the greatest ability to protect its interests even after losing in court. And although the Court has not announced a formal framework for this approach, a close reading of the cases reveals that it involves three basic steps.

The first step requires deciding whether the least harm principle even applies. As I've suggested throughout the book, the least harm principle is an approach specifically for deciding *hard cases*. Thus, in each of the disputes discussed above, the Court has grappled with a difficult question on which both sides possess strong legal arguments. That is no accident. It is only when a case is hard—when the Constitution and traditional tools of legal interpretation fail to point to a single, clear answer—that a substantial risk of judicial error arises. And it is only this risk of error—and the accompanying risk of unwarranted human suffering—that justifies the Court's desire to do the least harm possible by asking whether one side possesses superior post-defeat options.

An example can help to show why. Suppose California were to file a lawsuit arguing that its large population entitles it to an extra senator in the next session of Congress. Progressives can surely think of political reasons why they might prefer that result. Some may even articulate principled reasons why, in a popular democracy, the Senate ought to be designed in just that way. (Consider that Senate Democrats in 2021 represented roughly forty-three million more Americans than Senate Republicans, yet both sides held the same number of Senate seats.)[44]

But of course that is not how our Constitution is designed. Article I, Section 3, provides that "the Senate of the United States shall be composed of two Senators each from each State." For the Court to override that clear command would be lawless, no matter how much one might like the result—and no matter how difficult it would be for persons injured by the correct outcome to avoid their harms. (There is, for example, no way for California to obtain greater Senate representation because Article V of the Constitution explicitly forbids amendments that would deprive a state of "its equal suffrage in the Senate.") The least harm principle's first analytic step thus cabins its reach. Where the Constitution is clear, it governs—end of story.

Of course, in a number of society-altering cases, the Constitution isn't clear. This point is so widely recognized across the legal spectrum that it isn't controversial. Princeton professor Keith Whittington, a noted conservative originalist, admits, for instance, that in some cases "the language that the founders used may be unavoidably vague" such that originalism will be incapable of providing a "determinate meaning."[45] Georgetown professor Randy Barnett, a libertarian originalist, agrees that "the original meaning of the text may not always determine a unique rule of law to be applied to a particular case."[46] University of Chicago professor David Strauss argues that the earlier decisions on which living constitutionalist judges are supposed to base their rulings will sometimes fail to "dictate a result," such that a judge will need to make a contested choice about what is "more fair" or "more in keeping with good social policy."[47] Harvard law professor Richard Fallon, another noted liberal scholar who rejects originalism, has acknowledged that in many hard cases, there exists an "apparent tendency of different kinds of arguments [pointing] to divergent results."[48]

What to do in these cases where one's preferred interpretive theory fails to determine a legal question is thus the whole ballgame. I have argued that the Court's usual approach—of refusing to acknowledge legal difficulty and instead overconfidently announcing definitive winners and losers—has had real costs, not just for losing groups but also for the Court's legitimacy. By admitting what all serious legal scholars know to be true, that some Supreme Court cases are in truth objectively difficult, the least harm principle offers a more promising approach.

To be sure, judges will not always agree that a given case is "hard" such that the least harm principle should apply. A case that seems hard to one justice may strike another as straightforward. But the justices need not agree on this threshold question for the least harm principle to work: it is enough for those justices who *do* think a case is hard to rely on it. This is a familiar approach across the law. Courts routinely use similar threshold inquiries in contexts as diverse as contract disputes and administrative law, where judges can disagree over an initial threshold question (is the contract or statute ambiguous?) yet still go on to apply a clear decision rule.[49]

The second step in the Supreme Court's least harm decisions is to identify the harms each side would suffer upon defeat. The Court has done so with great deference to the parties themselves, largely accepting each side's description of its own harm. Thus, for example, the Court accepted at face value President Trump's claim that he would suffer "diversion, stigma, and harassment" if he were to lose in *Vance,* before explaining how state and federal law afforded him other ways to protect against those injuries.[50] The Court likewise accepted Joe and Joyce Cruzan's description of the harm their daughter would suffer in defeat: ruling against her would create the risk of an "erroneous decision not to terminate" her life despite her desire to reject the "forced administration of life-sustaining medical treatment."[51] This deferential approach is consistent with the least harm principle's driving motivation: a desire to respect, rather than denigrate, each side's legitimate interests in truly difficult cases.

There are, however, two somewhat trickier issues implicit in the identification of the harms on each side of a case. One issue concerns the matter of whose harms count in the Court's analysis. Theoretically, the Court could limit its focus to just the named parties in the case, ignoring the harms of similarly situated persons or entities. Yet Supreme Court decisions announce broad propositions of law that affect entire groups, not just the individual parties who happen to come before it. The Court has accordingly asked about the harms those entire groups might suffer and how they may avoid them in turn. When the Court considered the plight of undocumented children in *Plyler v. Doe,* for instance, it did not limit its consideration to the specific children whose parents had challenged Texas's law, nor did it ask about the harms that would befall only the particular school officials who had been named as defendants. It instead noted how all of the affected undocumented children would suffer educational losses and how residents across the state had legitimate interests in ensuring the quality of Texas's public schools. Professors Charles Barzun and Michael Gilbert have wisely described this as an approach that focuses on the "real parties in interest" to the case.[52]

Another complication involves the possibility that lawyers may get creative in describing their clients' harms in order to manipulate the least harm approach. Suppose, for example, that lawyers in the *Cruzan* case had defined Nancy's harm more abstractly, as the state's unwanted interference in her life. Or suppose those lawyers had defined her harm in such a technical and legalistic way that it could *never* be avoided—something like "the loss of the Nancy's right to make an end-of-life decision with less than clear and convincing evidence." On either of these definitions, the post-defeat ability to adduce new evidence of Nancy's end-of-life wishes wouldn't redress her harm because the state would have still interfered with her decision making, and the state would have still used the clear and convincing evidence standard.

Fortunately, the Court's actual approach suggests meaningful limits to such lawyers' games. To start, the parties must define their harms in specific rather than abstract terms. This means that vague and generic harm definitions—such as one's desire to be free from "state interference"—won't do. In the *Cruzan* case, there is no mystery as to the specific harm Nancy would actually face in defeat: the "state interference" at issue was Missouri's refusal to terminate her life-sustaining treatment. That is the most specific account of the harm Nancy would suffer, and so that is the harm the Court analyzed under the least harm principle.

In addition, lawyers may not characterize their clients' harm as the Court's bare refusal to adopt the very legal argument they are asserting. Prohibiting circular harm definitions makes sense because people do not go to the Supreme Court to vindicate their desire for certain technical legal arguments to appear in dusty legal casebooks. They go to the Court because of the concrete effects those arguments will have on their lives. So that is how the litigants must define their harms. In the *Cruzan* case, the concrete harm Nancy faced upon defeat was her inability to terminate medical treatment despite her likely wishes, and so that is the harm the Court grappled with.

The least harm principle's third and final step is to identify which side will be better able to avoid its harms in the event that the Court rules against it. The most crucial observation about this step is what it is not: it is not an invitation for the Court to weigh which side's harms are more severe or more important. The whole point of the least harm principle is to recognize that in the difficult cases that divide society, the stakes are immense on both sides—which means that both sides will suffer significant harm if they lose. Moreover, those harms will typically involve conflicting, subjective values rather than easily quantifiable losses. There is no way to objectively determine, for example, whether denying Missouri the ability to protect against the wrongful termination of life will be more harmful than denying Nancy Cruzan's wish to terminate her treatment absent clear evidence. Choosing one side on matters of such profound moral disagreement is more likely to inflame than heal divisions among our people.[53]

The principle's last step thus focuses on a categorically different question: whether one side possesses greater ability to avoid its harms than the other. That is why each of the cases discussed so far has focused so much on the various responses that litigants possess after defeat, such as President Trump's alternative legal challenges to New York's subpoenas, the Cruzans' ability to find new evidence of Nancy's end-of-life wishes, and religious employers' ability to seek exceptions from Title VII under other sources of law. The idea is straightforward. If judges cannot locate a clear answer in the Constitution or their preferred interpretive theories, and if they cannot objectively compare the severity of harms on each side, then they should shift the ground of decision to something they *can* compare: the availability of other avenues for protecting each side's interests.

In the least harm decisions discussed above, the Court has assessed two different kinds of strategies by which losing groups may do so. One kind involves returning to the democratic process to secure new legislative action. Thus, for example, the Court explained in *Espinoza* that Montana residents who oppose the use of public dollars at religious schools can advocate the elimination of the state's voucher program. The Court likewise explained in *Mazars* that Congress could still obtain the information it needed to enact money-laundering and ethics laws through narrower presidential subpoenas or subpoenas to other sources. One can think of responses of this kind as "public avoidance" strategies insofar as they require action from public officials.[54]

A second kind of post-defeat response involves "private avoidance" in the sense that losing groups can sometimes protect their interests on their own, without any need to change public laws. The Cruzans' ability to find new evidence of Nancy's end-of-life wishes is a textbook example, but so too is the option that other individuals possessed to avoid a similar fate in the future: executing a will with specific end-of-life instructions. Similarly, religious employers upset in the aftermath of *Bostock*'s pro-LGBTQ reading of federal antidiscrimination law could advance arguments for exceptions rooted in existing law without any additional action from government officials. In an era in which legislatures are often gridlocked—especially on nationally divisive matters—private avoidance strategies are especially important in their ability to minimize harm in feasible and attainable ways. By focusing our attention on these options, the least harm principle offers an important reminder to the justices and public alike: often, solutions to difficult societal conflicts are best when they come from the people themselves, not the courts or a government official sitting on high.

The chapters so far have painted the least harm principle in its most favorable light, illustrating its ability to break through difficult cases in situations where one side clearly possesses superior options for avoiding its harm. The next chapter explains how this decisional approach advances important values to the benefit of the Supreme Court and the public writ large.

However, it won't be obvious in every case whether one side is better able to avoid its harm than the other. In these cases, identifying the better harm avoider may be every bit as difficult as the task of determining the law's meaning. Is the least harm principle still a useful approach when this is true? I explore this important question at the end of the next chapter, in the context of one of constitutional law's most difficult and divisive issues: abortion.

7
Rebuilding Trust

The most unexpected moment in my year clerking at the Supreme Court happened in the middle of an oral argument. It did not involve a gotcha question from one of the justices or some eloquent speech made by an oral advocate. It did not even involve a particularly noteworthy case.

Near the end of the oral argument in a dry dispute over attorneys' fees in patent cases, a man stood up in the public audience section at the back of the courtroom. But he did not shuffle quietly out of the room, as courtroom officials and other audience members expected. He stood there waiting, almost respectfully, for a pause in the back-and-forth between the justices and the lawyer at the podium.

Then, he spoke.

"I rise on behalf of the vast majority of the American people who believe that money is not speech, corporations are not people, and our democracy should not be for sale to the highest bidder! Overturn *Citizens United!*"

A swarm of Supreme Court police officers rushed to arrest the man. The justices watched with visible discomfort, uncertain whether he had been acting alone. (A second protester was indeed in the room covertly videotaping the event, against the Court's official rule forbidding cell phones, but he never revealed himself. The following year, eight protesters would interrupt another oral argument session by chanting, one after the other, "Overturn *Citizens United*!" and "Money is not speech!")

Order was eventually restored, and Chief Justice Roberts cracked a joke. The oral argument resumed. Evidence of the protest was eventually expunged from both the oral argument audio file and the official Court transcript. To anyone who hadn't been there, it might have seemed as though nothing unusual had ever happened.

Yet when the argument ended, an excited murmur filled the courtroom. Two things were clear to everyone in attendance. First, we had just witnessed a historic moment: a rare public disturbance of the Supreme Court's solemn and methodical mode of conducting business. And second, many people were not happy about *Citizens United.* Not one bit.

To understand the public's outrage over *Citizens United* is to understand the first of three important reasons why the least harm principle can rebuild public trust in the Supreme Court. The problem with the decision wasn't simply that many people consider it deeply harmful to our democracy. The problem was also that the Court left the public no way to avoid those harms.

In September 2009, Gallup surveyed the American public about their impressions of the Supreme Court. A near record-high 61 percent of respondents reported approving of the Court's work.[1] Three months later, the Court held in *Citizens United* that corporations enjoy a First Amendment right to make unlimited expenditures out of their general corporate treasuries to influence elections.

The following September, Gallup conducted another poll. It found the Court's approval rating had dropped by a staggering ten points. There's little mystery as to why: the public was deeply upset about *Citizens United* and its implications for our democracy. Eighty percent of Americans, including overwhelming majorities in both political parties, opposed the ruling shortly after it was issued.[2] Its sweeping effects on our democracy became even clearer after the presidential election cycle of 2012, during which torrents of money were spent on attack ads funded by obscurely named super-PACs (political action committees). And the Court's approval rating suffered further in the years to come, remaining below 50 percent in the next twelve Gallup polls.

Why did *Citizens United* change so many Americans' views of the Supreme Court? The simplest explanation is that the American people loathed the idea of wealthy corporate barons buying off politicians, drowning out the voices of ordinary Americans, and skewing public policy to favor the wealthiest 1 percent. Because the ruling moved the United States a large step closer to this unsavory state of affairs, the Court lost the public's trust.

While there is a good deal of force to this account, it misses a major piece of the puzzle. The problem with *Citizens United* isn't just that most Americans disagreed with the outcome. It's that the Court rushed so unnecessarily to the rescue of large, wealthy corporations that already enjoyed many channels through which to influence our politics. And in doing so, it left virtually no way forward for ordinary Americans struggling to be heard amid a sea of wealthy donors.

Why did *Citizens United* leave the public no ways to curtail corporate influence over our nation's elected officials? Surprisingly, it's not because of a lack of political will. In 2002, federal lawmakers enacted a bipartisan law limiting corporate spending on elections for the very purpose of ensuring that our leaders would remain responsive to ordinary voters. Those were the limits the Supreme Court struck down in *Citizens United.* Yet because the Court did so as a broad matter of constitutional law, Congress and the states were forbidden to respond by reenacting similar limits on corporate electioneering.

After the decision, the only options for reasserting the primacy of the public's voice were to amend the Constitution or to somehow persuade the Court to change its mind. Given the requirement of both a two-thirds supermajority of Congress and a three-fourths supermajority of states to amend the Constitution, the former option is virtually impossible. So that leaves the latter: the public can attempt to pressure the Court to change its mind about *Citizens United* by relentlessly attacking it. This, of course, is just what the public has done, in ways both overt (such as by protesting at the Court itself) and less so (such as by registering disapproval in opinion polls). Public trust in the Court collapsed after *Citizens United,* in other words, largely because that ruling violated the least harm principle. Rather than recognizing the legal difficulty of the case and ruling in a way that left the losing side some options moving forward, the Court confidently declared that the First Amendment entitles corporations to spend on elections without limit.

Now contrast *Citizens United* against another case in which the Court reached a politically unpopular outcome but followed the least harm principle. *Mazars* is a decent example. As I noted earlier, a supermajority (60 percent) of Americans disagreed with the Court's refusal to hold President Trump accountable by compelling his accounting firm to turn over his financial records to Congress. But unlike what happened after *Citizens United,* public approval rose after *Mazars.* Some of this, of course, likely owed to other major decisions issued in the 2019–20 term. Yet the fact that the public didn't display similar levels of outrage over *Mazars* also owed to the Court's careful effort to leave the losing side options: Congress remained free to issue narrower subpoenas to Trump's accounting firm and other sources to obtain the information it needed to legislate. In fact, two years after the Supreme Court decided *Mazars,* a lower court sided with Congress in upholding narrow aspects of its subpoenas that the court considered necessary for investigating proposed government ethics laws.[3]

I want to suggest that the divergent public responses to the Supreme Court after *Citizens United* and *Mazars* are no accident. The reason the public expressed such profound disapproval of the Court after *Citizens United* is that the Court left the people no other way to effectuate change. The same was not true after *Mazars* because the Court itself provided a blueprint for Democratic lawmakers to obtain relevant private records.

A similar explanation describes the Court's steady public support after its landmark ruling in *Cruzan*. In 1990, the year *Cruzan* was decided, the vast majority of Americans expressed support for the right to die with dignity.[4] By ruling against Nancy Cruzan's desire to exercise that right, *Cruzan* diverged from popular opinion. Yet the Court's approval actually increased in *Cruzan*'s aftermath, with 48 percent expressing "a great deal" or "quite a lot" of confidence in February 1991, up two points from levels reported in 1989.[5] Although other factors likely played a role in this increase, the development further illustrates how the least harm principle can help protect the Court's public legitimacy. Rather than assail a Court that rejected a popular right to die, supporters of that right simply secured legislation authorizing living wills—and Nancy Cruzan's parents found additional evidence of their daughter's wishes.

When the Supreme Court ensures that the losers in high-profile, divisive disputes have other ways to get what they want, there is far less reason for them to doubt the Court's legitimacy—and little reason to engage in all-out warfare on the Court as an institution. The least harm principle's very mechanism for deciding hard cases thus offers a direct antidote to the Court's declining public trust because it channels losing groups' disappointment into productive responses. The principle also reinvigorates the essential democratic norms of mutual toleration and forbearance because losing groups who are left with reasonable options have less need to attack their political opponents. Why obliterate our opponents or fight to overthrow the political system when there exists a different solution that works within the usual channels of change?

All of this allows us to see how the least harm principle could have led to a more productive outcome in *Citizens United.* The principle's first step requires asking whether the case is hard. I think it is: the legal question is actually far more difficult than either side would like to admit. Opponents of the ruling often complain about the Court's extension of the individual right to free speech to corporations. Yet corporations are simply one form through which individual persons gather in pursuit of a common purpose. It isn't clear why First Amendment rights should disappear when people join together for some expressive end. Thus, for example, when Virginia enacted a law in 1956 prohibiting the NAACP from soliciting clients to bring school desegregation lawsuits, the Court rejected the state's argument that the NAACP's corporate status eliminated its right to free speech. "Though a corporation," the Court wrote, the NAACP "may assert [the First Amendment] on its own behalf."[6]

Yet recognizing that corporations can enjoy free speech rights does not end the case. The right to free speech is not absolute. This explains why government can punish someone who shouts "Fire!" in a crowded movie theater. Even at the founding, the general understanding was that lawmakers could restrict speech for the public good.[7] Yet the "public good" can be awfully difficult to define. The underlying constitutional question in *Citizens United* is thus far from easy.

Given this difficulty, *Citizens United* would have been an appropriate case for the least harm principle. Under that principle, the Court would have evenhandedly acknowledged the important interests on both sides of the case before ruling against the side with the strongest ability to protect its interests after defeat. The Court's actual ruling violated this principle, however, by leaving those who support limits on corporate influence with no power to protect their interests absent a constitutional amendment. Yet a ruling in the other direction would have left corporations at least two significant options for participating in political advocacy, thus redressing their harm.

First, under the law then in force, corporations were free to engage in express campaign advocacy using segregated funds contributed by stockholders, corporate executives, and their families. These individuals could contribute up to $5,000 to fund electioneering activities each year, an amount that, for a large corporation, can add up quickly.[8] So even if *Citizens United* had upheld the ban against campaign expenditures out of general treasury funds, corporations could have remained major donors.

Second, corporations had considerable lobbying influence through which they could move for changes to federal campaign finance limits. Furthermore, unlike ordinary Americans who would have to fight for a constitutional amendment to overrule an adverse ruling, a loss for the corporations would have simply meant that the federal spending limits were legally permissible, without blocking future political efforts to raise or even repeal them. Such a ruling would have left corporations free to lobby lawmakers for modest legislative changes like increasing the $5,000 limit on individual corporate donations or permitting a moderate amount of spending out of general treasury funds. This latter position might have been especially attractive because it would have allowed small issue-oriented corporations some ability to fund election activities without unleashing a tidal wave of corporate spending.

Regrettably, the Supreme Court never engaged in this least harm analysis. Blinded by overconfidence in its ability to uncover a single, correct answer in our 230-year-old Constitution, it ended the democratic debate over corporate campaign finance limits. Corporations won; ordinary Americans lost. But the Court's credibility suffered, too—in large part because it failed to leave the losing side meaningful options for redress.

The major society-altering cases that make it to the Supreme Court have come to resemble all-or-nothing warfare.

Consider, for instance, the arguments made in *Janus v. AFSCME, Council 31,* a landmark case decided in 2018 that affected public sector unions around the nation. The plaintiff in the case, Mark Janus, was a child support specialist employed by the State of Illinois. State law required Janus's union, the American Federation of State, County, and Municipal Employees, to bargain on Janus's behalf for better wages and benefits and to represent him in case his employer took action against him. To make up for that duty, state law also required Janus to pay a "fair share fee" for those services—in his case, a monthly fee of $44.58. But like many Americans, Janus was ideologically and politically opposed to labor unions. So he sued, claiming that the monthly dues payment violated his First Amendment right to free speech.

The Supreme Court ultimately ruled in Janus's favor. In truth, the legal question at the heart of the case is a difficult one on which both sides have reasonable arguments. For one thing, the unions have a strong argument that monthly fair share fees don't implicate the right to free speech to begin with. Such fees, after all, do not prohibit employees like Janus from saying anything; Janus was at all times perfectly free to express his opposition to the union. Nor do such fees compel Janus to express any message he disagrees with. For his part, Janus has a forceful response that his compelled fees would be used to support the *union*'s speech, even on political matters with which he deeply disagrees. So his expressive interests are quite arguably implicated when he is forced to fund a message that he finds objectionable. But if that's true, then the same argument can be made about taxes, which are often used to fund government speech that some taxpayers disagree with. For all these reasons, the First Amendment question in *Janus* was far from easy.

What I want to focus on here, however, is the deeply hostile arguments that Janus and the union advanced in their competing briefs to the Supreme Court. Janus's lawyers argued that the framers "would have been aghast at governments regimenting their workforces into involuntary, artificially-powerful factions for petitioning the government for a greater share of scarce public resources."[9] The public sector union responded by proclaiming that workers like Janus have "no right to object to conditions placed upon the terms of employment," even "including those which restrict[] the exercise of constitutional rights."[10] As Justice Alito asked at oral argument, "When I read your brief I saw something I thought I would never see in a brief filed by a public employee union, and that is the argument that . . . public employees have no free speech rights. Where do you want us to go with that?"[11]

Really? Framers "aghast" at the notion of workers joining together to negotiate higher wages and better health care? Public employees with "no right" to object to restrictions on their constitutional rights? For its part, the Court only added to this heated rhetoric. Writing for the majority to strike down the Illinois fair share fee law, Justice Alito denounced the unions for taking a "windfall" of "many billions of dollars" away from employees like Janus.

Consider, too, the argument advanced in *Masterpiece Cakeshop v. Colorado Civil Rights Commission,* also decided in 2018. The owner of Masterpiece Cakeshop, Jack Phillips, refused to bake a cake for a gay couple's wedding because of his religious opposition to same-sex marriage. That choice, however, violated a Colorado antidiscrimination law forbidding storefronts to discriminate based on sexual orientation. The question before the Supreme Court was whether Phillips possessed a First Amendment free speech right not to comply with the state's antidiscrimination law. Yet again, the parties' arguments before the Court reflected not respect for their opponents but disdain. Phillips's lawyers asserted that, in defending Colorado's antidiscrimination law, the gay couple had failed to advance even a "plausible reading of the First Amendment."[12] The couple responded by belittling the notion that Phillips enjoyed any kind of expressive interest to begin with, mocking Phillips's claim that his wedding cakes were works of art entitled to protection as "far-fetched" and "misguided."[13]

Cases like *Janus* and *Masterpiece Cakeshop* are now the norm. In our increasingly diverse society, rights routinely come into conflict.[14] The union's right to have the financial support of those for whom it fights for higher wages conflicts with the individual's right not to subsidize speech with which he disagrees. A baker's right to religious exercise clashes with a gay couple's right to equal treatment. A responsible gun owner's right to bear arms for self-defense meets a concerned parent's right to send her children to public school free from the fear of a mass shooting. A pregnant person's right to reproductive autonomy smashes into the state's interest in protecting unborn children. And on and on.

Columbia law professor Jamal Greene has observed that high-profile constitutional disputes of this sort have taken on the character of a "battle between those who are of constitutional concern and those who are not." Too often, the battle is ugly. Greene has lamented that this constitutional warfare "coarsens us, and by leaving us farther apart at the end of a dispute than we were at the beginning, it diminishes us."[15]

The Supreme Court's overconfidence bears a large share of the blame for this development. When the Court acts as though each case is susceptible to a single correct legal solution, knowable by the justices alone through their arcane tools of lawyerly deduction, it is only natural for contestants to disparage and denigrate even the most reasonable claims of their opponents. Litigants can win, after all, either by persuading the Court that their position is correct or by showing how their opponent's position is worthy of ridicule. And the more we ridicule our political opponents, the more we see them as enemies to be vanquished rather than fellow Americans with whom we hold good-faith disagreements.

The least harm principle's second virtue is its ability to transcend this hostile zero-sum rhetoric. When the Court decides hard cases based on the parties' relative ability to avoid the harms of an adverse ruling, justices are able to write more tolerant opinions that affirm both sides' legitimate interests and arguments. Just as significantly, the least harm principle creates incentives for the parties themselves to be more conciliatory to their opponents.

Start with how the principle would change the tenor of the Court's opinions. When justices believe their duty is to confidently deliver the one and only correct answer to pressing societal disputes, it is no surprise that their opinions are so dismissive of the losing side. Recall, for example, Justice Alito's accusation that the advocates who challenged Arizona's voting rules in *Brnovich v. Democratic National Committee* were engaged in a "radical project" aimed at overriding the text of the Voting Rights Act. Obliterating the arguments and interests advanced by litigants with whom one disagrees is time-honored tradition for lawyers. It is, however, a dangerous exercise for the nine lawyers on the Supreme Court. Disparaging people's deeply held positions on high-profile issues inevitably breeds antipathy.

The least harm principle offers a different way forward. By shifting the ground of decision away from esoteric, lawyerly arguments over originalism and complex webs of evolving precedent, the principle frees the Court of the perception that its duty is to declare a clear legal victor in constitutional battles that may more closely resemble a draw. It thus empowers the Court to write in a peacemaking rather than combative register.

Chief Justice Rehnquist's least harm opinion in *Cruzan* is a perfect example. Far from declaring Nancy Cruzan's parents "radical" for wishing to terminate their daughter's treatment, Rehnquist respectfully noted that "no doubt is engendered by anything in [the case's] record but that Nancy Cruzan's mother and father are loving parents." "If the State were required by the United States Constitution to repose a right of 'substituted judgment' with anyone," he continued, "the Cruzans would surely qualify."[16]

This is how our Supreme Court should speak to the losing groups in major, divisive cases if it wishes to maintain their trust. It is no coincidence that the Court treated the losing side with such respect in a decision that relied on the least harm principle: the principle invites precisely this respectful tone. The very condition that triggers the principle's application is, after all, the presence of a difficult legal question. And once the Court openly acknowledges this fact, there is no longer any need to belittle the losing side's legal or moral position. The least harm principle thus enables the justices to admit an important truth: in many high-profile cases, both sides have strong arguments.

Humbly admitting when a case is "hard" is honest, and honesty is always its own virtue. By embracing it, though, the Court can also foster mutual toleration between opposing litigants—a crucial democratic norm that is sorely lacking in America today. After all, when the Court sincerely affirms the validity of arguments and interests on both sides of a case (as it did in *Cruzan*), each side more easily sees the humanity in the other's position. Social science evidence from contexts as varied as religious and workplace conflict shows that the ability to acknowledge the strength of opposing viewpoints increases levels of tolerance and trust.[17]

In addition to encouraging the Court to write in more tolerant and constructive ways, the least harm principle encourages the same of competing litigants. To see how, start with the arguments litigants invariably make when the Court decides hard cases by confidently declaring one and only one side to be legally correct: litigants argue not only that their own position is correct but that their opponents are entitled to no constitutional regard. But when the Court determines winners and losers based on the options each side would have after defeat, the entire argumentative terrain changes. No longer is there value in belittling our opponents' constitutional status. The best way to prevail in a hard case is instead to point to constructive solutions. That is because the party that can identify the most effective way for its opponent to avoid its harm outside the Court is the party that will prevail inside it.

I admit that I am speculating somewhat when I claim that the least harm principle will produce this more constructive mode of argument. The Supreme Court has used least harm reasoning to decide a fair number of cases, as we have seen. But it has done so inconsistently and informally. And because the Court has not openly announced the least harm principle as a framework for future decisions, litigants do not always know to train their arguments on the alternative solutions that their opponents may employ if they lose.

In my view, though, this is a powerful reason why the Court should openly embrace the least harm framework for deciding all hard cases. Doing so would put litigants on notice of the importance of making arguments about each side's ability to mitigate the harms of defeat. That, in turn, would transform the arguments before the Court from zero-sum battles (in which lawyers have every reason to demean their opponents' constitutional claims) to debates over each side's options for securing its interests without the Court's intervention. The least harm principle, in other words, can help transform the aim of legal arguments at the Court from tearing our opponents down to finding other ways for them to get what they need. That's about as hopeful an image as one can imagine for today's Supreme Court.

The least harm principle possesses a third important virtue. It can enhance the Supreme Court's legitimacy by reducing the public's perception that the Court is merely engaged in partisan politics.

In chapter 2, I discussed the public's growing belief that the Court is driven by politics rather than law, and I argued that judicial partisanship is indeed an important factor behind the Court's declining levels of trust. But I also argued that partisanship alone is an insufficient explanation. It is the force-amplifying effect of overconfidence bias that has raised partisanship to such problematic levels.

The least harm principle addresses this problem at the root. By humbly acknowledging the difficulty of many prominent legal disputes, it alleviates the pressure on the Court to overconfidently declare a singular constitutional answer in hard cases. Instead, the Court compares the competing litigants' ability to avoid the harms of an adverse ruling. Critically, these least harm assessments are highly nuanced and turn on the particular facts in each case. Consider, for example, how two disputes involving identical subpoenas to President Trump, *Mazars* and *Vance,* resulted in divergent outcomes based on the different ability that Congress and New York prosecutors had to avoid their harms.

The result is a mode of deciding hard cases that is not politically predictable: whether the progressive or conservative side prevails will turn less on the justices' political priors and more on the alternatives each side enjoys for securing its interests. A quick glance at the least harm rulings the Court has already made confirms this fact. In some cases, such as *Cruzan, Mazars,* and *Espinoza* (the Montana school voucher dispute), the conservative position prevailed because the progressive side had superior options for avoiding harm. In other cases—*Vance, Bostock* (the LGBTQ discrimination case), and *Plyler* (the case concerning public education for undocumented immigrants)—the conservative side had stronger options for avoiding harm, so the Court ruled for the progressive position. By leading to a mixed bag of outcomes, the principle would aid the Court in refuting charges of rank partisanship.

• • •

Each of the three virtues I've described so far—providing losing groups with productive responses, producing a more constructive mode of constitutional argument, and reducing partisanship—can be seen in least harm decisions where one side has clearly superior strategies for avoiding its harm. But what about cases where this isn't true? Sometimes the question of which side possesses better post-defeat responses will be just as difficult as the first-order question of what the law requires. In such cases, it is fair to wonder if a contested decision based on the least harm principle will be just as problematic as a contested decision based on originalism or living constitutionalism.

This counterargument is actually even stronger than it seems. Recall that part of the problem when judges decide difficult cases under originalism and living constitutionalism is the influence of partisan motivated reasoning. Yet there is every reason to think the cognitive biases that afflict traditional theories of legal interpretation will also apply if the justices shift to a least harm analysis. When the justices evaluate each side's strategies for avoiding harm, in other words, we should expect them to do so with a thumb on the scale in favor of their preferred outcomes.

There is one important countervailing factor, however. Unlike with originalism or living constitutionalism, a justice applying the least harm principle will face partisan motivations that cut in competing directions. In one direction, justices will face subconscious pressure to rule for their favored groups by deeming the other side's post-defeat options more effective. Yet partisan pressure will also push in the other direction because the justices may prefer to identify powerful options for the groups they favor, not the groups they don't.

A case like *Bostock,* the LGBTQ employment discrimination dispute, illustrates this crosscutting dynamic. Recall that Justice Gorsuch's majority opinion ruled that Title VII's prohibition against workplace sex discrimination also encompasses discrimination based on sexual orientation and transgender identity. Conservative commentators were surprised and disappointed at Gorsuch's opinion, viewing it as a departure from his avowedly conservative credentials.

In keeping with those credentials, let us suppose that Gorsuch subconsciously preferred an outcome in which Title VII did not protect LGBTQ workers. One would expect, then, that in deciding which side possesses superior harm-avoidance strategies, partisan motivated reasoning would have swayed Gorsuch to rule against the workers, perhaps on the ground that they retained the post-defeat option of lobbying for express state or federal antidiscrimination protections. But partisan motivated reasoning would also cut the other direction: it is only by ruling in *favor* of the LGBTQ workers that Gorsuch's opinion was able to describe the series of legal arguments that religious employers could raise to avoid Title VII's requirements in future cases—arguments that Gorsuch declared deserving of "careful consideration."

Still, the most intellectually honest assessment is to admit that in cases where competing sides possess harm-avoidance strategies of similar ease and efficacy, the third virtue I've identified in this chapter—reducing partisanship at the Supreme Court—is unlikely to materialize. In such cases, it's likely that, over time, a conservative Court will find that progressive groups have stronger post-defeat responses than conservatives, leading to more rulings in favor of conservative litigants. (The opposite would surely be true for a liberal Court.) So partisanship will still be on display, only in a different way: rather than influencing the Court's pronouncements of who possesses what constitutional rights, it will lead the justices to conclude that certain, less-favored groups possess stronger options for reducing the harms they would suffer after defeat.

Even when this happens, though, the least harm principle would continue to serve important virtues. A least harm Court would still candidly acknowledge the strength of each side's legal arguments, furthering the value of mutual toleration. It would still encourage competing litigants to focus on solutions—other ways their opponents can protect their interests outside of court—rather than denigrating one another. And it would still identify responses that losing groups can pursue after defeat that are more productive than assailing the Court or their opponents. If partisanship is inevitable when the justices confront culturally and politically salient issues, in other words, perhaps the best option is to choose an approach that generates benefits for society even assuming that partisan reasoning will take its toll. That is something the least harm principle can plausibly accomplish.

To see how, let us consider how the least harm principle would apply in one of the most contentious issues in all of constitutional law: whether the Constitution protects the right to abortion. (I'll discuss the approach that a majority of justices actually took on this issue in *Dobbs v. Jackson Women's Health Organization* in the next chapter.)

For a justice committed to doing the least harm possible, the threshold issue is whether the constitutional right to abortion amounts to a hard question. The simplest version of the legal argument against a constitutional right to abortion is that because the word "abortion" appears nowhere in our founding document, no such right can exist.

It's a deceptively simple argument. And it's susceptible to a forceful response. True, there is no express right to an abortion in the Constitution. Yet neither does the Constitution expressly mention countless other important rights that are deeply held in our society. Take, for example, the right to send one's children to a private school. That right also appears nowhere in the Constitution. Yet that did not stop the Supreme Court from striking down an Oregon law that compelled all children to attend the state's public schools in the case of

Pierce v. Society of Sisters in 1925. The Constitution, *Pierce* held, vests "parents and guardians" with the right to "direct the upbringing and education of children under their control" because that right is implicit in the "liberty" guaranteed to parents under the Fourteenth Amendment Due Process Clause.[18] Without *Pierce,* present-day enrollment in private schools would be a fraction of its current figure (six million), roughly 80 percent of whom are enrolled in religious schools. Little wonder that conservative Justices Samuel Alito and Neil Gorsuch described *Pierce* in glowing terms in 2021, celebrating the case for recognizing that "[i]n our society, parents, not the State, have the primary authority and duty to raise, educate, and form the character of their children."[19]

Unless abortion opponents are willing to cast aside the parental right to direct the upbringing of their children, refuting the right to an abortion will require more than the mere observation that the Constitution does not mention it in explicit terms. The Constitution, after all, *does* guarantee the express right to "liberty" in the Fourteenth Amendment Due Process Clause. That was the source of the parental right recognized in *Pierce*. And it is just as plausibly the source of the right to an abortion. For just as the term "liberty" implies a sphere of deeply personal family decisions that the state cannot invade—decisions like how to educate one's children—so too could that sphere encompass one's deeply personal choice whether to carry a fetus to term. What is more, the right to abortion could also fit within the core concept of "liberty" as freedom from bodily restraint. By compelling a pregnant person to carry a child to term, the state exercises dominion over the person's body against their wishes.

There is accordingly a reasonable textual argument that the right to an abortion is encompassed by the "liberty" guaranteed by the Fourteenth Amendment. Yet the argument is hardly ironclad. The amendment guarantees that liberty may not be deprived without *due* process. So how much process is "due"? The Court's decision in *Pierce* stands for the proposition that no amount of process would be sufficient to deny a parent's liberty interest in sending their child to private school. Is the same true when the liberty at issue is the right to choose an abortion? The Constitution's text is utterly silent.

Grand constitutional theories are just as riddled with uncertainty. As to originalism, the honest assessment is that there is historical evidence to support both sides of the debate. Prominent originalist scholars such as Stanford professor Michael McConnell have argued that the Fourteenth Amendment's original meaning encompasses any right that individuals enjoyed in a substantial majority of states for a substantial period of American history.[20] That original understanding would seem consistent with a right to abortion for at least some of early pregnancy. When the Constitution was enacted in 1787, every American state freely allowed abortion at any point before quickening, or the first sign of fetal movement that typically occurs between the sixteenth and eighteenth weeks of pregnancy.[21] After quickening, however, abortion was generally punishable as a misdemeanor.[22]

The originalist argument against abortion responds that, by the time the Fourteenth Amendment was adopted in 1868, many states had changed their laws so as to prohibit abortions even before quickening.[23] So at that moment in time, more members of the American public would have understood abortion to be outside the realm of constitutional protection. Yet even this impression is complicated by the fact that a number of states still retained the quickening distinction—as many as twenty-one of the thirty-seven states then in the union.[24] Furthermore, public discussion had begun to emerge suggesting that abortion was indeed thought of by some as an inalienable right. In 1853 the author of a popular book argued, for example, that the pregnant person alone "has a right to decide whether she will continue the being of the child she has begun"; although "moral, social, [and] religious obligations should" weigh on her, "she alone has the supreme right to decide."[25] Is this a substantial enough body of evidence to give rise to a constitutional right? To ask the question is virtually to invite partisan motivated reasoning.

Living constitutionalism is just as indeterminate. If the question is whether, in light of precedent and modern values, most Americans *today* would understand the Due Process Clause's vague reference to "liberty" to encompass a right to abortion, no consensus exists. As of June 2021, 49 percent of Americans identify as pro-choice, compared to 47 percent who identify as pro-life (though these numbers were flipped as recently as 2019).[26] A combined 61 percent of respondents believe abortion should be legal under "all" or "most" circumstances, compared to a combined 37 percent who believe it should be illegal in "all" or "most" cases.[27] That sounds like a substantial majority in favor of legalizing the procedure. Yet another poll found that a plurality of Americans supported a ban on abortion after fifteen weeks: 48 percent supported such a law, while 43 percent opposed it.[28] That is not the stuff of an evolving societal consensus in either direction. Like so many other questions at the Court, the abortion debate is *hard*. And that's true from virtually every perspective—moral, historical, and legal.

The least harm principle's second step would therefore kick in, requiring the Court to identify the harms that both sides would suffer from an adverse ruling. The key here is to be deferential to both sides' genuine accounts of their interests, as that is what the Court has done in earlier least harm opinions. Defenders of state abortion bans will argue that a ruling against them will result in the deaths of many innocent unborn children. While some will disagree with this description, a justice applying the least harm principle could not. That is because many pro-life advocates sincerely believe that personhood begins at the moment of conception. On the other side of the case, those who challenge state abortion bans will argue that such bans deprive pregnant individuals of control over their bodies, forcing them to carry fetuses to term much like state-compelled incubators. The challengers will also point to evidence that abortion bans substantially increase maternal mortality rates because of the increase in pregnancy-related deaths, thus causing the loss of many innocent lives.[29]

All of these harms are of the utmost significance. It is impossible to say that one side's interest is weightier than the other without relying on a deeply subjective value judgment. The least harm principle would accordingly call for a third and final step: a comparison of each side's ability to avoid its harm should it lose in court.

Start with a ruling against the right to abortion. As we have seen in *Dobbs*'s actual aftermath, more than a dozen states have outlawed abortion access as a result.[30] In those states, pregnant people seeking to terminate their pregnancy have two kinds of options for how to respond. One set includes efforts to change the law—what I've called "public avoidance" strategies. But these efforts face an uphill political reality. At the state level, it is exceedingly unlikely that Republican lawmakers would reverse course in the deeply conservative states that enact abortion bans. At the federal level, pro-choice groups would need to win not just the White House and a majority of both houses of Congress but also enough Senate seats to override or eliminate the Senate filibuster. In fact, the filibuster stopped Senate Democrats from passing just such a bill in February 2022. What is more, even if enough senators could be persuaded to eliminate the filibuster for an abortion rights bill, it is an open question whether the Court itself would agree that Article I of the Constitution grants Congress the power to do so (I discuss this more in chapter 9).

Pregnant people seeking to terminate a pregnancy have therefore attempted a second kind of response, one involving private avoidance strategies that do not require public officials to change the law. On this approach, some pregnant individuals still have a reasonable ability to obtain an abortion—namely, wealthy patients who are able to pay to travel to another state where the procedure remains lawful. Even that, however, is the subject of some uncertainty, because some antiabortion states are actively considering restrictions on interstate travel to obtain abortion care. And quite apart from whether such restrictions are ultimately enacted, less affluent patients would still find the travel-for-care response highly impractical. Not only is it expensive to pay for air travel, lodging, and ground transportation—consider the plight of low-income minors who discover they are pregnant—but many working-class Americans do not have paid time off from work or ready access to childcare.

And so to avoid all of these life-changing consequences, some less privileged pregnant persons may make a different kind of choice altogether: they may attempt to terminate a pregnancy through unsupervised self-care or using some other dangerous method. Globally, abortions cause between 8 and 11 percent of all maternal deaths in countries where the procedure is illegal.[31] That is roughly 30,000 deaths each year. So an adverse ruling will result in some number of pregnant people in America dying. True, the percentage of abortion-related deaths might be somewhat lower in a nation like the United States, where health care is of somewhat higher quality. But at a minimum, many patients will be hospitalized after complications from their unsafe abortions—a serious harm of its own. By way of example, in Brazil, where abortion is illegal, 200 women die each year but approximately 250,000 are hospitalized.[32]

What about the options on the other side? If the Court were to rule against the pro-life position and strike down abortion bans under the least harm principle, such groups would have two primary responses for preventing their harm: the deaths of innocent unborn children. Neither response can be described as especially costless to implement.

To understand these options, begin with the evidence on the actual effect of laws criminalizing abortion. Such laws, it turns out, do not eliminate abortion so much as make it inconvenient. One recent study compared abortion rates in countries where the procedure is legal against rates in countries where it is banned; the latter showed only a modest decrease in actual abortion rates. Whereas 40 percent of unintended pregnancies ended in an abortion in countries where the procedure is broadly legal, 36 percent of such pregnancies ended in an abortion in countries that banned it.[33] This reduction—10 percent on a proportional basis—is not zero. But it is also clear that criminal abortion bans do not altogether stop what pro-life groups view as the purposeful termination of human life.

The question, then, is whether there are other strategies pro-life groups could pursue that would make equal or even greater headway in reducing the number of abortions and thus protecting fetal life. Research shows two: offering free, universal contraception and providing more generous social support structures to low-income prospective parents. These strategies address abortion in a completely different way: by reducing the *demand* for the procedure rather than punishing suppliers. A recent study performed at Washington University in St. Louis showed that offering women free birth control (such as IUDs, implants, birth control pills, patches, and rings) reduced unplanned pregnancies so sharply that abortion rates fell by "62 to 78 percent compared to the national rate."[34] That is many multiples more effective than a law punishing abortion providers. Increasing access to contraception is also vastly more popular. Whereas 46 percent of Americans believe abortion is "morally wrong," just 4 percent think the same about contraception.[35]

With respect to the social safety net, a study performed by Professor Laura Hussey found that in states like Texas, where the public holds a pro-life attitude, participation by low-income women in federal welfare benefits reduced the likelihood of abortion by almost 16 percent compared to similar women who did not receive those benefits.[36]

This finding also makes intuitive sense: if the choice whether to carry a child to term depends significantly on a parent's belief in their ability to provide for the child, then it stands to reason that actually helping parents provide for their children would influence reproductive preferences.

While both of these post-defeat options would accomplish pro-life groups' goal of reducing the number of abortions, it is also fair to acknowledge that both responses would be quite costly. Some of the most effective forms of contraception, such as IUDs and implants, can cost as much as $800.[37] For patients who lack insurance (or whose insurance does not cover these devices), a state would have to subsidize the cost to make contraception truly available. The costs of improving the social safety net for new, low-income parents would be even higher—current monthly federal welfare benefits for a single parent and single child range from $146 (in Mississippi) to $862 (in New Hampshire).[38]

The least harm principle's ultimate question is thus difficult to answer. It is hard to say with confidence that pro-life groups would have clearly superior options for avoiding their harms after defeat than pro-choice advocates would have for avoiding theirs—or vice versa. And where the harm avoider comparison is so close, the question is especially susceptible to motivated reasoning: progressive jurists will be more likely to think that pro-life groups should just enact more generous contraception and social safety net programs, while conservative jurists will think that pregnant people should just travel out of state for care or mobilize for a federal statutory abortion right.

Yet even if a conservative Court were to rule against an abortion right for this reason, that would still be an improvement over the current state of affairs for supporters of reproductive autonomy. For one thing, a ruling based on least harm concerns would openly recognize the crucial liberty interest that individuals have in choosing whether to carry a pregnancy to term as well as the significant harms that will be generated by denying that interest. For another, declaring that supporters of abortion rights may avoid their harms by advocating for a federal right-to-abortion statute or supporting interstate travel for patients who seek abortion care would offer them important strategies for securing abortion rights after their defeat. As we will see next chapter, the Court's actual opinion in *Dobbs* did neither.

Deciding the abortion issue under the least harm principle would be beneficial for another reason. A Court that thinks it can solve the issue conclusively using its usual legalistic tools, such as by identifying a singular answer based on eighteenth- and nineteenth-century historical arguments, is more likely to boldly declare an absolutist, all-or-nothing answer. In actuality, though, there are many rules the Supreme Court could recognize that would fall somewhere in between upholding *Roe v. Wade* and allowing states to ban abortion at any point in pregnancy. A Court applying the least harm principle would be able to consider these middle-ground positions.

To see how, consider the fifteen-week abortion ban that was at issue in *Dobbs*. Recall that under this Mississippi law, abortion would be criminally proscribed if performed after fifteen weeks, unless the procedure is performed due to a medical emergency or severe fetal abnormality. Recall also that the vast majority of abortions in America are performed before the fifteen-week mark; somewhere around 95 percent of all procedures (with a number of the remaining 5 percent performed later due to medical emergency or fetal abnormality).[39] The upshot is that replacing *Roe*'s fetal viability rule, which requires states to allow abortions until twenty-four weeks in pregnancy, with a fifteen-week rule, would leave the losing side with a plausible post-defeat response. Many pregnant people who would otherwise wait until after fifteen weeks to obtain the procedure could still choose before that time.

On the flip side, it is fair to say that allowing states to ban abortion only after fifteen weeks would not leave pro-life groups completely satisfied. That is because requiring states to allow abortions *before* fifteen weeks would still produce real harms from their perspective. But recall that such groups would still have the two other options for reducing the number of abortions: providing universal contraception and improving the social safety net for parents of young children. A least harm opinion would mention these options as plausible alternatives that remain open for disappointed pro-life advocates.

By pointing to both sides' options moving forward, a least harm approach to the abortion issue could affirm the significant interests on both sides of the case without leaving either side hopeless in defeat. Speaking personally, I confess that this outcome would be disappointing from a policy perspective. Replacing *Roe*'s twenty-four-week viability rule with a fifteen-week rule would produce significant hardship for many people (think of low-income, minor children who do not realize they are pregnant until after fifteen weeks). But I have no illusion that the Constitution unambiguously enshrines my every policy preference. The constitutional right to abortion poses a genuinely difficult legal issue, even if I don't think it is a hard policy one. Because the Court has no choice but to decide these difficult legal questions, the best it can do is decide them with a sincere awareness of the harmful consequences on both sides—and a commitment to leaving losing groups with ways to respond.

Because the private deliberations of the justices are rarely disclosed to the public, we may never know how close the Court came to embracing a least harm approach in *Dobbs*. But there is some reason to suspect that it was within reach. In April, before Justice Alito's draft opinion was leaked, the *Wall Street Journal* ran an eye-opening editorial insinuating that the Chief Justice was "trying to turn another Justice" to "find a middle way."[40] Ultimately, of course, the Chief did not succeed. But his solo concurring opinion in *Dobbs* is significant because of how it would have resolved the abortion issue: not through a shrill declaration that *Roe* was "egregiously wrong" but by paying careful attention to the options that pregnant people would have retained if Mississippi's fifteen-week ban were upheld.

The Chief Justice began his concurring opinion by observing that "the woman's right to choose to terminate her pregnancy" should "extend far enough to ensure a reasonable opportunity to choose." On the other hand, because of the state's important interest in protecting fetal life, the Chief also took the view that the woman's right should "not extend any further." And when it came to demarcating how much time was enough to count as a reasonable opportunity to choose, the Chief considered how pregnant people could respond to avoid their harms if a fifteen-week rule were to go into effect—precisely the analysis called for under a least harm approach. "Pregnancy tests are now inexpensive and accurate," he noted, and "safe and effective abortifacients . . . are now readily available, particularly during those early stages." Thus, while the Chief recognized that some abortions currently take place after the fifteen-week mark, he suggested that many of those procedures could still "take place earlier if later abortions were not a legal option."[41]

The Chief Justice's concurrence reflected the least harm principle in yet another important way: it forthrightly acknowledged the legal difficulty of the abortion issue. "Both the [majority] opinion and the dissent display a relentless freedom from doubt on the legal issue that I cannot share," the Chief admitted. He continued: "I am not sure, for example, that a ban on terminating a pregnancy from the moment of conception must be treated the same under the Constitution as a ban after fifteen weeks." Such candor must be applauded for the message it sends to our divided society: sometimes, our debates are heated not because the other side is acting in bad faith, but because there is no easy answer. And given that fact, sometimes the best the Supreme Court can do is ensure that both sides have meaningful ways to minimize their harms moving forward.[42]

Sadly, the *Dobbs* majority undertook none of the Chief's measured analysis. No other justice joined his opinion. Instead, the five other conservatives signed onto an alarmingly overconfident opinion. As much as anything, it is that overconfidence—along with the certitude on display in other important recent decisions—that bodes ill for the future of the Supreme Court.

8
Backsliding

When Chief Justice John Roberts announced on July 9, 2020, that the Supreme Court would begin its summer recess, he had good reason to be optimistic. The Court had deftly navigated a series of difficult and controversial disputes involving presidential subpoenas, immigration, LGBTQ rights, and school vouchers, and it would soon record its highest public approval rating in more than a decade. Broad majorities of Republicans and Democrats expressed support for the Court.[1]

Roberts deserved much of the credit. Not only had he built surprising coalitions of Democrat- and Republican-appointed justices across a range of divisive issues, but he'd done so in rulings that left losing groups little cause for outrage because they retained meaningful options for protecting their interests. In the words of CNN legal analyst Joan Biskupic, the end of the 2019–20 term left little doubt that "John Roberts was in charge."[2]

But by the time Chief Justice Roberts gaveled the Court into session for the start of the 2020–21 term just three months later, a great deal had changed. Justice Ruth Bader Ginsburg had died, President Trump had nominated Amy Coney Barrett to fill her seat, and the Republican-controlled Senate had rushed to confirm Barrett before the presidential election of 2020. And once Barrett was confirmed, the Chief Justice found that he was no longer the Court's median vote, meaning he had less leverage to steer his colleagues away from harmful rulings.

With the Chief no longer in clear command, the 2020–21 term was rocky. In some cases, the justices coalesced around moderate rulings that ensured losing groups would possess means for redress. In others, the new conservative supermajority ignored the harmful effects of its decisions, exposing losers to difficult-to-avoid consequences. And by the time the next term came around, in 2021–22, the five conservative justices to the Chief's right had seized control, issuing stridently overconfident decisions on a range of major issues, including blockbuster opinions on abortion and gun safety.

In New York City, life as its residents knew it ended on March 20, 2020. State officials had confirmed the city's first case of Covid-19 on March 1, and in less than three weeks, the virus had spread to more than eight thousand city residents. The scene in some hospitals was "apocalyptic"; at one point a refrigerated truck was stationed outside Elmhurst Hospital in Queens to store the bodies of the dead.[3] So on March 20, then-Governor Andrew Cuomo announced an order banning any nonessential gathering of any number of people for any reason. Restaurants closed, subway trains became eerily vacant, and people sheltered in place, uncertain of the future. The city that never sleeps ground to a halt.

The virus hit a peak in mid-April, with 8,021 new cases reported on the single day of April 15.[4] But owing significantly to the state's lockdown measures, the disease soon began to retreat. By late May, new daily case counts had fallen to the low hundreds. The state relaxed its restrictions on public gatherings, including its rules governing places of public worship: such places were permitted to reopen at 25 percent of their physical capacity.

But the respite was fleeting. Cases in New York City began to rise again in early October, leading the governor to issue a new executive order on October 6, 2020. That order divided the city into three "zones" depending on Covid case levels. In red zones, all nonessential gatherings were canceled; essential businesses were permitted to remain open; and houses of worship were effectively subjected to a limit of ten persons.[5] In orange zones, nonessential gatherings of up to ten persons were permitted; essential business and some nonessential businesses were allowed to open; and houses of worship could admit up to twenty-five persons. Less stringent rules applied in yellow zones, where Covid-19 cases were the lowest.

The Roman Catholic Diocese of Brooklyn sued the state, arguing that the red and orange zone rules violated the Free Exercise Clause. The core problem, the diocese argued, was that it was being treated worse than comparable businesses. Certain businesses deemed "essential" by the state, such as large retail stores, acupuncture facilities, garages, and chemical and electronic manufacturing facilities, were allowed to admit unlimited numbers of people. Yet houses of worship, which many would also call "essential," were limited to attendance by no more than ten or twenty-five persons. The state responded that places of worship were actually being treated *better* than many comparable businesses that posed similar public health risks such as concerts and theaters, which were forbidden to open at all.[6]

Given these reasonable arguments on both sides of the case, how was the Supreme Court to resolve this dispute? The Court had long struggled with this problem, leading to deep division over the meaning of the Free Exercise Clause. It had ruled previously that a law like New York's would not violate the clause—and would thus be upheld—so long as it was "neutral," meaning that it did not single out places of worship for harsher treatment.[7] But neutral compared to what? If churches were put in a class with theaters and concert venues, New York's law was better than neutral because houses of worship could at least open for some attendees. But if churches were like retail stores, acupuncture facilities, and other "essential" places, the law treated them worse.

In light of these complexities, the Supreme Court struck a reasonable balance. It accepted the diocese's argument that a ruling against it would inflict a significant burden upon the religious exercise rights of persons of faith, who would be banned from attending in-person services. It also agreed that the state unquestionably had a compelling interest in slowing the spread of Covid-19. But a ruling against the state's red and orange zone rules would not prevent it from reducing that spread so much as require it to do so in a different way: the state could tie "maximum attendance at a religious service" to a percentage based on "the size of the church or synagogue" rather than to strict ten- or twenty-five-person caps.[8] For smaller houses of worship, the two approaches would yield a roughly similar result. (Twenty-five percent of a building with a one-hundred-person capacity, for instance, would still be twenty-five people.) Yet many of the diocese's churches could seat several hundred or even a thousand people. Was it really more dangerous to let those facilities seat a fraction of their capacity (while observing strict masking and distancing requirements) than to let a retail store or acupuncturist admit an unlimited number of customers?

The Court's ruling in *Roman Catholic Diocese v. Cuomo* understandably drew criticism from those concerned about the spread of Covid-19. Yet nestled within the ruling was a set of arguments with far greater public health implications. Just two weeks after the Court issued that opinion, the Food and Drug Administration gave emergency approval for Pfizer's Covid-19 vaccine. And as production of the vaccine ramped up in 2021, the crucial public health question was whether states and localities could require individuals to get vaccinated. In theory, *Roman Catholic Diocese*'s ruling against New York's public health measures might have spelled disaster for supporters of vaccine mandates. But one of the Court's leading conservatives, Justice Neil Gorsuch, wrote a concurring opinion in the case explaining that he saw something meaningfully different about vaccine laws—a difference best understood through the lens of the least harm principle.

Gorsuch began his discussion of vaccine mandates by describing a precedent from 1905, *Jacobson v. Massachusetts,* in which the Supreme Court upheld a state law requiring individuals to do one of three things: get a smallpox vaccine, pay a $5 fine, or apply for an exemption on religious or medical grounds. Supporters of New York's red and orange zone restrictions had cited *Jacobson* in support of their effort to limit attendance at houses of worship. But Gorsuch found this unpersuasive because *Jacobson* was importantly different. Unlike New York's law, which effectively banned "all traditional forms of worship," with no exemptions available for adversely affected parties, Gorsuch emphasized that the law challenged in *Jacobson* gave affected persons three options: "accept the vaccine, pay the fine, or identify a basis for exemption."[9] To Gorsuch, the vaccine mandate was constitutionally permissible, unlike New York's capacity limits for houses of worship, precisely because its effect was "avoidable" by those who didn't want to comply.[10] That is the least harm principle in a nutshell.

Justice Gorsuch's decision to preemptively support similarly crafted vaccine mandates proved crucial. Federal courts rejected numerous constitutional attacks against vaccine requirements imposed by state and local governments, many of which have exemption provisions similar to those at issue in *Jacobson.*[11] (The Supreme Court did invalidate an Occupational Safety and Health Administration vaccine requirement for large businesses in January 2022, but not for constitutional reasons: the Court held that the administration lacked the statutory authority to impose it. By that point in time, however, 86.7 percent of American adults had already received at least one shot, including 95 percent of the most vulnerable population, those above the age of sixty-five.)[12]

Some have worried that the availability of vaccine exemptions might undermine public health efforts to vaccinate as many people as possible, but that hasn't been borne out by experience. The public university where I teach, for instance, offers just such an exemption: as a condition of enrollment or employment, students and employees must either provide proof that they've been vaccinated or apply for an individual medical or religious exemption. To date, 98 percent of persons have been vaccinated, just 1 percent have sought and obtained an approved exemption, and another 1 percent are either in the process of getting vaccinated or applying for an exemption.[13] The U.S. Navy has reported a similar figure, with roughly 99.5 percent of active duty members obtaining the vaccine and just a handful requesting an exemption or losing their jobs.[14] Far from serving as a loophole by which politically motivated individuals could evade the vaccine requirement, the religious exemption has been reserved for persons who can prove a sincere religiously based objection, as supported by a track record of rejecting other similar vaccinations and medical treatments.[15] No major religion has objected to the vaccine; Pope Francis even described getting it as the "moral choice" because it saves others' lives.[16]

These sensible vaccine measures, permitted under Justice Gorsuch's least harm reasoning, have had far greater effect in mitigating the spread of Covid-19 than any negative effect that *Roman Catholic Diocese* had in replacing New York's strict twenty-five-person attendance limits with percentage limits tied to physical capacity.[17] By pointing a way forward in these difficult cases, the least harm principle has helped the Supreme Court strike a reasonable balance on constitutional rights during an unprecedented public health crisis.

Alas, the Court failed to follow this principle on a different Covid-related issue in the 2020–21 term: mail-in voting. The states prepared for the presidential election of 2020 in a time of mounting danger. That June, they reported a combined total of roughly twenty thousand new cases each day. By November 2, on the eve of the election, that number had grown to more than ninety thousand. Because vaccines had yet to be approved, public health authorities understood that indoor, in-person voting would pose grave dangers for individuals, particular the elderly and immunocompromised.

Few states presented dangers more striking than Wisconsin. The number of cases in the state had exploded by more than 1,000 percent, from a few hundred a day at the start of June to more than four thousand a day in November. And a study of the health effects of in-person voting during Wisconsin's primaries that spring had already shown a relationship between in-person voting and Covid infection: for every 10 percent increase in in-person voting that a Wisconsin precinct experienced compared to its counterparts, that precinct suffered an 18.4 percent increase in positive test rates within three weeks.[18] And that was *before* case counts in the state increased by tenfold.

Given all of this, many Wisconsin voters made the sensible decision to request mail-in ballots for the November election. But the deluge of such requests produced its own complication: the surge overwhelmed state election officials and the United States Postal Service, such that the typical mail-in ballot would take *two weeks* to go from a Wisconsin clerk's office to a voter and back for counting, even if the voter filled and mailed out the ballot instantly upon receipt.[19] Recognizing similar delays, more than twenty states had voluntarily extended their deadlines for the receipt of mail-in ballots, promising to count any ballot *postmarked* by election day, even if it arrived a few days afterward.[20] But Wisconsin did not. So a group of voters and organizations sued in federal district court, arguing that the state's refusal to count ballots that had been cast on or before election day would violate the constitutional right to vote.

The district court sided with the challengers. Crucial to its conclusion was its finding that mail delays and backlogs in requests for mail-in ballots would create a "near certainty of disenfranchising tens of thousands" of Wisconsin voters.[21] To prevent that from happening, the court ordered a modest remedy: any ballot that was lawfully cast by election day would be counted so long as it was received within six days of the polls closing. But the Republican-controlled Wisconsin legislature appealed the case all the way up to the Supreme Court. On October 26, just a week before the election, the Supreme Court ruled in the state's favor on a party-line, six-to-three vote.

The Court's decision to reject the six-day extension for the receipt of mail-in ballots flatly contradicted the least harm principle. Unlike with Covid public health measures and vaccines, where the Court ensured that losing litigants retained options for redress, the decision in the Wisconsin case left losers with no reasonable options for avoiding their harms. The Court's ruling forced many Wisconsin voters to make an unenviable choice: either cast their ballots diligently by mail and risk having their votes go uncounted through no fault of their own, or vote in-person at indoor polling places and risk contracting a deadly disease.

A ruling in the other direction, however, would have left the state with an obvious way to avoid *its* harm—its claimed concern for announcing election results as quickly and accurately as possible after election day. Wisconsin could do what several other states did: segregate ballots received after Election Day for separate tabulation.[22] Keeping these ballots separate would allow officials to calculate and report the margin of all ballots received on election day as soon as possible, permitting an accurate report of received votes no matter whether the later-arriving ballots could change the outcome. Doing so would also permit challenges to the late-arriving ballots because of any alleged improprieties. Indeed, Wisconsin already had exactly such a procedure for separately tabulating provisional ballots, which could be counted up to three days after election day.[23] The district court's six-day extension would have simply represented a modest expansion of an approach the state had already taken. Yet the Supreme Court never considered the availability of this obvious alternative.

The Covid cases show how the 2020–21 term was uneven in following the least harm principle. The 2021–22 term, by contrast, was not—and not in a good way. On case after case and issue after issue, from climate change to church-state separation and to the rights of Native peoples, the Court consistently ruled without any concern for losing groups' ability to protect their interests after defeat.[24] Nowhere was this clearer than on two of the biggest issues of the day: abortion and guns.

I touched on *Dobbs v. Jackson Women's Health Organization,* the case that overturned *Roe v. Wade,* at the end of chapter 7. I noted that there are strong legal arguments on both sides of the issue. In defense of the right to abortion, the choice whether to carry a pregnancy to term is surely the kind of intensely personal decision that belongs within what the Court has previously called a "realm of personal liberty which the government may not enter."[25] After all, while the word "abortion" does not itself appear in the Constitution, the word "liberty" does. And that term, the dissenting justices forcefully argued in *Dobbs,* must "gain[] content from the long sweep of our history and subsequent judicial precedents," lest the Constitution be found not to protect the right to contraception or the rights to interracial and same-sex marriage.[26] When you add these arguments to the force of stare decisis, or the Court's general rule of "standing by things decided," one can see why so many have fervently pressed the case for reaffirming *Roe* in its entirety.

One can also see the arguments for an approach like the Chief Justice's, which would have permitted Mississippi's fifteen-week ban while simultaneously upholding the right to a "reasonable opportunity to choose" an abortion. Given the immense stakes on each side of the case, there is something to be said for drawing a line in a place where both sides still have meaningful options for avoiding their harms. The Chief's approach of drawing the line at fifteen weeks rather than twenty-four (as required under *Roe*) would at least leave pregnant women a meaningful period of time in which to exercise their right to choose. The Chief's approach was open to other critiques, to be sure. For instance, why fifteen weeks? Would twelve weeks be enough time for a pregnant person to choose? Ten? The answers are hardly clear.

In the end, the *Dobbs* majority followed neither the Chief's nor the dissent's reasoning. It criticized the Chief's "reasonable opportunity" approach as lacking a "principled basis."[27] And it rejected the dissent's view that the Constitution "gains content from the long sweep of our history and from subsequent judicial precedents" on the ground that it would "impose[] no clear restraints on . . . the exercise of raw judicial power."[28] After all, if all that is needed to create a new constitutional right is a Supreme Court decision that can serve later as a content-creating "judicial precedent," what is to stop any group of five justices from creating any right they find personally desirable and then bootstrapping from it to reach more and more self-serving outcomes? If you are a progressive, imagine five justices recognizing a new free speech right for homophobic business owners to discriminate against customers on the basis of sexual orientation and then extending that ruling to license more and more discriminatory conduct. This possibility is no mere abstraction: precisely such a case is pending in the Court, and I discuss it in the next chapter.

Instead of these approaches, the majority thought that the entire abortion issue could be conclusively resolved with just the right lawyerly tool: an assessment of how abortion was regulated by the states more than 150 years ago. The majority thus reasoned that the right to abortion could only be found to exist if it was "deeply rooted in the Nation's history and tradition."[29] And to answer that question, the majority engaged in a very specific inquiry, asking whether at the time of the adoption of the constitutional provision at issue in 1868 (the Fourteenth Amendment), the states criminally punished abortion throughout pregnancy. If the answer was yes, the majority reasoned, then the "liberty" protected by the Fourteenth Amendment could not include a right to abortion.

There are problems with this approach, not least the fact that it would freeze in place the rights that did (and did not) exist at a time when women were categorically excluded from the right to vote and when few women could own property or enter into contracts. Against that backdrop, to ask whether women enjoyed the right to an abortion in 1868, when the Fourteenth Amendment was ratified, is to fall victim to the worst kind of historical fallacy: presentism, or the anachronistic assumption that present-day ideas existed at a much earlier point in time.

Just as fundamentally, for the five justices in the majority to believe that they could answer a question as legally complex and morally freighted for millions of Americans as the right to abortion, simply by cracking open enough eighteenth- and nineteenth-century legal treatises, displays staggering overconfidence.

The cost of this overconfidence is plain to see in the majority's shoddy and partisan motivated historical analysis. Justice Alito declared that the "most important historical fact" in his entire opinion was "how states regulated abortion when the Fourteenth Amendment was adopted."[30] He then asserted that when the amendment was adopted, "three-quarters of the States, 28 out of 37, had enacted statutes making abortion a crime" at all points in pregnancy. He even repeated that precise claim, nearly verbatim, four times in the opinion, and included a twenty-two-page appendix (longer than most Supreme Court majority opinions!) listing every state that had supposedly banned all abortions.[31] It was on the strength of this supposedly decisive fact that Alito declared, without a shadow of doubt, that *Roe v. Wade* was "egregiously wrong from the start."

Alito's "most important historical fact," however, was no fact at all. Several of the states in his twenty-eight-state count did not actually ban abortion throughout pregnancy and instead continued a centuries-old rule under which women could terminate their pregnancy at any point before quickening, or the first noticeable movement of the fetus, often at roughly sixteen to eighteen weeks in gestation. For example, Alabama was on Alito's list even though the Alabama Supreme Court held in 1857 that the state's abortion ban only punished providers who perform a procedure after quickening; abortions before quickening remained legal.[32] Alito counted Oregon even though the state's own prosecutors declared in open court that Oregon's abortion law only prohibited abortion of a "quick fetus."[33] He counted two states—Nebraska and Louisiana—that consciously limited their bans to abortions performed via noxious poisons, drugs, or potions, while continuing to permit safer surgical procedures. He even cited a Virginia abortion statute enacted in 1848 when that very law was repealed ten months later and replaced with a different law that an antiabortion physician criticized for failing to prohibit procedures before quickening.[34]

For Alito to declare *Roe*'s basic recognition of an abortion right—which earned the votes of a bipartisan supermajority of Supreme Court justices over a two-decade period—"egregiously wrong" when his own historical analysis was so riddled with errors is as jaw-dropping as it is disheartening. Overconfidence is squarely to blame for it. Overconfidence in their legal conclusion also explains the majority's utter disregard for the thousands of pregnant people harmed by its ruling—and their lack of options for coping with this enormous defeat. The majority expressed this lack of concern bluntly: "[E]ven if we could foresee what will happen" across society after *Dobbs,* "we would have no authority to let that knowledge influence our decision."[35]

Sadly, *Dobbs*'s harmful effects did not take long to materialize. Just days after the decision, for example, a pregnant ten-year-old rape victim was denied access to an abortion under an Ohio ban that went into effect because of *Dobbs.*[36] Although the girl was eventually able to travel to Indiana to obtain the procedure, even that option will likely be unavailable in the months ahead as Indiana works to enact its own abortion ban—and as antiabortion states contemplate restrictions on travel across state lines for abortion care. By ignoring the harmful consequences of these laws on pregnant people, *Dobbs* was the furthest thing from a least harm ruling.

The conservative justices were equally unconcerned with the harms wrought by their decision in another major case decided in June 2022, just one day before *Dobbs. New York State Rifle & Pistol Association v. Bruen* concerned a New York gun safety measure that limited the concealed public carry of firearms to only those who can demonstrate a "special need" to carry a gun for self-defense. (Under New York law, the open carrying of firearms is categorically prohibited.) Thus, New York permitting authorities would not award a concealed carry license based on a generic fear of crime; an applicant was required to show a concrete danger particularized to their personal circumstances. Two individuals (both members of the New York State Rifle & Pistol Association) applied for, but were denied, concealed carry licenses. They sued, arguing that New York's limitation of public carry licenses to only those with a "special need" violated the Second Amendment right to keep and bear arms.

Few constitutional provisions provoke feelings as intense—and as conflicting—as the Second Amendment. And few provisions pose more difficult interpretive questions. Does the amendment enshrine a right to keep and bear arms for personal self-defense? Read in isolation, one clause of the amendment seems to suggest "yes." The amendment's second half provides that "the right of the people to keep and bear arms, shall not be infringed." Why else would the people's right to bear arms be protected, if not for the purpose of self-defense?

The first clause of the Amendment offers a conflicting answer: "*A well-regulated Militia, being necessary to the security of a free State,* the right of the people to keep and bear arms, shall not be infringed." The italicized portion of the amendment appears to qualify the entire right to keep and bear arms, limiting it to those with a connection to the militia. This makes some historical sense, given that the American people had just fought a revolutionary war against a British crown that had attempted to disarm their militias. For this reason, the Supreme Court had long understood the amendment to guarantee a militia-related right to bear arms. In 1939, for example, the Court considered a challenge brought by a man convicted of transporting a short-barreled shotgun in violation of federal law. The man argued that this law violated the Second Amendment, but the Court disagreed. "In the absence of any evidence tending to show that possession or use of a 'shotgun having a barrel of less than eighteen inches in length' at this time has some reasonable relationship to the preservation or efficiency of a well regulated militia," the Court reasoned, "we cannot say that the Second Amendment guarantees the right to keep and bear such an instrument."[37]

All of this changed in 2008, however, when the Supreme Court decided *District of Columbia v. Heller*. In chapter 4 I explained how the Court in *Heller* recognized a right to keep a handgun in one's home for personal self-defense (rather than militia) purposes by drawing on hotly disputed historical materials. *Heller* only concerned the right to keep a gun inside one's home, however, so it did not answer the question at issue in *Bruen:* Does that same right extend to all law-abiding individuals outside the home, effectively constitutionalizing the right to publicly carry a firearm?

At first glance, the text of the amendment would seem to support such a right. The right at issue is not only to keep but also to "bear" arms—and there is little sense to a right to bear arms only within the safety of one's home. Yet who may bear such arms, and for what purpose? Again, the prefatory clause, which speaks of the importance of a militia, suggests that a person may bear arms only if doing so would be for some militia-related purpose. Like so many other questions arising out of our 230-year-old Constitution, a close textual analysis points up no definitive answer.

In *Bruen,* however, all six conservative justices found "little difficulty" locating an answer in a different place. To justify a regulation of the right to bear arms, the Court declared, "the government must demonstrate that the regulation is consistent with this Nation's *historical tradition* of firearms regulation."[38] Just as in *Dobbs,* in other words, the Court deemed irrelevant any consideration of the modern-day consequences of its ruling or whether losing groups possessed other options after defeat. All that mattered—in deciding whether millions of Americans would be free to enact laws protecting themselves from gun violence or to choose to carry a pregnancy to term—was what five members of the Court thought about arcane statutes adopted centuries ago.

This is overconfidence on steroids, and its price is evident from an evenhanded review of the *Bruen* majority's historical analysis. Faced with genuinely complex and conflicting historical materials, the majority did not honestly admit the lack of a clear answer: it succumbed instead to partisan motivated reasoning and mined those materials to support its preferred outcome. Thus, writing for the majority, Justice Thomas conceded that English law, the closest predecessor to American law at the founding, had long regulated the public carrying of arms. The Statute of Northampton, enacted in 1328, provided that people could not "ride armed by night nor by day, in Fairs, Markets . . . nor in no part elsewhere, upon pain to forfeit their Armour to the King, and their Bodies to Prison at the King's pleasure."[39] Yet Thomas rejected the significance of this statutory precedent for a remarkable reason: it had "little bearing on the Second Amendment adopted in 1791" because it was enacted "more than 450 years before the ratification of the Constitution." Reading that argument, one would assume Thomas's point to be that the Statute of Northampton was repealed long before the American founding, such that it could cast no light on what Americans would have thought about lawful firearms regulation in 1791. But that is not the case: the Statute of Northampton's prohibition against public carrying of arms *remained in force* at least into the late eighteenth century, even earning citations in leading treatises read throughout the American colonies.[40]

The majority also rejected the significance of roughly two dozen state limitations on public firearm carry enacted between the colonial era and the adoption of the Fourteenth Amendment. Thus, before and shortly after the founding, Massachusetts, New Hampshire, New Jersey, Virginia, and Tennessee all prohibited the carrying of arms in public where done "in fear" or "terror" of the people.[41] A number of states later enacted statutes altogether prohibiting concealed public carry, including Alabama, Louisiana, Georgia, Kentucky, and Tennessee.[42] And ten more states passed laws before 1868 making it more difficult for certain people to carry guns in public if they lacked a "reasonable cause to fear an assault or other injury, or violence to [their] person"—a close analog to New York's "special need" permitting requirement.[43]

Faced with this substantial history and tradition of public firearms regulation, Justice Thomas labored to distinguish away each law as insufficiently similar to New York's special need requirement. Some of the early statutes were inapposite, he argued, because they only prohibited "bearing arms in a way that spreads 'fear' or 'terror' among the people."[44] (Never mind that then, as now, many rational people would experience fear as a natural consequence of seeing a person bear *any* firearm in public.) And the laws limiting guns to people with "reasonable cause" to fear for their safety were insufficiently similar because they did not operate through a licensing requirement quite like New York's.[45] Instead, those laws required certain gunowners who lacked reasonable cause to fear for their safety to post a financial surety, or bond, that would be forfeited upon misuse of the firearm.

Was Justice Thomas right to conclude that all of these historic firearms restrictions are insufficiently analogous to New York's special need law? Or are the historic laws similar enough to uphold it? I want to be very clear about my answer: *I don't know*. I don't know because I do not think it is possible to discern a single, clear answer to the question of what exactly thousands of lawmakers across the different states were getting at hundreds of years ago when they passed a variety of laws limiting the public carrying of firearms—arms that, of course, barely resemble today's semiautomatic handguns. To hold that judicial conjecture about how closely those centuries-old laws resemble modern laws is not just the starting point but also the ending point of constitutional analysis is to replace democratically elected lawmakers' considered judgment with rule by black-robed fiat. Yet that is exactly what the *Bruen* majority accomplished when it reached its strident conclusion: "there is no historical basis for concluding that" the Second Amendment "permitted broad prohibitions on all forms of public carry."[46]

The worst part about *Bruen*'s new test for evaluating gun safety laws, however, is not what it turns on but what it excludes completely from judicial consideration: any concern for the momentous reasons why lawmakers might enact gun safety laws to begin with. Justice Thomas's opinion is unambiguous about this point: "to justify [a gun] regulation, the government may not" argue that "the regulation promotes an important interest."[47] That is so arresting that it deserves repeating: in all future Second Amendment challenges to local and state laws that reduce gun violence, it will be categorically irrelevant if a law is necessary to save lives.

A concrete example can help to prove the point. One of the most impactful laws that a state could enact to reduce the epidemic of gun violence in America without significantly burdening gun rights is a law limiting individuals to owning only "smart guns," or guns that use fingerprint or radio frequency technology to prevent unauthorized users from firing the weapon. (Such laws are politically unlikely today due to opposition from the gun lobby, but the example is worth playing out to see how far the *Bruen* test strays from the least harm principle.) If every gun in the nation were a smart gun, the result would be to save the lives of hundreds of children who accidentally shoot themselves, render inoperable hundreds of thousands of stolen firearms, and substantially reduce the forty-five thousand gun deaths in America each year.[48] Just as importantly, such a law would impose a relatively minor burden on lawful gun owners, all of whom would still be able to use their firearms for self-defense. And radio frequency technology—which can be integrated into a wearable bracelet or ring to activate a firearm when within a certain proximity—would be especially effective at limiting any inconvenience entailed by the law.

Under *Bruen*'s history and tradition test, however, a smart gun law would almost surely violate the Second Amendment. For obvious reasons, there is no history or tradition of eighteenth-century firearm regulations requiring guns to use radio frequency or fingerprint activation technology or anything analogous. So applying *Bruen*'s test, that would be the end of the analysis. None of the law's benefits—the lives of children and adults saved, the elimination of an entire market for stolen guns, and the minimal burden on gun owners—would be relevant.

An approach to gun safety laws grounded in the least harm principle would be far more sensible. Under it, the Court would start by admitting that the legal question is not susceptible to a single, clear answer: whether the Second Amendment protects an individual self-defense right or only a militia right is hotly contested. The Court would then recognize the substantial and deeply felt interests on both sides of the case: the desire of gun owners to be able to defend themselves, as well as the unquestionable interest of state lawmakers to reduce mass shootings and other violent crimes. (To the latter point, researchers have found that special need permitting limits like New York's reduced violent crime by roughly 13–15 percent compared to states in which public carry was not similarly restricted.)[49] Finally, the Court would resolve the case by asking which side would possess superior alternatives for avoiding the consequences of an adverse ruling.

In the context of a hypothetical smart gun law, this last step would cut in favor of upholding the regulation because gun safety proponents would have no plausible alternative for so effectively reducing the incidence of accidental shootings and shootings using stolen weapons. By contrast, responsible gun owners concerned with self-defense could continue to use smart guns for that purpose with little burden, particularly in the case of guns activated via radio frequency in one's watch, ring, or some other wearable. To be sure, some gun owners would be unable to afford the price of a new smart gun, which can cost as much as $900. So a smart gun requirement would stand a greater chance of being upheld if lawmakers were to take these gun owners' concerns into account, for example through a non-smart-gun buyback program and a temporary phase-in period during which non-smart-guns could be carried without punishment. This is yet another example of how deciding cases through the least harm principle would nudge legislatures toward reasonable compromises.

In the context of public carry restrictions like New York's "special need" requirement, the least harm principle's final step is admittedly a closer call. Start with the alternatives that would be available to gun owners if the Court had upheld New York's special need requirement. Although such persons would not be able to carry their guns in public, they would still be allowed to carry *nonlethal* self-defense weapons, such as stun guns (which can discharge a high-voltage shock upon direct contact) and tasers (which can shoot electrical probes over a distance). Indeed, the Court held in a little-noted opinion in 2016 that *Heller*'s right to possess a gun in self-defense encompassed a stun gun that a woman had used to prevent a physical assault by her ex-boyfriend.[50] Gun owners would also have the option to seek out legislation liberalizing gun restrictions, whether in statehouses or in Congress. Still, neither of these options is perfectly sufficient: a stun gun is likely less helpful than a handgun to deter or defend oneself against a heavily armed assailant, and efforts to convince blue state legislatures (or Congress) to relax gun permitting regimes seem likely to run into a variety of veto gates.

A similarly mixed picture is true for states like New York now that the Court has invalidated special need permitting limits. One response would be for states to require applicants for public carry permits to pass criminal and mental health background checks, to comply with firearms safety and training courses, and perhaps even to prove their possession of gunowners' liability insurance.[51] Another response would involve restricting firearm carry in certain sensitive places. Indeed, New York responded to *Bruen* by enacting a new law forbidding publicly carried firearms in educational institutions, places that serve alcohol, public transportation, entertainment venues, medical facilities, and other similar places.[52] Taken together, these alternatives would seem to yield *some* public safety benefit, though likely not as much as keeping guns off the streets altogether.

For these reasons, it is hard to conclude with certainty whether one side in *Bruen* would possess an obviously superior way to avoid the harm of an adverse ruling. Even still, a least harm ruling would have been preferable over an overconfident declaration that the law means one and only one thing. That is, from the perspective of gun safety proponents, an adverse ruling accompanied by the recognition that New York may still enact strict permitting requirements and ban guns in a range of sensitive places would be far better than a declaration that the Constitution's text and history guarantee a right to public firearm carry, full stop.

To his credit, Justice Kavanaugh attempted this kind of least harm move in a concurring opinion (joined by Chief Justice Roberts), which suggested that New York and other states may still employ upfront licensing requirements such as "fingerprinting, a background check, a mental health records check, and training in firearms handling" among "other possible requirements."[53] But Kavanaugh's (and the *Bruen* majority's) refusal to consider whether gun owners on the other side of the case would have had meaningful self-defense options short of publicly carrying a firearm is telling. Providing post-defeat alternatives to New York and other states concerned with gun violence was a mere afterthought. The *Bruen* majority's main thought was a bold announcement concerning the future of gun safety laws across the nation. Henceforth, the fate of those laws will be decided by the justices' ability to discern a singular historical tradition out of conflicting, centuries-old laws.

It is natural to read *Dobbs* and *Bruen* as evidence that the Court has abandoned the least harm principle that was used in several of the cases discussed earlier in the book. I am sympathetic to that conclusion, and I lament the backsliding that these more recent rulings represent, especially in comparison to the promising 2019–20 term discussed in chapter 6.

But the Court's fate is not sealed. Its damaged credibility need not be permanent. The key to saving it starts with the American people, who have always had the power to call the Court to account for its overconfidence. The next chapter discusses how.

9

The Crossroads

In December 1955, an unexpected author offered some unexpected praise in memory of a former colleague. "No man," he wrote in a tribute issue of the *University of Pennsylvania Law Review,* "ever served on the Supreme Court with more scrupulous regard for its moral demands than Mr. Justice Roberts."[1]

The author was Associate Justice Felix Frankfurter, whom FDR had appointed to serve as the intellectual leader of the New Deal Supreme Court. Frankfurter's praise for his late colleague Owen Roberts was most surprising given his earlier opinion of the man. In a private letter to Chief Justice Harlan Fiske Stone, Frankfurter had once complained of Roberts's "severe intellectual limitations."[2] Nor was he any more impressed with Roberts's backbone. After Roberts's famously unexpected vote to uphold the minimum wage in *West Coast Hotel v. Parrish*—the so-called switch in time because of its inconsistency with his earlier positions—Frankfurter complained that "everything that he now subscribes to he rejected not only June first last, but as late as October twelfth."[3] Other members of the Court held similarly dim views. When Roberts stepped down from the Court in 1945, his colleagues could barely muster a positive word in their customary retirement letter. Frankfurter described it as "the minimum of what you could write and say anything that wasn't ungracious."[4]

To swing from that appraisal to calling Roberts the justice most attuned to the Supreme Court's moral demands in its entire history is, to say the least, quite a change. Why did Frankfurter change his assessment so dramatically? He pointed to the six years he served with Roberts on the bench, writing in his tribute that "not until I became a colleague, and even then only after some time, did I come to realize . . . the qualities that he brought to the work of the Court." His listing of those qualities is revealing. What set Roberts apart had nothing to do with legal acumen, nothing to do with the ability to pore over dense texts in an effort to uncover the law's one, true meaning. Instead, Frankfurter wrote, it was Roberts's "humility engendered by consciousness of limitations, respect for the views of others whereby one's own instinctive reactions are examined anew, [and] subordination of solo performances to institutional interests" that made him "indispensable" to the Supreme Court.[5]

Over the Court's history, plenty of justices have possessed powerful minds, breathtaking mastery of rhetorical craft, and the tremendous confidence that often comes with professional success. The Ivy League–steeped Frankfurter admired these traits more than most.[6] But Owen Roberts? He won Frankfurter over with his humility.

Roberts's humility was more than a charming personal quality. It helped rescue the Supreme Court from a dire threat to its public legitimacy and shaped its jurisprudence for decades to come. Only an awareness of his own limitations enabled Roberts to admit that his earlier views about the constitutionality of the minimum wage and other economic regulations might have been wrong. And it was only his humble recognition of this potential for error that enabled him to see the value of the legal approach that eventually rescued the New Deal Court: the concept of deferring to democratically elected legislatures in hard cases. Not only did that approach recognize the Court's inability to discern a single clear legal answer to every pressing social controversy, but it also left losing business interests free to pursue redress through the ordinary legislative process.

Crucially, however, Roberts's changed views did not emerge out of thin air. They were activated by a forceful public response against an overconfident Court that had lost touch with American society. The story is worth retelling because it provides insight into the predicament facing today's Court—and how a motivated public can fight to inspire today's justices to embrace humility, much as Owen Roberts did, before it is too late.

In 1935 and 1936, in the midst of the Great Depression, the Supreme Court issued a pair of rulings that shook the nation. The first case, *Schechter Poultry Corporation v. United States,* invalidated the National Industrial Recovery Act, a major New Deal law that regulated industry, protected workers' right to unionize, and facilitated fair competition. The second case, *United States v. Butler,* struck down the Agricultural Adjustment Act, another landmark New Deal law that stabilized agricultural prices by curbing excess production. Both acts were passed as vital components of FDR's vaunted first hundred days in office, and they represented the administration's efforts to restore two of the most vital sectors of the economy. Yet with the stroke of a pen, the Supreme Court rendered both laws unenforceable, significantly hampering FDR's efforts to end the Depression.

The public responded by delivering the Court a stinging rebuke in three important ways. The first involved the election of 1936—a contest in which the Court's effort to kneecap the New Deal through decisions like *Schechter Poultry* and *Butler* was very much on the ballot. Voters were decisive. Not only did they reelect Roosevelt by a twenty-four-point popular vote margin (seven points greater than in 1932), but they also handed the House and Senate to Democrats with overwhelming supermajorities. It is impossible to overstate the significance of this electoral shift and what it meant for the Court. Indeed, Professors Dan Ho and Kevin Quinn have offered strong statistical evidence that this electoral outcome actually precipitated

Justice Owen Roberts's change of heart in voting to uphold New Deal laws.[7]

Second, the public also responded by supporting congressional efforts to pass new legislation in direct answer to the Court's earlier decisions. Thus, after the Court struck down the National Industrial Recovery Act, lawmakers passed the National Labor Relations Act to codify many of the earlier law's important labor union provisions. And after the Court invalidated the Agricultural Adjustment Act in 1936 because of the particular way in which it taxed agricultural processors, Congress enacted a new version of the same law in 1938, with an amendment that worked around the Court's earlier ruling. Put another way, neither Democratic lawmakers nor the people who voted for them took the Court's decisions as the final word; they kept working to find new legislative solutions to the problems facing society.

Third, another legislative proposal played a role in sending a message to the Court. Shortly after his dominant victory in the presidential election of 1936, Franklin D. Roosevelt proposed to add as many as six justices to the nine-member Court. The stated purpose of this plan, which carried the benign name "Judicial Procedures Reform Bill of 1937," was to increase the Court's efficiency by infusing it with more and younger manpower. (The bill technically afforded the president the power to appoint one new justice for each justice then over seventy years old.) But no one was fooled. The bill's true motivation was to ensure that the Court would uphold FDR's New Deal legislative programs against a flurry of constitutional challenges.

FDR's court-packing plan eventually died in Congress, but the key point for now is how the Court came to uphold the New Deal nonetheless. The standard story is that two of the six conservative-leaning justices—Owen Roberts and Charles Evans Hughes—changed their votes in direct response to it. The more centrist Hughes represents a somewhat easier case, since he had already voted with the liberal justices on important issues such as the minimum wage.[8] Hughes thus had less distance to travel in his move to the left, a pivot Professor Bruce Ackerman has attributed to his "constitutional statesmanship of the first order."[9]

For Roberts, the tale is more complicated. The popular account is that he held true to his conservative views until FDR publicly announced the court-packing plan, in February 1937. Then, worried about the consequences for the Court's reputation and legitimacy if the plan were approved, he abruptly changed his vote in a pair of key cases upholding a state minimum wage law in March (*West Coast Hotel v. Parrish*) and the federal National Labor Relations Act in April (*NLRB v. Jones & Laughlin Steel*).[10] Thus was born the famous quip "the switch in time that saved nine": by eliminating both the need and the political momentum for court-packing, Roberts's last-minute change of heart saved the nine-member Court.

Scholars debate the accuracy of this account. Among other things, there is evidence that Roberts had already cast his decisive vote to uphold the minimum wage in *West Coast Hotel* well before FDR publicly announced his court-packing plan.[11] Moreover, as I mentioned earlier, statistical evidence suggests that Roberts began shifting his votes to the left earlier, shortly after the Democrats' landslide election victory in 1936. What really motivated Roberts's change in judicial philosophies may have thus had less to do with FDR's threat to pack the Court and more with the public's decisive turnout in favor of New Deal Democrats. Even still, the court-packing proposal could have only added to the public pressure that Roberts (and Hughes) perceived, pushing them further toward a philosophy of deferring to the legislature.

Thus, faced with a recalcitrant Court in 1935 and 1936, the American people responded through a combination of voting en masse, convincing their lawmakers to pass new laws to circumvent the Court's most troubling decisions, and openly discussing structural Court reform. It worked: the Court mended its ways, adopting a humbler, more deferential approach to uphold every New Deal program challenged thereafter. This success can serve as a playbook for Americans concerned about the Court today.

The most important lesson the history of the New Deal Supreme Court teaches those who are worried about the direction of today's Court is to get out the vote—by which I mean not only showing up at the polls but donating to, and volunteering for, candidates in close House and Senate elections around the nation. This kind of nitty-gritty electoral mobilization is important in two ways: it can send the Court a direct message about the unsustainability of its current course, and it can create conditions for lawmakers to challenge the Court's most out-of-touch rulings.

I should pause to acknowledge the one-sided nature of what I am proposing. When I emphasize the importance of voting to send the Court a message, the reality is that because of our two-party system, I am talking about voting for, donating to, and otherwise supporting Democrats in contested House and Senate races. But not everyone who is worried about the Court's direction is a Democrat—a point worth making explicit. While a paltry 13 percent of Democrats reported a "great deal" or "quite a lot" of confidence in the Court in June 2022, the figure was only somewhat better among independents: 25 percent.[12] For the many independent voters who are concerned about the Court, however, a dilemma emerges. Reining in the Court may be one reason to vote for Democrats, yet there may be other reasons that cut in the opposite direction. How to weigh these competing considerations?

One answer is to think about the overarching goal of restoring the "middle" in American politics—a bigger-picture project that should be appealing to independents. One major reason the political center has been hollowed out is partisan gerrymandering, the rampant practice of Republican- and Democrat-controlled state legislatures drawing electoral maps to ensure that their party will retain a supermajority of the state's seats in Congress, even when they win only a minority of the state's popular vote. These maps carve out numerous "safe" districts that are so loaded with voters of a single party that the real contest is the primary election—where the candidate who can tack furthest to the extreme often wins.

The Supreme Court had an opportunity to invalidate partisan gerrymandering, but it declined to do so in 2019 in an important case called *Rucho v. Common Cause*. That decision did not eliminate an important strategy for eradicating partisan gerrymandering, however. Congress can still enact a statute requiring all states to create independent redistricting commissions responsible for drawing electoral maps, which would substantially reduce the number of noncompetitive seats and create conditions for centrist candidates to emerge across the nation. For an independent who thinks that having more moderate officials in *both* parties sounds like a good idea, though, only one party supports the kind of federal law that would bring it about: the Democrats, who included an independent redistricting commission requirement in a major voting rights bill that failed to secure passage in 2021 due to the Senate filibuster.

For these reasons, Americans across the political spectrum who are worried about the Supreme Court must take to the polls. Without such electoral pressure, the justices who rolled back reproductive autonomy rights and gun safety measures in June 2022 will see no reason to be humbler in their future efforts to rewrite the Constitution on topics such as contraception and same-sex marriage. *With* electoral pressure, by contrast, lawmakers can enact statutes that would directly attack some of the Court's most harmful rulings. Partisan gerrymandering is an important example: with enough votes in Congress, we can carve out from the Senate filibuster to remedy the Court's failure to curb gerrymandering through the kind of independent redistricting committee statute mentioned above. With enough votes in Congress, we can also carve out from the filibuster to protect voting rights, pass sensible gun safety laws, and enact a federal statutory right to abortion to remedy the Court's decision in *Dobbs*.

But as in 1937, Congress can also do more. It can send a more aggressive message to this Court by proposing deeper, structural reform of the Court itself. We've discussed court-packing at earlier points in this book, which is problematic as an actual policy proposal insofar as it would encourage tit-for-tat retaliation and even presage democratic collapse. Yet the aftermath of FDR's *unsuccessful* court-packing effort suggests that, in moments when the Court is deeply out of step with mainstream American values, the same democratic harms may not occur after *unrealized threats* to pack the Court if the justices respond to them with greater humility and moderation. For that reason, even if one is ultimately opposed to adding more justices to the bench, calls to pack the Court may remain important for strategic reasons. After all, if today's conservative justices were forced to choose between spending the rest of their careers on the minority of a packed and delegitimized Court or serving as power brokers on a more centrist Court that restores the public's confidence in the judiciary, some might prefer the latter—much as how Charles Evans Hughes and Owen Roberts responded in 1937.

But another court reform option may be more promising than court-packing, both as an actual policy goal and as a source of pressure on the Court: a practice known as "jurisdiction stripping."[13] The basic idea behind jurisdiction stripping is that Congress may enact a law that explicitly removes the Supreme Court's power to pass judgment on a particular kind of legal question. Take, for instance, a hypothetical statute that Congress could pass to eliminate partisan gerrymandering by requiring independent redistricting commissions. Although such a statute would eliminate Republican and Democrat gerrymanders alike, the reality is that Republicans control more state legislatures and thus benefit from the practice more.[14] Partisan motivated reasoning may thus lead the current conservative Supreme Court to find some way to strike down an independent redistricting commission law. So to prevent that possibility, Congress could include a provision in the statute declaring that the Supreme Court lacks jurisdiction, or the power of review, over the law. The constitutional basis for this is quite strong; Article III's second clause provides that the Court "shall have appellate Jurisdiction" subject to "*exceptions*" that "the Congress shall make." The Supreme Court ruled in 1869 that Congress could use its authority under this clause to strip the Court's jurisdiction over certain cases, and a robust body of literature supports that conclusion.[15]

If Congress were to use this power selectively to deem certain legal questions—such as statutory voting rights protections to which the conservative justices have been particularly hostile—outside the Supreme Court's power of review, the result could be to send the Court a targeted yet striking message: continuing down an overconfident path will lead to diminution of the Court's power. Importantly, this approach would not run into quite the same problem of escalating retaliation when Republicans regain control. True, Republicans would certainly have license to retaliate by stripping the Court of jurisdiction in future cases (though why they would do so when the Court is overwhelmingly conservative is an open question). But even if Republicans did strip the Court of power in other areas, that would not jeopardize the Court's integrity in the same way as increasing its size from nine to thirteen, and then to seventeen or even more members.

Jurisdiction stripping is thus a viable answer to a Court gone awry. Ultimately, however, it would be better to have a trusted, centrist, and publicly responsive Court than a powerless one. And on that front, the biggest takeaway from the history of the New Deal Court is that if voting, legislative action, and calls to reform the Court are going to succeed, it will be in a particular way: as reasons for the justices to bring their own behavior into line with public values. That, at least, is how Justice Owen Roberts responded when he humbly changed course and began voting to defer to Congress's New Deal legislation, earning Justice Felix Frankfurter's lasting admiration in the process. Our best hope for today's Supreme Court is for Chief Justice John Roberts and one other conservative to do the same.

Yet there is a complication. Even supposing that another conservative justice were to join the Chief in an effort to moderate the Court's rulings and thereby preserve its image, how will we know that they have chosen this route? In 1937, Roberts and Hughes were able to signal that they'd reached a détente through their votes in just a pair of important cases. They could do so because the entire controversy over the Court at the time essentially involved two legal issues: the constitutionality of federal and state economic regulations designed to protect working-class Americans. Those regulations may have spanned an array of fields, from the minimum wage to social security, organized labor, agricultural regulation, and beyond. But the same two questions existed in each dispute. Could Congress use its Article I authority to enact these economic measures? And could states enact the same laws consistent with the Fourteenth Amendment's guarantee of due process of law? When Roberts and Hughes answered "yes" to both questions, backtracking on contrary earlier rulings, those two outcomes made clear to all that they'd changed their minds in a durable fashion.

Today, the landscape of legal controversy is much wider. Economic issues remain contentious, including the role of organized labor. But the Court and society are also deeply divided over immigration, voting rights, reproductive autonomy, gun safety, the environment, religious freedom, antidiscrimination law, and other high-profile issues—all of which implicate divergent legal doctrines. There is no way for the Court to signal its desire for a lasting settlement through just one or two case outcomes.

We can, however, look at the Court's reasoning. As we have seen, the big move during the New Deal settlement was the Court's embrace of a particular judicial principle for deciding close cases—the doctrine of legislative deference. As Chief Justice Hughes put it for the Court in *West Coast Hotel,* "even if the wisdom of [a] policy be regarded as debatable and its effects uncertain, still the Legislature is entitled to its judgment."[16] The Court would rely on this humble rule—which it called the "presumption of constitutionality"—in dozens of subsequent rulings.[17] By formally and expressly adopting this legal principle, the New Deal justices, and Justices Hughes and Roberts in particular, committed themselves to a course of humble moderation in a way that earned the public's trust.

Today's Court can likewise signal its intentions through its reasoning. As in 1937, humility will be the first step. The Court must admit that it cannot discern clear answers to every dispute through lawyerly analysis alone. The second step is trickier, because the issues at stake are so different. The 1937 approach of deferring to legislatures won't work in the modern era: history is filled with examples of elected majorities running roughshod over vital personal freedoms. Neither conservatives nor liberals today are likely to support a world in which their preferred individual rights (such as religious freedom and gun rights for conservatives and reproductive autonomy and freedom from discrimination for liberals) are left to the mercy of politicians.

But the *instinct* behind the turn to legislative deference in 1937 remains instructive. That instinct was more than a simple desire to trust humbly in another body's judgment; it was to defer in a way that would leave the Court's rulings reasonably susceptible to correction by losing groups. As Justice Frankfurter explained it, "a decree of unconstitutionality by this Court is fraught with consequences [that are] enduring" because of how difficult it is to amend the Constitution. By contrast, a decision to defer to elected officials is not so fraught or enduring, because legislatures "can readily mend [their] ways, or the people may express disapproval by choosing different representatives."[18] Business groups that challenged economic regulations before the New Deal Court, and lost, sometimes succeeded in exactly this way, winning concessions at the legislative bargaining table.

The same instinct motivates the least harm principle. But unlike legislative deference, which views the lawmaking process as the sole mechanism through which losing groups may pursue their interests, the least harm principle recognizes that today's marginalized groups frequently lack the political clout to lobby state or federal lawmakers successfully, particularly in this moment of legislative dysfunction. For this reason, the least harm principle invites courts also to consider whether a losing group may protect itself *on its own,* through private conduct that requires no legislator's support. For example, in expressing his support for vaccine mandates that include narrow exemptions, Justice Gorsuch left those with documented medical and religious reasons a clear option for protecting their interests through their own private conduct. The same was true after *Cruzan,* when individuals seeking to avoid the tragic end-of-life controversy that befell Nancy Cruzan were able to execute living wills that clearly expressed their intentions.

In short, what American democracy needs to survive are compelling reasons for losing groups to continue playing within the rules of our system rather than fighting to tear it down. When the New Deal Supreme Court openly adopted a posture of legislative deference, it provided these kinds of reasons to business litigants, who remained able to lobby lawmakers for protection. By embracing the least harm principle today, the justices can do the same. By ensuring that losing groups retain post-defeat options for redress, they can defuse demands to radically transform the Court.

This, then, is the crossroads before the Court. Will it continue to overconfidently announce legalistic answers in the divisive cases before it, where those answers lean in a certain political direction due to partisan motivated reasoning? That is what the Court did in 2022, when it decided *Dobbs* and *Bruen,* the abortion and gun cases. Or will it humbly admit the limits of its own knowledge and rule with an eye toward doing the least harm possible? That is what the Court did as recently as 2020, in the Trump subpoena, DACA, and LGBTQ rights cases.

We will not have to wait long to find out. Several major cases are working their way to the Court with significant implications for its public legitimacy. I touch here on a few to underscore how much turns on the Court's decisional approach.

Two major disputes involve abortion in the aftermath of *Dobbs*. One concerns the ability of red states to restrict the ability of pregnant women to obtain care across state lines. As of this writing, for example, Missouri is actively considering laws that would impose liability for out-of-state abortions, including on individuals who help Missouri citizens travel out of state for such care.[19] A model statute drafted by the National Right to Life Committee would likewise punish anyone who assists a minor in traveling across state lines to obtain an abortion.[20] Are such laws permissible?

The legal question is surprisingly difficult. Harvard law professor Richard Fallon expressed "no hesitation in concluding that this question would be a difficult one that is not clearly resolved" by existing precedent.[21] In light of this uncertainty, there would be ample room for partisan motivated reasoning to rear its head, such that the conservative justices could rule yet again against those seeking to terminate a pregnancy based on contested historical propositions.[22]

A least harm approach would lead to a different outcome. If pregnant people residing in states that ban abortion are not able to obtain care across state lines, it will be virtually impossible for them to avoid the harmful consequences of that ruling: they will either have to carry an unwanted pregnancy to term or engage in dangerous self-care. By contrast, states that wish to protect fetal life would still retain two options that would be significantly more effective: provide basic income and childcare support to pregnant mothers so as to encourage them to carry their children to term, or provide universal contraception to reduce the number of unplanned pregnancies at the outset. A court concerned with doing the least harm possible would thus rule in favor of a right to obtain abortion care across state lines.

A similar kind of analysis applies to another looming abortion dispute: If Democrats were ever to win large enough majorities in the Senate and House, may Congress enact a federal statute codifying a right to abortion across America? Under current doctrine, the answer is "yes." That is because the Commerce Clause affords Congress broad power to enact laws that regulate "economic activity," which the Court has defined to encompass "the production, distribution, and consumption of a commodity."[23] The act of providing a medical service to a patient in exchange for money is a quintessential economic activity. So if Congress were to regulate it—for example, by making it illegal to deny a medical service to a pregnant patient on the ground that it would terminate the life of an unborn fetus (unless a physician has a medical or other reason for doing so)—such a law would be squarely within its power. What is more, this kind of a federal law would unquestionably preempt, or override, any contrary state abortion ban. Under the Constitution's Supremacy Clause, state laws that conflict with federal law must give way. A state abortion ban that forces providers to turn away patients who seek to terminate a pregnancy would conflict irreconcilably with a federal law forbidding them to do exactly that. So the federal law would prevail.

As *Dobbs* shows, however, an overconfident Court can overrule existing precedent. So no one should think a federal statute protecting the right to abortion would be safe from legal challenge. In particular, Justice Clarence Thomas is already on record arguing that the Court's entire Commerce Clause jurisprudence is incorrect because it fails to comport with how the word "commerce" was understood in 1787.[24] Prominent legal scholars, including Yale law professors Akhil Amar and Jack Balkin, have marshaled historical evidence to the contrary.[25] Still, if the conservatives were to answer the question of Congress's power to recognize a nationwide abortion right based on their legalistic assessment of founding era dictionaries and papers, it is quite possible they would adopt Thomas's more restrictive view.

The least harm principle would lead to a different course. After admitting that the founding era meaning of "commerce" is disputed and difficult to ascertain with confidence, it would acknowledge the intense, good-faith interests on both sides of the case: for supporters of the right to abortion, restoring reproductive autonomy in states that have banned abortion; for pro-life groups, protecting fetal life. It would then rule in favor of the side that would be least able to protect its interest should it lose. For those who support reproductive autonomy, precious few options would remain to ensure access to abortion in red states if a federal statutory abortion right is taken off the table, especially for low-income patients (and even more so if red states are permitted to restrict access to care across state lines). Such patients will be left with little choice but to carry an unwanted pregnancy to term or to engage in dangerous, unmedically supervised self-care. By contrast, those who are concerned with protecting fetal life would retain stronger options. Most notably, they would have the ability to repeal the federal abortion statute through the democratic process, by winning the White House and enough seats in Congress. And even failing that, they could still reduce abortion rates by supporting contraception and social supports for families with children.

Another looming dispute involves a voting rights case that one commentator has called "the biggest threat to U.S. democracy since January 6."[26] *Moore v. Harper* arises out of a lawsuit challenging the Republican-controlled North Carolina legislature's enactment of an extremely gerrymandered map in 2021. After exhaustively considering the evidence, the trial court in the case explained how this gerrymander distorted the votes of North Carolinians to ensure that Republicans would retain legislative control even when they lose the popular vote: "even when Democrats win statewide by clear margins," the court observed, Republicans would maintain "an outright majority in the state's congressional delegation, the State House, and the State Senate."[27] Based on this evidence, the North Carolina Supreme Court struck down the map as a violation of the state's constitutional guarantee that "all elections shall be free," which the court interpreted to require substantially equal voting power for all North Carolina voters.[28]

The Republican speaker of the North Carolina House of Representatives, Tim Moore, appealed this decision to the U.S. Supreme Court, which will decide the case in 2023. If Moore prevails, North Carolina's badly gerrymandered maps will be allowed to go into effect—as would similar maps in states across the nation. And our continued descent into extreme partisanship would continue.

The legal argument at the heart of *Moore v. Harper* is called the "independent state legislature" theory, or ISL. The theory holds that the Constitution's Elections Clause, which provides that the manner of holding congressional elections "shall be prescribed in each State by the *Legislature* thereof," actually means to deprive state supreme courts of any say whatsoever in ensuring that state legislatures are following their respective constitutions.[29] (The better conclusion is that the Elections Clause simply vests the initial authority to regulate elections with state legislatures, the most sensible lawmaking body, while continuing to subject those same legislatures to the usual demand of complying with their own constitutions.) The Supreme Court has repeatedly rejected the ISL argument, most recently in *Rucho v. Common Cause* itself, where it specifically declared that those concerned with gerrymandering could seek relief in state supreme courts.[30] So there are many problems with the ISL theory, and one hopes the Court will see it as an easy case and reject it out of hand. However, Justices Thomas, Alito, and Gorsuch have already expressed sympathy to the theory, so the outcome is not open-and-shut.

Even if the case were hard, however, the least harm principle would offer a clear reason to rule against the North Carolina partisan gerrymander. It is a mathematical fact that the side with the greatest ability to avoid its harm in a gerrymandering dispute is the one that seeks to get away with the gerrymander. That is because once a gerrymandered map is invalidated and a fair map is implemented in its place, the party that sought to gerrymander can still secure its ultimate interest—that of winning a majority of legislative seats—by winning slightly more than 50 percent of the statewide popular vote. (This number won't always be precise given random chance, but the basic idea is that if electoral maps are truly fair and competitive, then the party that wins the statewide popular vote should typically win a majority of seats.)

By contrast, if a gerrymandered map is upheld, the victims of that gerrymandering would have to win far greater than 50 percent of the statewide popular vote to have even a chance at a legislative majority. For example, North Carolina's Democratic candidates for the U.S. House of Representatives actually won the statewide popular vote by a nearly two-point margin over Republicans in 2012. Due to the state's pro-Republican gerrymandered maps, however, Democrats did not earn a majority of the state's thirteen seats in the House. Far from it:

Republicans actually won *nine* seats despite earning less than 48 percent of the popular vote. A least harm ruling would find this fact significant. If the Court genuinely cannot answer the legal question at hand, the least harmful outcome would be to rule against gerrymandering because the political party that is blocked from gerrymandering can still maintain its legislative majority by doing what it should have been doing all along: appealing to a majority of voters.

The least harm principle would also offer a powerful ground for deciding *303 Creative LLC v. Elenis,* another blockbuster case to be decided in 2023. The case concerns a lawsuit filed by Lorie Smith, a Christian woman who owns and operates a graphic design company called 303 Creative. As part of her business, Smith would like to design wedding websites for customers. But because of her religious views, she would not want to create such a website for a gay or lesbian couple. That choice, however, places Smith in violation of Colorado's antidiscrimination law, which forbids companies like 303 Creative from discriminating against a customer on the basis of sexual orientation. (The same law applied to the baker who refused to make a wedding cake for a gay couple in the *Masterpiece Cakeshop* case mentioned in chapter 7.) So Smith sued the state, arguing that any attempt to punish her for engaging in sexual orientation discrimination would violate her right to free speech.

No one should doubt the important and sincerely held interests on both sides of the case. Religious business owners like Smith surely possess a genuine desire to perform work consistent with their faith, just as gay and lesbian customers are entitled to equal treatment under the law. The free speech issues in the case are also nuanced: although Colorado has a very good reason for requiring Smith to design a website for a gay or lesbian couple, what it is requiring her to do is, at the end of the day, to engage in a certain kind of expression against her wishes.

If the Court hopes to find a way out of this difficult dilemma, the least harm principle would offer a promising approach. After recognizing the strong moral and legal arguments on both sides of the case, the principle would call for an assessment of each side's other options for avoiding its harm. Smith's harm is that she does not wish to design a wedding website that celebrates a form of marriage inconsistent with her religious beliefs. She can avoid that harm by subcontracting any such design request to a different graphic designer who would do the work instead. (Indeed, this kind of accommodation was used to solve a similar problem for county court clerks who did not want to personally sign same-sex marriage certificates after the Court's decision in *Obergefell v. Hodges.*) Importantly, embracing this accommodation would mean that no gay or lesbian couple has a right to force Smith *herself* to design a wedding website; what they are entitled to is nondiscriminatory provision of a website by Smith's company, whether by her, some other employee, or a contractor.

By contrast, a gay or lesbian couple's harm—the stigma of being labeled second-class citizens who can be denied equal service merely because of their sexual orientation—would be much harder to avoid. It is not enough to say that such couples can avoid discrimination by searching around to find providers who tolerate and are thus willing to serve them. After all, that "option" was also available to Black customers in the Jim Crow South, but no one would say it was sufficient to enable Black Americans to avoid the stigma of racial discrimination. So the Court would rule against Smith's free speech claim.

Across each of these pressing conflicts over abortion, voting rights, and LGBTQ discrimination, the least harm principle offers the Court a way to reach outcomes that losing groups can still do something about. It is also an approach the Court has used before with success across a range of other contentious disputes, as described in chapters 5 and 6. If the Court wishes to repair its battered credibility in the years ahead, returning to this approach would be far better than continuing to overconfidently announce all-or-nothing winners and losers.

Meanwhile, we the people needn't sit on the sidelines, hoping for the justices' better angels to win out. There are things we can do now, in addition to going to the polls.

First, we can disabuse ourselves of what Columbia law professor Henry Monaghan has called "constitution worship," the naive belief that our Constitution is "perfect" in the sense that it supplies clear and ideal solutions to every political disagreement.[31] Second, and relatedly, we can stop viewing the Supreme Court as the ultimate protector of our cherished rights. Taken together, these ideals leave us with the false impression that not only does our Constitution contain clear answers that can save us from every problem but that the Supreme Court is the white knight who will come along and do the saving.

That some Americans have this mentality is entirely understandable. Schoolchildren across the nation are taught how, at important moments in our history, the Supreme Court has stood up for the Constitution's proudest ideals. The Court's decision to strike down segregated public schools in *Brown v. Board of Education* is only the most obvious example. Everyone loves a good hero story, and scholars-in-robes who face down the scourge of white supremacy by unlocking our founding charter's sacred egalitarian values make for quite a tale.

Yet we can celebrate certain moments of our constitutional story without attributing anything close to perfection to the Constitution or Supreme Court. As a constitutional law professor, I try to identify the limitations of our Constitution and Court in every class I teach. But the process of recognizing these imperfections should start earlier. Middle and high school teachers can emphasize not just proud moments in our constitutional history, like *Brown,* but our constitutional failings, too. For each hero story like *Brown,* our Court and Constitution have also played a central role in some profound injustice, including returning freedmen and women to slavery, permitting the incarceration of more than one hundred thousand innocent Japanese Americans during World War II, and eliminating legal protections for children facing hazardous conditions in manual labor.[32] We should linger on these tragic stories, as painful as they may be, to better appreciate the dangers of overreliance on the Supreme Court. Neither it nor our Constitution is infallible.

The problem is not merely that today's Court lacks the proper ideological composition, such that all would be well if the justices would just vote in closer alignment with our own political viewpoints (whatever they might be). The problem is that this dream scenario is a false hope. The Constitution does not enshrine a laundry list of clear policy outcomes, whether conservative or liberal. On issue after issue, a singular, correct legal answer is hard to discern. Pretending otherwise is how we got to this precipice in the first place.

By openly acknowledging these hard truths, we can make important progress toward cultivating a broader culture of legal humility. When people are less quick to claim that the Constitution clearly supports their preferred policy outcomes on divisive social issues—and more willing to acknowledge that our conflicts often involve deeply contested value judgments with no clear answers—the result is to create vital space for the Court to do the same. Just as important, a culture of legal humility would help us realize that our disagreements with our fellow Americans should not be left to nine unelected lawyers to solve using arcane legal tools and an eighteenth-century document. Our problems are chiefly for *us* to solve, whether through the democratic process or through private efforts to protect our interests within existing norms.

Last, progressives and moderates must continue debating political responses if the conservative supermajority on the Court chooses to hand them a series of defeats from which there are no meaningful avenues for redress. By keeping structural Court reforms such as jurisdiction stripping and even court-packing on the table, the public can put pressure on the more institutionally minded conservative justices to hew closer to the middle.

For many, the time to break that glass may have already arrived. For others, perhaps not. Yet even the most optimistic progressive must identify a line that, if the Court were to cross it, would warrant responding with significant Court reform—all while recognizing that America's best hope is for that day never to arrive.

Our best hope is instead that, with enough public pressure, the Court recognizes the fragility of its position and that it responds, not with more confidence in its ability to pronounce the law, but with less. It is only with a greater sense of humility that the Court can remember that its decisions are not the final chapter in our constitutional story. After each ruling, the Court moves on to the next case. But losing groups—the people and organizations in the trenches who actually suffer the harmful consequences of defeat—will continue to fight for the rights and causes they hold dear. By consciously working to provide these groups meaningful options, the Court can ensure that the next chapters in our American story are constructive ones, where people work together in pursuit of shared interests rather than assailing our democratic order. A humbler Supreme Court can remind us, in other words, that when it comes to solving America's mounting problems, *we* are the ones we've been waiting for—not nine lawyers clothed in black robes.[33]

Notes

Introduction

1. *Stanford v. Kentucky,* 492 U.S. 361 (1989). The Court's death penalty jurisprudence was a frequent target of Scalia's in his public appearances. See, e.g., C-SPAN, "Interpreting the U.S. Constitution," https://www.c-span.org/video/?c4929700/user-clip-scalia-death-penalty.

2. See Matthew Tokson, "Supreme Court Clerks and the Death Penalty," *George Washington Law Review Arguendo* 89 (2020), https://ssrn.com/abstract=3541816.

3. Supreme Court Rule 10.

4. See, e.g., *W. Virginia v. Environmental Protection Agency,* 142 S. Ct. 2587, 2621 (2022) (Gorsuch, J., concurring) (arguing that this is an "easy case" for applying the Court's major questions doctrine); *Garland v. Dai,* 141 S. Ct. 1669, 1678 (2021) (Justice Gorsuch); *Gundy v. United States,* 139 S. Ct. 2116, 2121 (2019) (arguing that the delegation of power to the attorney general "easily passes constitutional muster") (Justice Kagan); *Virginia Uranium, Inc. v. Warren,* 139 S. Ct. 1894, 1917 (2019) (Roberts, J., dissenting) ("That should have made for an easy case."); *Carpenter v. United States,* 138 S. Ct. 2206, 2255 (2018) (Alito, J., dissenting) ("This should have been an easy case."); and *Collins v. Virginia,* 138 S. Ct. 1663, 1671 (2018) ("[T]his is an easy case.") (Justice Sotomayor).

5. Hal R. Arkes and Catherine Blumer, "The Psychology of Sunk Costs," *Organizational Behavior and Human Decision Processes* 35 (1985): 124–40.

6. See dansac,"Sunk Cost in Iraq and Vietnam: A Lesson in Economics," *Daily Kos,* Sept. 21, 2004, https://www.dailykos.com/stories/2004/9/21/52557/-.

7. Michela Del Vicario et al., "Modeling Confirmation Bias and Polarization," *Scientific Reports,* Jan. 11, 2017.

8. David Shariatmadari, "Daniel Kahneman: 'What Would I Eliminate If I Had a Magic Wand? Overconfidence,'" *Guardian,* July 18, 2015.

9. See Ryan W. Wohleber and Gerald Mathews, "Multiple Facets of Overconfidence: Implications for Driving Safely," *Transportation Research Part F: Psychology and Behaviour* 43 (2016): 265–78.

10. Michael Tomasky, "The Supreme Court's Legitimacy Crisis," *New York Times,* Oct. 5, 2018; Paul Waldman, "Yes, the Supreme Court Is Facing a Legitimacy Crisis. And We Know Exactly Whose Fault It Is," *Washington Post,* Sept. 24, 2018.

11. See Barry Friedman, *The Will of the People: How Public Opinion Has Influenced the Supreme Court and Shaped the Meaning of the Constitution* (New York: Farrar, Straus and Giroux, 2009), 196 (arguing that after 1937 and a series of new judicial appointments, the Court "wrote a new Constitution" rooted in deference to the legislature that was "widely hailed as the proper one").

12. William J. Brennan Jr., "The Constitution of the United States: Contemporary Ratification," delivered at Georgetown University Law Center, Washington, D.C., Oct. 12, 1985, reprinted in *South Texas Law Review* 27 (1986): 433–46, at 438.

13. See Aaron Tang, "The Supreme Court Flunks Abortion History," *Los Angeles Times,* May 5, 2022.

14. *Kennedy v. Louisiana,* 554 U.S. 407 (2008).

15. *Kennedy,* at 455 (Alito, J., dissenting).

16. Gallup News Service, "June Wave 1," June 23, 2022, https://news.gallup.com/file/poll/394118/20220623SupremeCourt.pdf.

17. See William K. Rashbaum and Benjamin Weiser, "D.A. Is Investigating Trump and His Company over Fraud, Filing Suggests," *New York Times,* Aug. 3, 2020.

18. For 2020 polling data, see Gallup, "Approval of the Supreme Court Is Highest Since 2009," https://news.gallup.com/poll/316817/approval-supreme-court-highest-2009.aspx.

19. *Brnovich v. Democratic National Committee,* 141 S. Ct. 2321 (2021); 52 U.S.C. § 10301(a).

20. *Shelby County v. Holder,* 570 U.S. 529 (2013).

Part One. The Problem

1. But see Randy Barnett, "Keep the Courts the Same," *New York Times,* Oct. 27, 2020.

2. See, e.g., Larry Kramer, "Pack the Courts," *New York Times,* Oct. 27, 2020.

3. Ariane de Vogue, "Conservatives with High Expectations Anxious for Justice Amy Coney Barrett to Show Her Hand," *CNN,* Mar. 24, 2021, https://www.cnn.com/2021/03/24/politics/amy-coney-barrett-conservatives/index.html.

4. According to one recent poll, a majority of Democrats, Republicans, and independents all agreed that the Court is "too mixed up in politics." Kathy Frankovic, "How Republicans and Democrats View the Supreme Court," *YouGov,* July 8, 2019, https://today.yougov.com/topics/politics/articles-reports/2019/07/08/republicans-democrats-supreme-court-poll.

5. See, e.g., Steven G. Calabresi, "End the Poisonous Process of Picking Supreme Court Justices," *New York Times,* Sept. 22, 2020 (libertarian-conservative law professor advocating Supreme Court term limits to improve the judicial nomination and confirmation process); and Bloomberg Law, "Supreme Court Term Limits Endorsed by Major Progressive Group," Aug. 3, 2020 (same support from progressive Center for American Progress), https://news.bloomberglaw.com/us-law-week/supreme-court-term-limits-endorsed-by-major-progressive-group.

6. Josh Gerstein, "Senate Committee Approves Legislation to Put Supreme Court Hearings on Camera," *Politico,* June 24, 2021 (describing bipartisan support for Supreme Court transparency legislation).

Chapter 1. Distrust and Democracy

1. See *Reynolds v. Sims,* 377 U.S. 533 (1964) (one person, one vote); and *Harper v. Virginia State Board of Elections,* 383 U.S. 663 (1966) (poll taxes).

2. See *Keyishian v. Board of Regents,* 385 U.S. 589 (1967) (protecting members of the Communist Party); *National Socialist Party of America v. Village of Skokie,* 432 U.S. 43 (1977) (siding with neo-Nazi demonstrators in Skokie, Ill.); and *Texas v. Johnson,* 491 U.S. 397 (1989) (upholding right to burn the American flag).

3. *Marbury v. Madison,* 5 U.S. 137 (1803).

4. *Gong Lum v. Rice,* 275 U.S. 78 (1927) (permitting exclusion of a child of Chinese ancestry from a Mississippi public school).

5. Allegra Kirkland, "Just Last Week Hatch Said Obama Won't Nominate a 'Moderate' Like Garland," *Talking Points Memo,* Mar. 16, 2016, https://talkingpointsmemo.com/livewire/hatch-last-week-obama-wont-pick-moderate-garland.

6. Katie Wadington, "Then and Now: What McConnell, Others Said About Merrick Garland in 2016 vs. After Ginsburg's death," *USA Today,* Sept. 19, 2020, https://www.usatoday.com/story/news/politics/2020/09/19/what-mcconnell-said-merrick-garland-vs-after-ginsburgs-death/5837543002/.

7. Russell Berman, "Republicans Abandon the Filibuster to Save Neil Gorsuch," *Atlantic,* Apr. 6, 2017, https://www.theatlantic.com/politics/archive/2017/04/republicans-nuke-the-filibuster-to-save-neil-gorsuch/522156/.

8. In the presidential election of 2016, for example, among the 21 percent of all voters who answered an exit poll stating that the Supreme Court was the "most important factor" for their vote, 56 percent voted for Trump compared to 41 percent for Clinton. See Jane Coaston, "Polling Data Shows Republicans Turned Out for Trump in 2016 Because of the Supreme Court," *Vox,* June 29, 2018, https://www.vox.com/2018/6/29/17511088/scotus-2016-election-poll-trump-republicans-kennedy-retire.

9. See Jamie Crooks and Samir Deger-Sen, "We Were Clerks at the Supreme Court. Its Legitimacy Is Now in Question," *New York Times,* Oct. 25, 2020 (describing how Kennedy rejected the "swing" justice label).

10. See Staci Zaretsky, "We See a Pride Parade Float in Justice Kennedy's Future," *Above the Law,* Sept. 3, 2013, https://abovethelaw.com/2013/09/we-see-a-pride-parade-float-in-justice-kennedys-future/.

11. See, e.g., *Carhart v. Gonzales,* 550 U.S. 124 (2007) (upholding the federal Partial-Birth Abortion Ban Act).

12. See, e.g., Amelia Thomson-DeVeaux, "Justice Kennedy Wasn't a Moderate," *FiveThirtyEight,* July 3, 2018, https://fivethirtyeight.com/features/justice-kennedy-wasnt-a-moderate/; and Andrew Cohen, "Anthony Kennedy Was No Moderate," *New Republic,* June 27, 2018.

13. Aaron Tang, "An Open Letter: Justice Kennedy, Please Stay on the Supreme Court," *National Law Journal,* Dec. 26, 2016, https://www.law.com/nationallawjournal/almID/1202775447553/An-Open-Letter-Justice-Kennedy-Please-Stay-on-the-Supreme-Court/; Ruth Marcus, "If You're Reading This Justice Kennedy, Please Don't Retire," *Washington Post,* Feb. 3, 2017; Editorial Board, "Please Stay, Justice Kennedy. America Needs You," *New York Times,* Apr. 28, 2018.

14. Todd Purdum, Jodi Wilgoren, and Pam Belluck, "Court's Nominee's Life Is Rooted in Faith and Respect for Law," *New York Times,* July 21, 2005.

15. See Thomson-DeVeaux, "Justice Kennedy Wasn't a Moderate."

16. *NFIB v. Sebelius,* 567 U.S. 519 (2013).

17. Adam Liptak, "After Ruling, Roberts Makes a Getaway from the Scorn," *New York Times,* July 2, 2012.

18. *Parents Involved in Community Schools v. Seattle School District No. 1,* 551 U.S. 701, 748 (2008).

19. Faith Karimi, "It's Now Illegal in Georgia to Give Food and Water to Voters in Line," *CNN,* Mar. 26, 2021, https://www.cnn.com/2021/03/26/politics/georgia-voting-law-food-drink-ban-trnd/index.html.

20. Joan Biskupic, *The Chief: The Life and Turbulent Times of Chief Justice John Roberts* (New York: Basic Books, 2019).

21. "Democratic Lawmakers, Liberal Groups Rally Against Brett Kavanaugh, Trump's Supreme Court Nominee," *PBS,* July 9, 2018, https://www.pbs.org/newshour/politics/democratic-lawmakers-liberal-groups-rally-against-brett-kavanaugh-trumps-supreme-court-nominee.

22. Ninety-one percent, according to one C-SPAN poll. See C-SPAN/PSB, "Supreme Court Survey: Agenda of Key Findings," August 2018, 5, https://static.c-span.org/assets/documents/scotusSurvey/CSPAN%20PSB%202018%20Supreme%20

Court%20Survey%20Agenda%20of%20Key%20Findings%20FINAL%2008%20 28%2018.pdf; see also p. 7 (only 48 percent can name a single justice or more).

23. Politico Staff, "Full Transcript: Christine Blasey Ford's Opening Statement to the Senate Judiciary Committee," *Politico,* Sept. 26, 2018, https://www.politico.com/story/2018/09/26/christine-blasey-ford-opening-statement-senate-845080.

24. Melissa Healy, "Must Reads: Here's What Experts Who Study Sexual Violence Say About the Credibility of Christine Blasey Ford's Testimony," *Los Angeles Times,* Sept. 28, 2018.

25. "Brett Kavanaugh's Opening Statement: Full Transcript," *New York Times*, Sept. 27, 2018.

26. One Democratic senator, Joe Manchin, voted to confirm Kavanaugh. One Republican senator, Lisa Murkowski, registered her opposition to Kavanaugh but voted "present" to cancel out the missed yea vote from her Republican colleague Steve Daines, who was away at his daughter's wedding in Montana.

27. CNN/SSRS study, Oct. 8, 2018, http://cdn.cnn.com/cnn/2018/images/10/08/rel9a.-.kavanaugh.pdf.

28. Washington Post–ABC News poll, Oct. 8–11, 2018, at 11, https://apps.washingtonpost.com/g/page/politics/washington-post-abc-news-poll-oct-8-11-2018/2340/.

29. Supreme Court Press Release, Sept. 18, 2020, https://www.supremecourt.gov/publicinfo/press/pressreleases/pr_09-18-20; Rand Paul (@RandPaul), "My thoughts and prayers are with the family of Ruth Bader Ginsburg tonight . . .," Twitter, September 17, 5:19 p.m., https://twitter.com/randpaul/status/1307111939697446917; "Statement from the President on the Passing of Supreme Court Associate Justice Ruth Bader Ginsburg," Sept. 18, 2020, https://trumpwhitehouse.archives.gov/briefings-statements/statement-president-passing-supreme-court-associate-justice-ruth-bader-ginsburg/.

30. Mitch McConnell, "McConnell Statement on the Passing of Justice Ruth Bader Ginsburg," Sept. 18, 2020, https://www.republicanleader.senate.gov/newsroom/press-releases/mcconnell-statement-on-the-passing-of-justice-ruth-bader-ginsburg.

31. Wadington, "Then and Now."

32. Since 1970, only one justice was confirmed in shorter time than the twenty-seven days it would eventually take the Republican-controlled Senate to confirm Barrett: John Paul Stevens, whom President Gerald Ford nominated in 1975 (and who was confirmed within thirteen days). See Barbara Sprunt, "How Amy Coney Barrett's Confirmation Would Compare to Past Supreme Court Picks," *NPR,* Oct. 1, 2020, https://www.npr.org/sections/supreme-court-nomination/2020/10/01/916644231/how-a-barrett-confirmation-would-compare-to-past-supreme-court-timelines.

33. Mark Sherman, "Barrett Cites 'Ginsburg Rule' That Ginsburg Didn't Follow," *AP News,* Oct. 13, 2020, https://apnews.com/article/gay-rights-ruth-bader-ginsburg-confirmation-hearings-amy-coney-barrett-us-supreme-court-b970417abe65977bc8031856aa769eda.

34. John Bresnahan and Burgess Everett, "No Apologies: McConnell Says Barrett a 'Huge Success for the Country,'" *Politico,* Oct. 27, 2020, https://www.politico.com/news/2020/10/27/no-apologies-mcconnell-barrett-success-country-432828.

35. Gary Langer, "Most Say Wait on Ginsburg Seat, While Opposing Packing the Court: Poll," *ABC News,* Sept. 25, 2020, https://abcnews.go.com/Politics/wait-ginsburg-seat-opposing-packing-court/story?id=73239784.

36. Crooks and Deger-Sen, "We Were Clerks"; John F. Harris, "The Supreme Court Is Begging for a Legitimacy Crisis," *Politico Magazine,* Oct. 29, 2020, https://www.politico.com/news/magazine/2020/10/29/supreme-court-begging-for-legitimacy-crisis-433573; Ian Millhiser, "How an Anti-Democratic Constitution Gave America Amy Coney Barrett," *Vox,* Oct. 26, 2020, https://www.vox.com/2020/10/26/21534358/supreme-court-amy-coney-barrett-constitution-anti-democratic-electoral-college-senate.

37. Harris, "Supreme Court Is Begging."

38. Alexandria Ocasio-Cortez (@AOC), "Expand the court," Twitter, Oct. 26, 2020, 5:13 p.m., https://twitter.com/aoc/status/1320881248861126663.

39. Jamelle Bouie, "Down with Judicial Supremacy!," *New York Times,* Sept. 22, 2020.

40. Ryan Cooper, "Democrats Have a Better Option Than Court Packing," *Week,* Sept. 22, 2020, https://theweek.com/articles/938865/democrats-have-better-option-than-court-packing.

41. Petition for Certiorari in *Dobbs v. Jackson Women's Health Organization* at 5.

42. American College of Obstetricians and Gynecologists, "Second Trimester Abortion," June 2013, https://www.acog.org/clinical/clinical-guidance/practice-bulletin/articles/2013/06/second-trimester-abortion.

43. Natasha Ishak, "In 48 Hours of Protest, Thousands of Americans Cry Out for Abortion Rights," *Vox,* June 26, 2022, https://www.vox.com/2022/6/26/23183750/abortion-rights-scotus-roe-overturned-protests.

44. Jamelle Bouie, "The Supreme Court Is the Final Word on Nothing," *New York Times,* July 1, 2022.

45. Data drawn from Gallup, "Supreme Court," https://news.gallup.com/poll/4732/supreme-court.aspx.

46. Gallup, "Supreme Court."

47. Gallup, "Supreme Court."

48. I use the term "legitimacy" here to in line with what Professor Richard Fallon has described as "sociological legitimacy." See Richard H. Fallon Jr., *Law and Legitimacy at the Supreme Court* (Cambridge, Mass.: Harvard University Press, 2018), 21 (defining sociological legitimacy as whether the public views the Court as worthy of respect).

49. Steven Levitsky and Daniel Ziblatt, *How Democracies Die* (New York: Crown, 2018), 102, 106.

50. Adam Liptak, "Supreme Court Rejects Texas Suit Seeking to Subvert Election," *New York Times,* Dec. 11, 2020.

51. See Supreme Court Order List, Dec. 11, 2020.

52. See Liptak, "Supreme Court Rejects Texas Suit" ("Judge after judge in case after case ruled that the evidence was not persuasive, credible or anywhere near enough to give Mr. Trump the extraordinary relief he requested").

53. Daniel Politi, "Poll: 82 Percent of Trump Voters Say Biden's Win Isn't Legitimate," *Slate,* Dec. 13, 2020, https://slate.com/news-and-politics/2020/12/poll-trump-voters-biden-win-not-legitimate.html.

54. Ahiza Garcia, "Mike Huckabee: I Will Not Accept Gay Marriage Ruling by 'Imperial Court,'" *Talking Points Memo,* June 26, 2015, https://talkingpointsmemo.com/livewire/mike-huckabee-gay-marriage-decision.

55. David Jackson, "Trump Blasts DACA Decision, Asking if People Get the Impression 'The Supreme Court Doesn't Like Me?,'" *USA Today,* June 18, 2020.

56. Ariane de Vogue, "Chief Justice Roberts Rebukes Chuck Schumer for Comments About Kavanaugh and Gorsuch," *CNN,* Mar. 4, 2020, https://www.cnn.com/2020/03/04/politics/schumer-roberts-threats-supreme-court/index.html.

57. See Joshua Braver, "Court-Packing: An American Tradition?," working paper, 12–32, https://papers.ssrn.com/sol3/papers.cfm?abstract_id=3483927.

58. The unusual ticket comprising members of different parties owed to the exigencies of the presidential election of 1864, in which Lincoln Republicans sought to form an alliance with War Democrats like Johnson. Although Johnson opposed secession, he was also far less supportive of Reconstruction—a major source of conflict between him and the Republican Congress.

59. Braver, "Court-Packing," 33.

60. Braver, "Court-Packing," 32.

61. See Katie Galgano, "Venezuela's Story: Democratic Paths to Authoritarianism," *Real Clear World,* Feb. 24, 2021, https://www.realclearworld.com/articles/2021/02/24/venezuelas_story_democratic_paths_to_authoritarianism_661643.html.

62. Editorial Board, "Venezuela's Sham Election," *New York Times,* May 21, 2018.

63. Levitsky and Ziblatt, *How Democracies Die,* 81.

64. Dylan Matthews, "Court-Packing, Democrats' Nuclear Option for the Supreme Court, Explained," *Vox,* Sept. 22, 2020, https://www.vox.com/2018/7/2/17513520/court-packing-explained-fdr-roosevelt-new-deal-democrats-supreme-court; Benjamin Novak and Patrick Kingsley, "Hungary Creates New Court System, Cementing Leader's Control of Judiciary," *New York Times,* Dec. 12, 2018.

65. Marc Santora and Helene Bienvenu, "Hungary Election Was Free but Not Entirely Fair, Observers Say," *New York Times,* Apr. 9, 2018.

66. Levitsky and Ziblatt, *How Democracies Die,* 77.

67. Gallup, "Congress and the Public," https://news.gallup.com/poll/1600/congress-public.aspx.

68. Gallup, "Americans Remain Distrustful of Mass Media," Sept. 30, 2020, https://news.gallup.com/poll/321116/americans-remain-distrustful-mass-media.aspx.

Chapter 2. The Partisanship Trap

1. See, e.g., Randall Kennedy, "Politicians in Robes," *Nation,* Oct. 5, 2020; and Linda Greenhouse, "Law in the Raw," *New York Times,* Nov. 12, 2014 (admitting that she "surrender[s]" to the charge that the Supreme Court is "just a collection of politicians in robes"); Eric Segall, "Supreme Court Justices Are Not Really Judges," *Slate,* Nov. 14, 2014, https://slate.com/news-and-politics/2014/11/supreme-court-justices-are-not-judges-they-rule-on-values-and-politics-not-the-law.html.

2. Carl Hulse, "Political Polarization Takes Hold of the Supreme Court," *New York Times,* July 5, 2018.

3. Neal Devins quoted in Hulse, "Political Polarization Takes Hold."

4. See Lee Epstein, William M. Landes, and Richard A. Posner, *The Behavior of Federal Judges: A Theoretical and Empirical Study of Rational Choice* (Cambridge, Mass.: Harvard University Press, 2013); and Jeffrey A. Segal, Lee Epstein, Charles M. Cameron, and Harold J. Spaeth, "Ideological Values and the Votes of U.S. Supreme Court Justices Revisited," *Journal of Politics* 57 (1995): 812–23.

5. Quinnipiac University Poll, "Nearly 7 in 10 Favor a Limit on How Long SCOTUS Justices Can Serve," at 15, May 18, 2022, https://poll.qu.edu/images/polling/us/us05182022_uirc64.pdf.

6. Jill Lepore, "Party Time," *New Yorker,* Sept. 10, 2007.

7. Lepore, "Party Time."

8. Lepore, "Party Time."

9. Bruce Ackerman and David Fontana, "How Jefferson Counted Himself In," *Atlantic*, March 2004.

10. Lepore, "Party Time."

11. Edward J. Larson, *A Magnificent Catastrophe: The Tumultuous Election of 1800, America's First Presidential Campaign* (New York: Free Press, 2007).

12. Kathryn Turner, "The Midnight Judges," *University of Pennsylvania Law Review* 109 (1961): 494–523, at 516.

13. Turner, "Midnight Judges," 521. A separate last-minute law enacted by the Federalists on February 27, 1801 (just four days before Adams's final day in office), created three additional judgeships in the District of Columbia. Adams would eventually appoint William Marbury to one of those judgeships, though Marbury's commission went fatefully undelivered before the conclusion of Adams's term. Marbury eventually sued, giving rise to the Supreme Court's famous decision establishing the power of judicial review in *Marbury v. Madison*.

14. 2 Stat. 89, Section 3, https://govtrackus.s3.amazonaws.com/legislink/pdf/stat/2/STATUTE-2-Pg89.pdf.

15. Ellsworth sent his letter on October 16, 1800. See Oliver Ellsworth to John Adams, Oct. 16, 1800, Letters Received and Other Loose Papers, Adams Papers, Massachusetts Historical Society, Boston. Adams endorsed his receipt of that letter, "Rcd. Dec. 15, 1800."

16. R. Kent Newmyer, *John Marshall and the Heroic Age of the Supreme Court* (Baton Rouge: Louisiana State University Press, 2001), 142.

17. Kathryn Turner, "The Appointment of Chief Justice Marshall," *William and Mary Quarterly*, 3rd ser., 17 (1961): 143–63, at 162.

18. Thomas Jefferson to John Dickinson, Dec. 19, 1801, in *The Writings of Thomas Jefferson,* edited by Andrew A. Lipscomb and Albert Ellery Bergh, vol. 10 (Washington, D.C.: Thomas Jefferson Memorial Association, 1903), 302.

19. Thomas Jefferson to Abigail Smith Adams, June 13, 1804, online at https://rotunda.upress.virginia.edu/founders/default.xqy.

20. Newmyer, *John Marshall and the Heroic Age,* 143.

21. Newmyer, *John Marshall and the Heroic Age,* 142. Historian Kathryn Turner concurs in this assessment. See Turner, "Appointment of Chief Justice Marshall," 157–58 ("At no time was Marshall's personal loyalty to the President questioned").

22. Newmyer, *John Marshall and the Heroic Age,* 143.

23. See *McCulloch v. Maryland,* 17 U.S. 316 (1819) (giving broad interpretation to the Necessary and Proper Clause); and *Gibbons v. Ogden,* 22 U.S. 1 (1824) (broad construction of the Commerce Clause).

24. See *Cohens v. Virginia,* 19 U.S. 264 (1821); and *Martin v. Hunter's Lessee,* 14 U.S. 304 (1816).

25. Consider, for example, the impeachment of Justice Salmon Chase in 1804. Although Chase was eventually acquitted in the Senate, the episode suggests that the Court's prominent stature in American politics was hardly a preordained conclusion. See Robert G. McCloskey, *The American Supreme Court* (Chicago: University of Chicago Press, 1960), 45–46. Another low point occurred in 1832, when the State of Georgia seemed likely to defy the Court's controversial decision in *Worcester v. Georgia,* 31 U.S. 515 (1832), and President Andrew Jackson threatened not to enforce it. See Charles Warren, *The Supreme Court in United States History, 1789–1835,* 2nd ed., vol. 1 (Boston: Little, Brown, 1926), 257.

26. Michael J. Klarman, "How Great Were the 'Great' Marshall Court Decisions?," *Virginia Law Review* 87 (2003): 1111–84, at 1153.

27. John Jay to John Adams, Jan. 2, 1801, in *The Correspondence and Public Papers of John Jay,* ed. Henry P. Johnston, vol. 4 (New York: G. P. Putnam's Sons, 1890), 284, 285 (emphasis added).

28. Alexis de Tocqueville quoted in Edward S. Corwin, *John Marshall and the Constitution: A Chronicle of the Supreme Court* (New Haven: Yale University Press, 1921), 196.

29. Corwin, *John Marshall and the Constitution,* 195; see also Klarman, "How Great Were the 'Great' Marshall Court Decisions?," 1154 (arguing that "by the time of Marshall's death in 1835, the Court's stature had grown tremendously").

30. Klarman, "How Great Were the 'Great' Marshall Court Decisions?," 1181.

31. Klarman, "How Great Were the 'Great' Marshall Court Decisions?," 1179.

32. See generally Jeff Shesol, *Supreme Power: Franklin Roosevelt vs. the Supreme Court* (New York: W. W. Norton, 2010), 12–13.

33. *Lochner v. New York,* 198 U.S. 45, 57 (1905).

34. Professor David Bernstein has argued that the New York law actually reflects an effort by powerful interests—including labor unions and established bakeries—to drive out smaller bakeries often owned by less politically influential immigrants. See David Bernstein, *Rehabilitating Lochner: Defending Individual Rights Against Progressive Reform* (Chicago: University of Chicago Press, 2011), 24.

35. *Adkins v. Children's Hospital,* 261 U.S. 525 (1923) (invalidating state minimum wage law); *Hammer v. Dagenhart,* 247 U.S. 251 (1918) (invalidating federal child labor regulation); *Coppage v. Kansas,* 236 U.S. 1 (1915) (invalidating state law that prohibited yellow-dog contracts, or contracts barring workers from joining a union).

36. FDR quoted in Shesol, *Supreme Power,* 9.

37. See *Home Building and Loan Association v. Blaisdell*, 290 U.S. 398 (1934); and *Nebbia v. New York*, 291 U.S. 502 (1934).

38. Shesol, *Supreme Power*, 143.

39. See, e.g., Shesol, *Supreme Power*; Gregory A. Caldeira, "Public Opinion and the Supreme Court," *American Political Science Review* 81 (1987): 1139–53; and William E. Leuchtenburg, *The Supreme Court Reborn: The Constitutional Revolution in the Age of Roosevelt* (New York: Oxford University Press, 1996).

40. Noah Feldman, *Scorpions: The Battles and Triumphs of FDR's Great Supreme Court Judges* (New York: Twelve, 2010), 110.

41. Feldman, *Scorpions*, 111–12.

42. Feldman, *Scorpions*, 160.

43. Feldman, *Scorpions*, 113.

44. Feldman, *Scorpions*, 201.

45. Feldman, *Scorpions*, 203.

46. Barry Friedman, *The Will of the People: How Public Opinion Has Influenced the Supreme Court and Shaped the Meaning of the Constitution* (New York: Farrar, Straus and Giroux, 2009), 234.

47. Karlyn H. Bowman and Andrew Rugg, comps., *Public Opinion on the Supreme Court*, AEI Public Opinion Studies, American Enterprise Institute, June 2012, 67.

48. See Neal Devins and Lawrence Baum, "Split Definitive: How Party Polarization Turned the Supreme Court into a Partisan Court," Supreme Court Review (2016): 301–65, at 313 (explaining how, based on Martin-Quinn judicial ideology scores, the Court came "closest to a full split between Republican and Democratic appointees in the 1941–1944 Terms").

49. Bowman and Rugg, *Public Opinion on the Supreme Court*.

50. Gallup, "Approval of U.S. Supreme Court Down to 40%, a New Low," Sept. 23, 2021, https://news.gallup.com/poll/354908/approval-supreme-court-down-new-low.aspx.

51. Caldeira, "Public Opinion and the Supreme Court," 1147 (showing plurality support for the court-packing plan in four polls conducted in March 1937).

52. There is some evidence that Roberts actually changed his vote in *Jones & Laughlin Steel* not in response to FDR's court-packing plan but rather instead after seeing the decisive election results of 1936. See Marian C. McKenna, *Franklin Roosevelt and the Great Constitutional War: The Court-Packing Crisis of 1937* (New York: Fordham University Press, 2002), 435–37.

53. See Caldeira, "Public Opinion and the Supreme Court," 1148.

54. "The Wagner Decision," *Nation*, Apr. 17, 1937.

55. "Editorial Comment on Decisions by Supreme Court. Tribunal Declared to Have Given Answer to Roosevelt," *St. Louis Post Dispatch,* Mar. 30, 1937.

56. Barry Friedman, "The History of the Countermajoritarian Difficulty, Part Four: Law's Politics," *University of Pennsylvania Law Review* 148 (2000): 971.

57. See Bowman and Rugg, *Public Opinion on the Supreme Court.*

58. Justin McCarthy, "Gallup Vault: Gloomy Outlook During the Great Depression," Gallup, Oct. 22, 2019, https://news.gallup.com/vault/267656/gallup-vault-gloomy-outlook-during-great-depression.aspx.

59. McCarthy, "Gallup Vault."

60. See George Dangerfield, *The Awakening of American Nationalism, 1815–1828* (New York: Harper and Row, 1965), 1–5.

61. Friedman, *Will of the People,* 79.

62. To be sure, the Democratic-Republican Party itself grew more amenable to national power over time. But states' rights opposition to the Marshall Court was present—and dangerous—throughout. See, e.g., McCloskey, *American Supreme Court,* 64 (pointing out that after the Court's decision in *Cohens v. Virginia,* "hardly a session of Congress went by without a proposal to modify, in one way or another, the doctrine of judicial control"—threats that "were serious enough to alarm the Court and its friends").

63. Adam Chilton, Daniel Epps, Kyle Rozema, and Maya Sen, "Designing Supreme Court Term Limits," *Southern California Law Review* 95 (2022).

64. Fix the Court, "An Outline of a Supreme Court Term Limits Statute," https://fixthecourt.com/2020/09/tl-statute/ (proposing that "for a time, the Supreme Court may comprise more than nine justices").

65. See GovTrackUs, "With Kavanaugh Vote, the Senate Reaches a Historic Low in Democratic Metric," https://govtrackinsider.com/with-kavanaugh-vote-the-senate-reaches-a-historic-low-in-democratic-metric-dfbof5fa7fa.

Chapter 3. Overconfidence

1. *Lawrence v. Texas,* 539 U.S. 558 (2003); Oral Argument Transcript in *Shelby County v. Holder.*

2. AP, "Scalia: Abortion, Death Penalty 'Easy Cases,'" *CBS News,* Oct. 5, 2012, https://www.cbsnews.com/news/scalia-abortion-death-penalty-easy-cases/.

3. Tim Grieve, "Scalia on Detainee Rights: 'Give Me a Break,'" *Salon,* Mar. 27, 2006, https://www.salon.com/2006/03/27/scalia_14/.

4. *Braxton v. United States,* 500 U.S. 344 (1991).

5. Lydia Brashear Tiede, "The Impact of Federal Sentencing Guidelines and Reform: A Comparative Analysis," *Justice System Journal* 30 (2009): 35n1.

6. Congressional Research Service, "Federal Sentencing Guidelines: Background, Legal Analysis, and Policy Options," Mar. 16, 2009, https://www.everycrsreport.com/files/20090316_RL32766_53fd2d15dbbbddf179a847479b463cdab8e867ef.pdf.

7. *Longoria v. United States,* 141 S. Ct. 978 (mem.).

8. *Longoria,* 141 S. Ct. 978.

9. *Braxton,* 500 U.S. at 347.

10. Compare *United States v. Rogers,* 129 F.3d 76, 80–81 (2d Cir. 1997) (per curiam) (permitting the government to withhold a sentencing reduction where the defendant moves to suppress evidence), with *United States v. Price,* 409 F.3d 436, 443–44 (D.C. Cir. 2005); *United States v. Marquez,* 337 F.3d 1203, 1212 (10th Cir. 2003); and *United States v. Kimple,* 27 F.3d 1409, 1414–15 (9th Cir. 1994) (all holding that the government cannot withhold the sentencing reduction).

11. See Cass R. Sunstein, *Simpler: The Future of Government* (New York: Simon and Schuster, 2013).

12. See "Two Federal Judges on How They Interpret the Constitution," We the People Podcast, Oct. 19, 2019, National Constitution Center, https://constitutioncenter.org/news-debate/podcasts/two-federal-judges-on-how-they-interpret-the-constitution.

13. "Two Federal Judges on How They Interpret the Constitution."

14. Daniel Kahneman, *Thinking, Fast and Slow* (New York: Farrar, Straus and Giroux, 2011), 13–14.

15. Don A. Moore, *Perfectly Confident: How to Calibrate Your Decisions Wisely* (New York: HarperCollins, 2020), 8.

16. Moore, *Perfectly Confident,* 8.

17. Moore, *Perfectly Confident,* 8.

18. Moore, *Perfectly Confident,* 6.

19. Moore, *Perfectly Confident,* 22.

20. Captain Edward Smith quoted in Pedro C. Ribeiro, "Sinking the Unsinkable: Lessons in Leadership," *ASK Magazine,* Aug. 2, 2012.

21. *"Titanic" Disaster: Report of the Committee of Commerce, U.S. Senate,* S. Rep. No. 806, 62nd Cong., 2nd sess., May 12, 1912, online at https://www.titanicinquiry.org/USInq/USReport/AmInqRep01.php.

22. Ribeiro, "Sinking the Unsinkable."

23. M. Podbregar et al., "Should We Confirm Our Clinical Diagnostic Certainty by Autopsies?," *Intensive Care Medicine* 27 (2001): 1750–55.

24. Itzhak Ben-David, John R. Graham, and Campbell R. Harvey, "Managerial Miscalibration," *Quarterly Journal of Economics* 128 (2013): 1547–84.

25. Dominic D. P. Johnson, *Overconfidence and War: The Havoc and the Glory of Positive Illusions* (Cambridge, Mass.: Harvard University Press, 2004), 4.

26. Moore, *Perfectly Confident,* 23.

27. Moore, *Perfectly Confident,* 23.

28. See, e.g., Arezow Doost, "The Misdiagnosis Ended Up Costing Her, Her Life: A Texas Family's Warning for All Parents," KXAN Investigates, Oct. 4, 2020, updated Mar. 15, 2021, https://www.kxan.com/investigations/the-misdiagnosis-ended-up-costing-her-her-life-a-texas-familys-warning-for-all-parents/.

29. Al Kamen, "Powell Changed Vote in Sodomy Case," *Washington Post,* July 13, 1986.

30. Linda Greenhouse, "Black Robes Don't Make the Justice, but the Rest of the Closet Might," *New York Times,* Dec. 4, 2002.

31. "Chief Justice Roberts Statement: Nomination Process," United States Courts, https://www.uscourts.gov/educational-resources/educational-activities/chief-justice-roberts-statement-nomination-process.

32. Dan M. Kahan, "Foreword: Neutral Principles, Motivated Cognition, and Some Problems for Constitutional Law," *Harvard Law Review* 125 (2011): 1–77, at 7.

33. Ziva Kunda, "The Case for Motivated Reasoning," *Psychological Bulletin* 108 (1990): 480–98.

34. Among the Catholic justices, only Justice Sotomayor has voted consistently in favor of same-sex marriage and the right to an abortion.

35. Nathan P. Kalmoe and Lilliana Mason, "Lethal Mass Partisanship: Prevalence, Correlates, and Electoral Contingencies," paper presented at the NCAPSA American Politics Meeting, January 2019, https://www.dannyhayes.org/uploads/6/9/8/5/69858539/kalmoe___mason_ncapsa_2019_-_lethal_partisanship_-_final_lmedit.pdf.

36. Toby Bolsen et al., "The Influence of Partisan Motivated Reasoning on Public Opinion," *Political Behavior* 36 (2014): 235–62.

37. *United States v. Palomar-Santiago,* 141 S. Ct. 1615 (2021).

38. See, e.g., *California v. Texas,* 141 S. Ct. 2104 (2021); *King v. Burwell,* 576 U.S. 988 (2015); and *NFIB v. Sebelius,* 567 U.S. 519 (2012).

39. Eta S. Berner and Mark Graber, "Overconfidence as a Cause of Diagnostic Error in Medicine," *American Journal of Medicine* 121 (2008): S2–23.

40. Kahneman, *Thinking, Fast and Slow,* 264.

41. See generally Eric Berger, "The Rhetoric of Constitutional Absolutism," *William and Mary Law Review* 56 (2015): 667–758.

42. Quoted in Melvin I. Urofsky, *Louis D. Brandeis: A Life* (New York: Schocken Books, 2009), 836.

43. *Meier ex rel. Meier v. Sun International Hotels, Ltd.*, 288 F.3d 1264, 1267 (11th Cir. 2002).

44. "Family's Suit Revived Against Island Resort," *South Florida Sun-Sentinel*, Apr. 24, 2002.

45. "Justice Elena Kagan on the Career of Justice Ruth Bader Ginsburg," C-SPAN, Feb. 3, 2014, https://www.c-span.org/video/?317570-1/women-law-justice-ruth-bader-ginsburg.

46. *Ford Motor Company v. Montana Eighth Judicial District*, 141 S. Ct. 1017, 1039 n.5 (2021) (Gorsuch, J., concurring in the judgment) (slip op. at 10–11 & n.5).

47. Kahneman, *Thinking, Fast and Slow*, 242.

48. See Kahneman, *Thinking, Fast and Slow*, 219; and Philip E. Tetlock, *Expert Political Judgment: How Good Is It? How Can We Know?* (Princeton, N.J.: Princeton University Press, 2005).

49. Kahneman, *Thinking, Fast and Slow*, 263.

50. Richard A. Posner, "Foreword: A Political Court," *Harvard Law Review* 119 (2005): 32–102, at 56.

51. "The Law School Class of 1952," 125 Stanford Stories, No. 31, Stanford|125, https://125.stanford.edu/the-law-school-class-of-1952/.

52. Bob Stump quoted in Jeffrey Rosen, "A Majority of One," *New York Times*, June 3, 2001.

53. Rosen, "Majority of One"; see also Cass R. Sunstein, *One Case at a Time: Judicial Minimalism on the Supreme Court* (Cambridge, Mass.: Harvard University Press, 1999).

54. See, e.g., *Webster v. Reproductive Health Services*, 492 U.S. 290 (1989) (Scalia, J., concurring in part) ("Similarly irrational is the new concept that Justice O'Connor introduces into the law in order to achieve her result.").

55. Rosen, "Majority of One."

56. *Grutter v. Bollinger*, 539 U.S. 306, 343 (2003).

57. Rosen, "Majority of One."

58. Evan Thomas, *First: Sandra Day O'Connor* (New York: Random House, 2019), 340.

59. Thomas, *First*, 402.

60. See, e.g., *Gonzales v. Raich*, 545 U.S. 1 (2005) (Thomas, J., dissenting) (arguing that the Court's Commerce Clause jurisprudence is "at odds with the constitutional design").

61. See, e.g., *Everson v. Board of Education of Ewing Township*, 330 U.S. 1, 5 (1947).

62. *Elk Grove Unified School District v. Newdow,* 542 U.S. 1 (2004) (Thomas, J., concurring in the judgment).

63. Jeffrey Rosen, "If Scalia Had His Way," *New York Times,* Jan. 8, 2011.

64. Jeffrey Toobin, *The Oath: The Obama White House and the Supreme Court* (New York: Doubleday, 2012), 173.

65. Evan Caminker, "Thayerian Deference to Congress and Supreme Court Supermajority Rule: Lessons from the Past," *Indiana Law Journal* 78 (2003): 73–122, at 74.

66. See Keith E. Whittington, "Judicial Review of Congress Database," https://scholar.princeton.edu/kewhitt/judicial-review-congress-database.

67. Kenneth W. Starr, "The Supreme Court and Its Shrinking Docket: The Ghost of William Howard Taft," *Minnesota Law Review* 90 (2006): 1363–85, at 1369.

68. Keith Carlson, Michael A. Livermore, and Daniel Rockmore, "A Quantitative Analysis of Writing Style on the U.S. Supreme Court," *Washington University Law Review* 93 (2016): 1461–1510, at 1478 and n.91.

69. Adam Liptak, "Justices' Opinions Grow in Size, Accessibility and Testiness, Study Finds," *New York Times,* May 4, 2015.

70. In particular, the law explicitly states that "[t]he extent to which members of a protected class [e.g., Black representatives] have been elected to office in the State or political subdivision is one circumstance which may be considered." 52 U.S.C. 10301(b).

71. *Brnovich v. Democratic National Committee,* 141 S. Ct. 2321, 2341, 2361–62 (2021).

72. Kahan, "Neutral Principles," 60.

73. Oral Argument Transcript in *Northwest Austin Municipal Utility Dist. No. One v. Holder.*

74. Babylonian Talmud, Tractate Sanhedrin 17a ("We have learned by tradition that sentence must be postponed till the morrow in hope of finding new points in favor of the defense").

75. Michael J. Klarman, "How Great Were the 'Great' Marshall Court Decisions?," *Virginia Law Review* 87 (2003): 1111–84, at 1172–73.

76. Klarman, "How Great Were the "Great" Marshall Court Decisions?," 1168, 1178–79.

77. *Marbury v. Madison,* 5 U.S. 137 (1803).

78. *Cohens v. Virginia,* 19 U.S. 264 (1811).

79. See generally Jamal Greene, "The Meming of Substantive Due Process," *Constitutional Commentary* 31 (2016): 253–94 (describing contours of the debate).

80. *Lochner v. New York,* 198 U.S. 45, 53 (1905).

81. *Lochner,* at 57.

82. *Lochner,* at 70, 71, 58.

83. *West Coast Hotel v. Parrish,* 300 U.S. 379 (1937).

84. *West Coast Hotel,* at 398, 399.

85. *United States v. Carolene Products,* 304 U.S. 144, 153–54 (1939).

86. See the Taft-Hartley Act of 1947, which rolled back many of the seminal protections extended to organized labor in the National Labor Relations Act of 1935.

87. Robert G. McCloskey, *The American Supreme Court* (Chicago: University of Chicago Press, 1960), 125.

88. *Brown v. Allen,* 344 U.S. 443 (1953) (Jackson, J., dissenting)

Chapter 4. The Times They Were a Changin'

1. Keith E. Whittington, "Judicial Review of Congress Database," https://scholar.princeton.edu/kewhitt/judicial-review-congress-database. Note that Whittington codes one case as invalidating a congressional law in 1939, *NLRB v. Fansteel Metallurgical Corp.,* 360 U.S. 240 (1939). That case, however, did not actually strike down any federal statutory provision. Instead, it merely noted that *if* Congress had drafted a law forcing "employers to retain persons in their employ regardless of their unlawful conduct," such a law would raise a serious "question of . . . constitutional validity." Yet in the very next sentence, the Court made clear that "we find no such expression in the cited [statutory] provision." 360 U.S. at 255.

2. Heather Rodriguez, "The Quiet 'Riot,'" blog post, Texas A&M University, Mar. 19, 2018, https://liberalarts.tamu.edu/blog/2018/03/19/the-quiet-riot/.

3. "Negro Riot at Millican," *Dallas Herald,* July 25, 1868.

4. Rodriguez, "Quiet 'Riot.'"

5. *Smith v. Allwright,* 321 U.S. 649, 656 (1944).

6. Chad Garrison, "The Mystery of Lloyd Gaines," *Riverfront Times* (St. Louis, Mo.), Apr. 4, 2007.

7. Garrison, "Mystery of Lloyd Gaines."

8. *Poe v. Ullman,* 367 U.S. 497, 499–500 (1961).

9. *Griswold v. Connecticut,* 381 U.S. 479 (1965).

10. Brief of Respondents in *Bolling v. Sharpe,* 347 U.S. 497 (1954), 1952 WL 47258 at *63.

11. Robert G. McCloskey, *The American Supreme Court* (Chicago: University of Chicago Press, 1960), 129.

12. *Grovey v. Townsend,* 295 U.S. 45 (1935).

13. *Smith v. Allwright*, 321 U.S. 649 (1944).

14. *Missouri ex rel. Gaines v. Canada*, 305 U.S. 337 (1938).

15. *West Virginia State Board of Education v. Barnette*, 319 U.S. 624, 648 (1943) (Frankfurter, J., dissenting).

16. J. Harvie Wilkinson III, *Cosmic Constitutional Theory: Why Americans Are Losing Their Inalienable Right to Self-Governance* (New York: Oxford University Press, 2012). Others have written similarly powerful critiques of academic efforts to identify unifying theories of constitutional law. See, e.g., Daniel A. Farber and Suzanna Sherry, *Desperately Seeking Certainty* (Chicago: University of Chicago Press, 2004); and Mark Tushnet, *Red, White, and Blue: A Critical Analysis of Constitutional Law* (Cambridge, Mass.: Harvard University Press, 1988).

17. *Griswold*, at 482.

18. *Griswold*, at 509–10 (Black, J., dissenting).

19. Paul G. Kauper, "Penumbras, Peripheries, Emanations, Things Fundamental and Things Forgotten: The *Griswold* Case," *Michigan Law Review* 64 (1965): 235–58, at 244.

20. Harry H. Wellington, "Common Law Rules and Constitutional Double Standards: Some Notes on Adjudication," *Yale Law Journal* 83 (1973): 221–311, at 294.

21. John Hart Ely, *Democracy and Distrust: A Theory of Judicial Review* (Cambridge, Mass.: Harvard University Press, 1980), 103.

22. Robert H. Bork, *The Tempting of America: The Political Seduction of the Law* (New York: Simon and Schuster, 1990).

23. Laurence H. Tribe, "The Puzzling Persistence of Process-Based Constitutional Theories," *Yale Law Journal* 89 (1980): 1063.

24. Bruce A. Ackerman, "Beyond Carolene Products," *Harvard Law Review* 98 (1985): 713–46.

25. See Jeffrey R. Dudas, "In the Name of Equal Rights: 'Special' Rights and the Politics of Resentment in Post–Civil Rights America," *Law and Society Review* 39 (2005): 723–57, at 725.

26. Lawrence B. Solum, "Originalism Versus Living Constitutionalism: The Conceptual Structure of the Great Debate," *Northwestern Law Review* 113 (2019): 1243–96, at 1249.

27. See Noah Feldman, *Scorpions: The Battles and Triumphs of FDR's Great Supreme Court Judges* (New York: Twelve, 2010), 145.

28. *Griswold*, at 522 (Black, J., dissenting).

29. See Bork, *Tempting of America*.

30. *Griswold*, at 520 (Black, J., dissenting).

31. *United States v. Miller,* 307 U.S. 174, 178 (1939).

32. William J. Brennan Jr., "The Constitution of the United States: Contemporary Ratification," delivered at Georgetown University Law Center, Washington, D.C., Oct. 12, 1985, reprinted in *South Texas Law Review* 27 (1986): 433–46.

33. David A. Strauss, "Foreword: Does the Constitution Mean What It Says?," *Harvard Law Review* 129 (2015): 2–61.

34. David A. Strauss, *The Living Constitution* (New York: Oxford University Press, 2010), 38.

35. Strauss, "Does the Constitution Mean What It Says?"

36. Benjamin N. Cardozo, *The Nature of the Judicial Process* (New Haven: Yale University Press, 1921), 83–84.

37. Michael J. Klarman, "An Interpretive History of Modern Equal Protection," *Michigan Law Review* 90 (1991): 213–318, at 252.

38. One prominent originalist scholar, former federal judge Michael McConnell, has argued that originalism can also be reconciled with *Brown v. Board of Education.* See Michael W. McConnell, "The Originalist Case for *Brown v. Board of Education,*" *Harvard Journal of Law and Public Policy* 19 (1995): 457–64.

39. *Kennedy v. Louisiana,* 554 U.S. 407, 414 (2008).

40. *Kennedy v. Louisiana,* at 407.

41. Stuart Banner, *The Death Penalty: An American History* (Cambridge, Mass.: Harvard University Press, 2002), 23.

42. *Kennedy v. Louisiana,* at 438.

43. See, e.g., Lawrence B. Solum, "The Interpretation-Construction Distinction," *Constitutional Communication* 27 (2010): 95–118; Randy Barnett, "Interpretation and Construction," *Harvard Journal of Law and Public Policy* 34 (2011): 65–72; and Keith E. Whittington, *Constitutional Construction: Divided Powers and Constitutional Meaning* (Cambridge, Mass.: Harvard University Press, 1999), 5–9.

44. Brennan, "Constitution of the United States."

45. AP, "Scalia."

Part Two. The Solution

1. Daniel Kahneman, *Thinking, Fast and Slow* (New York: Farrar, Straus and Giroux, 2011), 239.

2. Learned Hand, "Liberty Lies in the Hearts of Men and Women," speech presented May 21, 1944, in *Our Nation's Archive: The History of the United States in Documents,* ed. Erik Bruun and Jay Crosby (New York: Black Dog and Leventhal, 1999), 658.

Chapter 5. What We Do When We Don't Know

1. See generally Shepherd Center, "Anoxic and Hypoxic Brain Injury," https://www.shepherd.org/patient-programs/brain-injury/about/anoxic-hypoxic-brain-injury.

2. Cleveland Clinic, "Cerebral Hypoxia," https://my.clevelandclinic.org/health/diseases/6025-cerebral-hypoxia.

3. See *Cruzan v. Director, Missouri Department of Health,* 497 U.S. 261 (1990).

4. *Cruzan by Cruzan v. Harmon,* 760 S.W.2d 408 (Mo. 1988).

5. William H. Colby, *Long Goodbye: The Deaths of Nancy Cruzan* (Carlsbad, Calif.: Hay House, 2002), 163.

6. Colby, *Long Goodbye.*

7. See Rachel Crosby, "Ex-Guardian Pleads Guilty to Exploitation, Theft," *Las Vegas Review-Journal,* Nov. 7, 2018.

8. Megan Brenan, "Record-Low 54% in U.S. Say Death Penalty Morally Acceptable," Gallup, June 23, 2020, https://news.gallup.com/poll/312929/record-low-say-death-penalty-morally-acceptable.aspx.

9. For a powerful account of how the Court's present approach exacerbates, rather than mediates, conflicting claims by competing litigants, see Jamal Greene, *How Rights Went Wrong: Why Our Obsession with Rights Is Tearing America Apart* (Boston: Houghton Mifflin, 2021).

10. "Charles E. Teel, Jr.," Obituary, Jan. 10, 2005, *Kansas City Star,* online at https://www.legacy.com/us/obituaries/kansascity/name/charles-teel-obituary?pid=3021762.

11. *Cruzan,* 760 S.W.2d at 411.

12. *Cruzan,* 760 S.W.2d at 426.

13. *Cruzan,* 497 U.S. at 278.

14. See William Blackstone, *Commentaries on the Laws of England,* 4 vols. (Oxford: Clarendon Press, 1765–69), 1:130 (defining "liberty" as "the power of locomotion, of changing situation, or removing one's person to whatsoever place one's own inclination may direct; without imprisonment or restraint, unless by due course of law").

15. See, e.g., Antonin Scalia, "Common-Law Courts in a Civil-Law System," in *A Matter of Interpretation: Federal Courts and the Law,* ed. Amy Gutmann (Princeton, N.J.: Princeton University Press, 1997), 24–25; and Laurence H. Tribe, *American Constitutional Law,* 3rd ed. (New York: Foundation Press, 2000), 1332–33.

16. Gayle Minard, "The History of Surgically Placed Feeding Tubes," *Nutrition in Clinical Practice* 21 (2006): 626–33.

17. Pew Research Center, "Views on End-of-Life Medical Treatments," Nov. 21, 2013, https://www.pewresearch.org/religion/2013/11/21/views-on-end-of-life-medical-treatments/.

18. *Cruzan,* 497 U.S. at 277.

19. *Cruzan,* at 277–78.

20. *Cruzan,* at 278.

21. *Cruzan,* at 280.

22. *Cruzan,* at 280, 281.

23. *Cruzan,* at 283.

24. *Cruzan,* at 283.

25. Matt Neal, "Pediatric Emergencies, Case #7," online at https://media.comsep.org/wp-content/uploads/2019/01/28163330/EmergencyCases.pdf.

26. See John Carney, "America Lost $10.2 Trillion in 2008," *Business Insider,* Feb. 3, 2009, https://www.businessinsider.com/2009/2/america-lost-102-trillion-of-wealth-in-2008.

27. See, e.g., David Ellis, "Wachovia Suffers Nearly $24 Billion Loss," *CNN Money,* Oct. 22, 2008, https://money.cnn.com/2008/10/22/news/companies/wachovia_results/index.htm.

28. See Tyler Cowen, "Bailout of Long-Term Capital: A Bad Precedent?" *New York Times,* Dec. 26, 2008.

29. Matthew Benjamin, "Americans Oppose Bailouts, Favor Obama to Handle Market Crisis," *Bloomberg.com,* Sept. 24, 2008.

30. Pew Research Center, "57% of Public Favors Wall Street Bailout," Sept. 23, 2008, https://www.pewresearch.org/politics/2008/09/23/57-of-public-favors-wall-street-bailout/.

31. David M. Herszenhorn, "Bush Administration Wants $700 Billion for Wall Street Bailout," *New York Times,* Sept. 21, 2008.

32. John Ashcroft quoted in Colby, *Long Goodbye,* 324.

33. PR Newswire, "Supreme Court Inching Toward 'Right to Life,' Says American Life League," June 25, 1990.

34. Colby, *Long Goodbye,* 320.

35. "Debate; States Must Permit the Right to Die," *USA Today,* June 27, 1990.

36. "Court Wrong in Saying It's Not Your Right to Die," *Palm Beach (Fla.) Post,* June 26, 1990.

37. Colby, *Long Goodbye,* 389.

38. *Cruzan,* 497 U.S. at 283.

39. *Cruzan,* at 322.

40. Colby, *Long Goodbye,* 334–35.

41. Colby, *Long Goodbye,* 335, 345.

42. Joy Hirsch, "Raising Consciousness," *Journal of Clinical Investigation* 115 (2005): 1102.

Chapter 6. The Least Harm Principle

1. Mark Sherman, "Supreme Court Postpones Arguments Because of Virus Outbreak," *AP News,* Mar. 16, 2020, https://apnews.com/article/664c5973c9d1cabea58fc33a1d50035a.

2. Justin McCarthy, "Approval of the Supreme Court Is Highest Since 2009," Gallup, Aug. 5, 2020, https://news.gallup.com/poll/316817/approval-supreme-court-highest-2009.aspx.

3. Stephen Jesse, Neil Malhotra, and Maya Sen, "What Do the American People Think About the 2020 Supreme Court Cases?," May 19, 2020, 5, SCOTUS-poll, online at https://projects.iq.harvard.edu/files/scotus-poll/files/scotuspoll-summary.pdf.

4. Kevin M. Kruse, "All the President's Taxes," *Esquire,* Apr. 14, 2017.

5. Kruse, "All the President's Taxes."

6. Pew Research Center, "Negative Views of Trump's Transition, amid Concerns About Conflicts, Tax Returns," Jan. 10, 2017, https://www.pewresearch.org/politics/2017/01/10/negative-views-of-trumps-transition-amid-concerns-about-conflicts-tax-returns/.

7. Tina Nguyen, "Eric Trump Reportedly Bragged About Access to $100 Million in Russian Money," *Vanity Fair,* May 8, 2017.

8. Robert S. Mueller III, *Report on the Investigation into Russian Interference in the 2016 Presidential Election,* vol. 1 (Washington, D.C.: Department of Justice, March 2019), 9, online at https://www.justice.gov/archives/sco/file/1373816/download.

9. Danny Hakim and William K. Rashbaum, "Did Trump Overvalue His Properties? Here's What We Know About the Inquiry," *New York Times,* Aug. 26, 2020.

10. See Lily Rothman, " 'I Am Not a Crook'; The Nixon Tax Story Rachel Maddow Just Compared to Trump," *Time,* Mar. 14, 2017.

11. Ebony Bowden, "Trump Slams 'Hideous Witch Hunt' After Judge Rejects Bid to Hide Tax Returns," *New York Post,* Aug. 20, 2020.

12. *Trump v. Vance,* 140 S. Ct. 2412, 2420 (2020).

13. Ben Protess and William K. Rashbaum, "Manhattan D.A. Subpoenas Trump Organization over Stormy Daniels Hush Money," *New York Times,* Aug. 1, 2019.

14. *Vance,* at 2424–25.

15. See *Vance,* at 2429 (noting, but declining to follow, Justice Clarence Thomas's separate opinion that was "based on the original understanding of the Constitution").

16. *Vance,* at 2430 (internal quotation marks omitted).

17. *Vance,* at 2427, 2430–31.

18. *Vance,* at 2430.

19. Reuters, "Factbox: Reaction to U.S. Supreme Court Decision on Trump Financial Records," July 9, 2020, https://www.reuters.com/article/uk-usa-court-trump-quotes-factbox/factbox-reaction-to-u-s-supreme-court-decision-on-trump-financial-records- idUSKBN24A2AX.

20. U.S. Const. art. I, § 8, cl. 18.

21. *Trump v. Mazars,* 140 S. Ct. 2019, 2031 (2020).

22. *Mazars,* at 2034.

23. *Mazars,* at 2033.

24. See Josh Chafetz, "Don't Be Fooled: Trump Is a Winner in the Supreme Court Tax Case," *New York Times,* July 9, 2020.

25. Reacting to the ruling, Democratic representative Carol Maloney, the chairwoman of a key oversight committee in Congress, issued the following statement: "I am disappointed that the Court remanded our case to the lower court for a review under a new standard for subpoenas for Presidential papers, but I am confident our Committee ultimately will prevail." "Chairwoman Maloney Issues Statement on Supreme Court Decision in *Trump v. Mazars,*" Press Release, July 9, 2020, https://oversight.house.gov/news/press-releases/chairwoman-maloney-issues-statement-on-supreme-court-decision-in-trump-v-mazars.

26. Elaine Duke, "Memorandum on Rescission of Deferred Action for Childhood Arrivals (DACA)," Sept. 5, 2017, https://www.dhs.gov/news/2017/09/05/memorandum-rescission-daca.

27. *Department of Homeland Security v. Regents of the University of California,* 140 S. Ct. 1891, 1910, 1913 (2020).

28. *Department of Homeland Security,* at 1905.

29. *Department of Homeland Security,* at 1914.

30. 42 U.S.C. § 2000e-2(a)(1).

31. Oral Argument Transcript in *Bostock v. Clayton County* at 8, online at https://www.supremecourt.gov/oral_arguments/argument_transcripts/2019/17-1618_7k47.pdf.

32. *Bostock v. Clayton County,* 140 S. Ct. 1731, 1753 (2020).

33. *Bostock,* at 1754.

34. Mont. Const. art. X, § 6(1).

35. *Espinoza v. Montana Department of Revenue,* 140 S. Ct. 2246, 2261 (2020).

36. Education Commission of the States, "50-State Comparison: Private School Choice," https://www.ecs.org/50-state-comparison-private-school-choice/. Note that an additional thirteen states have tuition tax credit scholarship programs through which individuals receive tax credits when they donate to private school scholarship organizations.

37. Andrew Coan, *Prosecuting the President: How Special Prosecutors Hold Presidents Accountable and Protect the Rule of Law* (New York: Oxford University Press, 2019), 55.

38. *Nixon v. United States,* 418 U.S. 683, 712, 713 (1974).

39. *Nixon,* at 715.

40. Stacy Teicher Khadaroo, "Alabama Immigration Law Leaves Schools Gripped by Uncertainty," *ABC News,* Sept. 30, 2011, https://abcnews.go.com/US/alabama-immigration-law-leaves-schools-gripped-uncertainty/story?id=14641343.

41. *Plyler v. Doe,* 457 U.S. 202, 220 (1982).

42. *Plyler,* at 229.

43. Jesse Bernal, "Highlights of the Education Reform Bill Passed by the 68th Texas Legislature, Second Called Session June 4–July 2, 1984," online at https://www.idra.org/wp-content/uploads/2018/07/Highlights-of-the-Education-Reform-Bill-Passed-by-the-68th-Texas-Legislature-Aug-1984.pdf.

44. Ian Millhiser, "Build Back Better Is the Latest Victim of America's Anti-Democratic Senate," *Vox,* Dec. 20, 2021, https://www.vox.com/2021/12/20/22846504/senate-joe-manchin-build-back-better-democrats-republicans-43-million.

45. Keith E. Whittington, "The New Originalism," *Georgetown Journal of Law & Public Policy* 2 599 (2004): 599–613.

46. Randy E. Barnett, "An Originalism for Nonoriginalists," *Loyola Law Review* 45 (1999): 611–54, at 645.

47. David A. Strauss, *The Living Constitution* (New York: Oxford University Press, 2010), 38.

48. Richard H. Fallon Jr., "A Constructivist Coherence Theory of Constitutional Interpretation," *Harvard Law Review* 100 (1987): 1189–1286, at 1191–92.

49. In contract law, courts first ask whether a contract term is ambiguous before deciding whether to construe the provision against the contract drafter (if it is ambiguous). Just as with the least harm principle, judges can disagree as to the threshold ambiguity determination yet still go on to apply the rule against the contract drafter. See, e.g., *Lamps Plus, Inc. v. Varela,* 139 S. Ct. 1407, 1417–19 (2019) (disagreeing with dissent's conclusion that *contra proferentem* ought to apply to arbitration clause at issue). A similar approach applies in the famous administrative law doctrine of *Chevron*

deference, where judges ask at Step 1 whether a statute is ambiguous. It is only if it is that judges go on to Step 2 where they defer to any reasonable interpretation adopted by an agency. See *Chevron v. N.R.D.C.*, 467 U.S. 837, 842–43 (1984).

50. *Vance,* 140 S. Ct. at 2425.

51. *Cruzan v. Director, Missouri Department of Health,* 497 U.S. 261, 279, 283 (1990).

52. Charles L. Barzun and Michael D. Gilbert, "Conflict Avoidance in Constitutional Law," *Virginia Law Review* 107 (2021): 1–56.

53. For a powerful defense of this kind of direct weighing, see Jamal Greene, *How Rights Went Wrong: Why Our Obsession with Rights Is Tearing America Apart* (Boston: Houghton Mifflin, 2021), 110 (defending an internationally accepted proportionality approach to judicial review that asks, among other questions, whether "the government's policy [is] seriously out of proportion to the burdens it imposes on rights?").

54. See Aaron Tang, "Harm-Avoider Constitutionalism," *California Law Review* 109 (2021): 1847–1912, at 1880.

Chapter 7. Rebuilding Trust

1. Gallup, "Supreme Court," https://news.gallup.com/poll/4732/supreme-court.aspx.

2. Gary Langer, "Citizens United Poll: 80 Percent of Americans Oppose Supreme Court Decision," *HuffPost,* April 19, 2010, https://www.huffpost.com/entry/citizens-united-poll-80-p_n_465396.

3. *Trump v. Mazars,* Case No. 19-cv-01136 (APM), Aug. 11, 2021, at *32, online at https://s3.documentcloud.org/documents/21041029/trump-v-mazars-memorandum-opinion.pdf.

4. Pew Research Center, "Strong Public Support for Right to Die," Jan. 5, 2006 (describing results of 1990 survey in which 73 percent rejected view that "doctors should always try to save a patient's life" and 55 percent agreed that persons have a "moral right to end life if they suffer great pain with no hope of improvement").

5. Gallup, "June Wave 1," June 23, 2022, https://news.gallup.com/file/poll/394118/20220623SupremeCourt.pdf.

6. *NAACP v. Button,* 371 U.S. 415, 428 (1963).

7. See Jud Campbell, "Natural Rights and the First Amendment," *Yale Law Journal* 127 (2017): 246–321.

8. See Federal Election Commission, "Limits on Contributions Received by the SSF," https://www.fec.gov/help-candidates-and-committees/taking-receipts-ssf/limits-contributions-received-ssf/.

9. Reply Brief for Petitioner Mark Janus, at 11.

10. Brief for Respondent American Federation of State, County, and Municipal Employees, Council 31, at 18.

11. Oral Argument Transcript in *Janus v. American Federation of State, County, and Municipal Employees, Council 31,* at 56, https://www.supremecourt.gov/oral_arguments/argument_transcripts/2017/16-1466_gebh.pdf.

12. Reply Brief of Petitioner Masterpiece Cakeshop, at 18.

13. Brief for Respondents Charlie Craig and David Mullins, at 19.

14. See Jamal Greene, *How Rights Went Wrong: Why Our Obsession with Rights Is Tearing America Apart* (Boston: Houghton Mifflin, 2021).

15. Jamal Greene, "Foreword: Rights as Trumps?," *Harvard Law Review* 132 (2018): 28–132, at 34.

16. *Cruzan v. Director, Missouri Department of Health,* 497 U.S. 261, 286 (1990).

17. See Daniel Rodriguez et al., "Religious Intellectual Humility, Attitude Change, and Closeness Following Religious Disagreement," *Journal of Positive Psychology* 14 (2018): 133–40, at 138 (describing how intellectual humility is positively correlated with increased tolerance for religious out-groups); and Bradley P. Owens, Michael D. Johnson, and Terence R. Mitchell, "Expressed Humility in Organizations: Implications for Performance, Teams, and Leadership," *Organization Science* 24 (2013): 1517–38, at 1530 (finding that leader-expressed humility in the workforce increased employee job engagement and satisfaction).

18. *Pierce v. Society of Sisters,* 268 U.S. 510, 534–35 (1925).

19. *Mahanoy Area School District v. B. L.,* 141 S. Ct. 2038, 2053 (Alito, J., concurring).

20. Michael W. McConnell, "The Right to Die and the Jurisprudence of Tradition," *Utah Law Review* (1997): 665–708, at 696.

21. James C. Mohr, *Abortion in America: The Origins and Evolutions of National Policy, 1800–1900* (New York: Oxford University Press, 1978), 3.

22. *Roe v. Wade,* 410 U.S. 113, 134–36 (1973).

23. See *Dobbs v. Jackson Women's Health Organization,* 142 S. Ct. 2228, 2253 (2022); and Aaron Tang, "After Dobbs: History, Tradition, and the Uncertain Future of a Nationwide Abortion Ban," *Stanford Law Review* (forthcoming 2023), https://papers.ssrn.com/sol3/papers.cfm?abstract_id=4205139.

24. Tang, "After Dobbs."

25. Thomas Low Nichols, *Esoteric Anthropology* (Port Chester, N.Y.: [N.Y. Stereotype Assoc.], 1853), 193.

26. Megan Brenan, "Record-High 47% in U.S. Think Abortion Is Morally Acceptable," Gallup, June 9, 2021, https://news.gallup.com/poll/350756/record-high-think-abortion-morally-acceptable.aspx.

27. Pew Research Center, "America's Abortion Quandary: 1. Americans' Views on Whether, and in What Circumstances, Abortion Should Be Legal," May 6, 2022, https://www.pewresearch.org/religion/2022/05/06/americans-views-on-whether-and-in-what-circumstances-abortion-should-be-legal/.

28. Catherine Lucey, "Support for 15-Week Abortion Ban Outweighs Opposition, WSJ Poll Finds," *Wall Street Journal,* April 1, 2022.

29. See Amanda Stevenson, "The Pregnancy-Related Mortality Impact of a Total Abortion Ban in the United States," *Demography* 58 (2021): 2019–28.

30. Nigel Chiwaya and Chantal Da Silva, "Map: 23 States Would Ban Abortion in Post-Roe America," *NBC News,* May 3, 2022, https://www.nbcnews.com/data-graphics/map-23-states-ban-abortion-post-roe-america-rcna27081.

31. Olga Khazan, "When Abortion Is Illegal, Women Rarely Die; But They Still Suffer," *Atlantic,* Oct. 11, 2018.

32. Khazan, "When Abortion Is Illegal."

33. Jonathan Bearak et al., "Unintended Pregnancy and Abortion by Income, Region, and the Legal Status of Abortion: Estimates from a Comprehensive Model for 1990–2019," *Lancet,* July 22, 2020.

34. Diane Duke Williams, "Access to Free Birth Control Reduces Abortion Rates," Washington University School of Medicine in St. Louis, Oct. 12, 2012, https://medicine.wustl.edu/news/access-to-free-birth-control-reduces-abortion-rates/.

35. See Brenan, "Record-High 47% in U.S. Think Abortion Is Morally Acceptable"; and Pew Research Center, "Where the Public Stands on Religious Liberty vs. Nondiscrimination: 4. Very Few Americans See Contraception as Morally Wrong," Sept. 28, 2016, https://www.pewresearch.org/religion/2016/09/28/4-very-few-americans-see-contraception-as-morally-wrong/.

36. Laura S. Hussey, "Is Welfare Pro-Life? Assistance, Abortion, and the Moderating Role of States," *Social Science Review* 85 (2011): 75–107, 92.

37. See Williams, "Access to Free Birth Control Reduces Abortion Rates."

38. Congressional Research Service, "The Temporary Assistance for Needy Families (TANF) Block Grant: Responses to Frequently Asked Questions," Mar. 31, 2022, https://sgp.fas.org/crs/misc/RL32760.pdf.

39. See American College of Obstetricians and Gynecologists, "Second Trimester Abortion," June 2013, https://www.acog.org/clinical/clinical-guidance/practice-bulletin/articles/2013/06/second-trimester-abortion.

40. Editorial Board, "Abortion and the Supreme Court: This Is the Moment for the Justices to Turn the Issue over to the Voters," *Wall Street Journal,* April 26, 2022.

41. *Dobbs,* at 2310 (Roberts, C.J., concurring in the judgment).

42. *Dobbs,* at 2312 (Roberts, C.J., concurring in the judgment).

Chapter 8. Backsliding

1. See Justin McCarthy, "Approval of the Supreme Court Is Highest Since 2009," Gallup, Aug. 5, 2020, https://news.gallup.com/poll/316817/approval-supreme-court-highest-2009.aspx.

2. Joan Biskupic, "Behind Closed Doors During One of John Roberts' Most Surprising Years on the Supreme Court," *CNN,* July 27, 2020, https://www.cnn.com/2020/07/27/politics/john-roberts-supreme-court-liberals-daca-second-amendment/index.html.

3. Michael Rothfeld et al., "13 Deaths in a Day: An 'Apocalyptic' Coronavirus Surge at an N.Y.C. Hospital," *New York Times,* Mar. 25, 2020.

4. See "New York City Coronavirus Map and Case Count," updated May 25, 2021, https://www.nytimes.com/interactive/2020/nyregion/new-york-city-coronavirus-cases.html.

5. See Executive Order No. 202.68, online at https://www.governor.ny.gov/sites/default/files/atoms/files/EO202.68.pdf.

6. *Roman Catholic Diocese of Brooklyn v. Cuomo,* 141 S. Ct. 63 (2020).

7. *Church of Lukumi Babalu Aye, Inc. v. Hialeah,* 508 U.S. 520, 533 (1993).

8. *Roman Catholic Diocese,* at 67.

9. *Roman Catholic Diocese,* at 71 (Gorsuch, J., concurring).

10. *Roman Catholic Diocese,* at 71 (Gorsuch, J., concurring).

11. The Court even upheld a Maine law requiring health care workers to obtain the vaccine and that permitted medical but not religious exemptions. Three justices—including Justice Gorsuch—dissented. See *Does #1–3 v. Mills,* 142 S. Ct. 17 (2021).

12. See Centers for Disease Control and Prevention, "Stay Up to Date, Interpretive Summary for January 28, 2022," https://www.cdc.gov/coronavirus/2019-ncov/covid-data/covidview/past-reports/01282022.html.

13. See "UC Davis COVID-19 Dashboard," https://campusready.ucdavis.edu/testing-response/dashboard.

14. Carolyn Crist, "23 Active-Duty Sailors Discharged Over Vaccine Refusal," WebMD, Jan. 27, 2022, https://www.webmd.com/vaccines/covid-19-vaccine/news/20220127/active-duty-sailors-discharged-vaccine-refusal.

15. See Phil McCausland, "Religious Exemptions to Vaccine Mandates Could Test 'Sincerely Held Beliefs,'" *CBS News,* Sept. 5, 2021.

16. Joshua J. McElwee, "Pope Francis Suggests People Have Moral Obligation to Take Coronavirus Vaccine," *National Catholic Reporter,* Jan. 11, 2021, https://www.ncronline.org/news/vatican/pope-francis-suggests-people-have-moral-obligation-take-coronavirus-vaccine.

17. See "A Proclamation on Advancing the Safe Resumption of Global Travel During the COVID-19 Pandemic," White House, Oct. 25, 2021, https://www.whitehouse.gov/briefing-room/presidential-actions/2021/10/25/a-proclamation-on-advancing-the-safe-resumption-of-global-travel-during-the-covid-19-pandemic/ ("The Centers for Disease Control and Prevention . . . has determined that the best way to slow the spread of COVID-19, including preventing infection by the Delta variant, is for individuals to get vaccinated.").

18. Chad D. Cotti et al., "The Relationship Between In-Person Voting and COVID-19: Evidence from the Wisconsin Primary," NBER Working Paper 27187, May 2020.

19. *Democratic National Committee v. Wisconsin State Legislature,* 141 S. Ct. 28, 40 (2020) (Kagan, J., dissenting).

20. McKenzie Sadeghi, "Fact Check: Mail-In Ballots Arriving After Election Day Will Count in Some States," *USA Today,* Oct. 30, 2020.

21. *Democratic National Committee v. Bostelmann,* 488 F. Supp. 3d. 776, 783 (W.D. Wisc. 2020).

22. See Jacob Shamsian, "Pennsylvania, Texas and Minnesota Are Setting Aside Some of Their Ballots in Case a Judge Throws Out the Votes; Here's Why," *Business Insider,* Nov. 6, 2020, https://www.businessinsider.com/why-pennsylvania-texas-minnesota-segregating-ballots-in-case-thrown-out-2020-11.

23. Ben Jordan, "Provisional Ballots to Add to Wisconsin's Election Totals," Nov. 4, 2020, updated Nov. 5, 2020, WTMJ-TV, https://www.tmj4.com/news/election-2020/provisional-ballots-to-add-to-wisconsins-election-totals; see also My Vote Wisconsin, "Provisional Ballots," https://myvote.wi.gov/en-us/Provisional-Ballots.

24. *West Virginia v. EPA,* 142 S. Ct. 2587 (2022); *Carson v. Makin,* 142 S. Ct. 1987 (2022); *Kennedy v. Bremerton School District,* 142 S. Ct. 2407 (2022); *Oklahoma v. Castro-Huerta,* 142 S. Ct. 2486 (2022).

25. *Planned Parenthood v. Casey,* 505 U.S. 833, 847 (1992).

26. *Dobbs,* at 2326 (joint dissent).

27. *Dobbs,* at 2281.

28. *Dobbs,* at 2260.

29. *Dobbs,* at 2242.

30. *Dobbs,* at 2267.

31. *Dobbs,* at 2242, 2248, 2253, 2256, 2285–93. Note that the appendix occupies pages 79–101 of the Court's published version of its opinion.

32. *Smith v. Gaffard,* 31 Ala. 45 (1857).

33. *State v. Dunn,* 53 Or. 304 (1909).

34. See R. H. Tatum, "A Few Observations on the Attributes of the Impregnated Germ," *Virginia Medical Journal* 6 (1856): 456.

35. *Dobbs,* at 2279.

36. Edward Helmore, "10-year-old Rape Victim Forced to Travel from Ohio to Indiana for Abortion," *Guardian,* July 3, 2022.

37. *United States v. Miller,* 307 U.S. 174, 178 (1939).

38. *New York State Rifle & Pistol Association v. Bruen,* 142 S. Ct. 2111, 2126 (2022).

39. Statute of Northampton, 2 Edw. 3, c. 3 (1328).

40. *Bruen,* at 2183 (Breyer, J., dissenting) (quoting William Blackstone, *Commentaries on the Laws of England,* vol. 4 [Oxford: Clarendon Press, 1769], 148–49 ("The offence of riding or going armed, with dangerous or unusual weapons, is a crime against the public peace, by terrifying the good people of the land; and is particularly prohibited by the Statute of Northampton.").

41. *Bruen,* at 2142–44.

42. *Bruen,* at 2145–47.

43. *Bruen,* at 2148–50.

44. *Bruen,* at 2145.

45. *Bruen,* at 2149.

46. *Bruen,* at 2145.

47. *Bruen,* at 2126.

48. See Center for American Progress, "Smart Guns: Technology That Can Save Lives," Mar. 29, 2022, https://www.americanprogress.org/article/smart-guns-technology-that-can-save-lives/.

49. John Donohue, Abhay Aneja, and Kyle D. Weber, "Right-to-Carry Laws and Violent Crime: A Comprehensive Assessment Using Panel Data and a State-Level Synthetic Control Analysis," *Journal of Empirical Legal Studies* 16 (2019): 198–247.

50. *Caetano v. Massachusetts,* 577 U.S. 411 (2016).

51. See Elinor Aspegen, "Northern California City Passes Law Requiring Gun Owners to Carry Liability Insurance," *USA Today,* July 1, 2021.

52. "Governor Hochul Signs Landmark Legislation to Strengthen Gun Laws and Bolster Restrictions on Concealed Carry Weapons in Response to Reckless

Supreme Court Decision," press release, July 1, 2022, https://www.governor.ny.gov/news/governor-hochul-signs-landmark-legislation- strengthen-gun-laws-and-bolster-restrictions.

53. *Bruen,* at 2161–62 (Kavanaugh, J., concurring).

Chapter 9. The Crossroads

1. Felix Frankfurter, "Mr. Justice Roberts," *University of Pennsylvania Law Review* 104 (1955): 311.

2. Justice Felix Frankfurter to Chief Justice Harlan Fiske Stone, Aug. 20, 1945, reel 64, Frankfurter Papers, Library of Congress.

3. Justice Felix Frankfurter to Justice Harlan Fiske Stone, Mar. 30, 1937, quoted in Michael E. Parrish, *Felix Frankfurter and His Times: The Reform Years* (New York: Free Press, 1982), 271.

4. Frankfurter to Stone, Aug. 20, 1945.

5. Frankfurter, "Mr. Justice Roberts," 311, 312–13.

6. See Brad Snyder, *Democratic Justice: Felix Frankfurter, the Supreme Court, and the Making of the Liberal Establishment* (New York: W. W. Norton, 2022); and H. N. Hirsch, *The Enigma of Felix Frankfurter* (New Orleans, La.: Quid Pro Books, 2014).

7. Daniel E. Ho and Kevin M. Quinn, "Did a Switch in Time Save Nine?," *Journal of Legal Analysis* 2 (2010): 69–113, at 102.

8. *Morehead v. New York, ex rel. Tipaldo,* 298 U.S. 587 (1936)

9. Bruce Ackerman, *We the People,* vol. 2, *Transformations* (Cambridge, Mass.: Harvard University Press, 1998), 484n47.

10. See John Q. Barrett, "Attribution Time: Cal Tinney's 1937 Quip, 'A Switch in Time'll Save Nine,'" *Oklahoma Law Review* 73 (2021): 229–42.

11. Laura Kalman, "Law, Politics, and the New Deal(s)," *Yale Law Journal* 108 (1999): 2165–2213, at 2174; see also Laura Kalman, *FDR's Gambit: The Court Packing Fight and the Rise of Legal Liberalism* (New York: Oxford University Press, 2022), 281.

12. Jeffrey M. Jones, "Confidence in the U.S. Supreme Court Sinks to Historic Low," Gallup, June 23, 2022, https://news.gallup.com/poll/394103/confidence-supreme-court-sinks-historic-low.aspx.

13. See Christopher Jon Sprigman, "Congress's Article III Power and the Process of Constitutional Change," *N.Y.U. Law Review* 95 (2020): 1778–1859.

14. Drew Desilver, "With Fewer State Governments Divided by Party Than in Years Past, GOP Has Edge in Redistricting," Pew Research, Mar. 4, 2021, https://www.pewresearch.org/fact-tank/2021/03/04/with-fewer-state-governments-divided-by-party-than-in-years-past-gop-has-edge-in-redistricting/.

15. *Ex Parte McCardle,* 74 U.S. (7 Wall.) 506 (1869). If it were also concerned about the lower federal courts invalidating its important legislative enactments, Congress could strip those courts of jurisdiction, too, given that lower courts are not constitutionally required at all. See Sprigman, "Congress's Article III Power," at 1802.

16. *West Coast Hotel v. Parrish,* 300 U.S. 379, 399 (1937).

17. See, e.g., *United States v. Carolene Products,* 304 U.S. 144, 148 (1939). The Court first used the phrase "presumption of constitutionality" to uphold a challenged law in a decision of 1931: *O'Gorman & Young, Inc. v. Hartford Fire Insurance Co.,* 282 U.S. 251, 257 (1931). But its use increased rapidly after 1937. See, e.g., *South Carolina State Highway Department v. Barnwell Bros.,* 303 U.S. 177, 195 (1938); *Carolene Products,* 304 U.S. 144 (1939); and *Madden v. Commonwealth of Kentucky,* 309 U.S. 83, 88 (1940).

18. *United States v. Lovett,* 328 U.S. 303, 319, 327 (1946) (Frankfurter, J., concurring).

19. See David S. Cohen, Greer Donley, and Rachel Rebouche, "The New Abortion Battleground," *Columbia Law Review* (forthcoming, 2023).

20. Cohen, Donley, and Rebouche, "New Abortion Battleground."

21. Richard H. Fallon Jr., "If Roe Were Overruled: Abortion and the Constitution in a Post-Roe World," *St. Louis University Law Journal* 51 (2007): 611–53, 632.

22. See Cohen, Donley, and Rebouche, "New Abortion Battleground," 30.

23. *Gonzales v. Raich,* 545 U.S. 1, 25–26 (2005).

24. *Gonzales,* at 58 (Thomas, J., dissenting) (arguing that because of its founding era meaning, the Commerce Clause empowers Congress only "to regulate the buying and selling of goods and services trafficked across state lines").

25. Akhil Reed Amar, *America's Constitution: A Biography* (New York: Random House, 2005), 107–8; Jack M. Balkin, "Commerce," *Michigan Law Review* 109 (2010): 1–51, at 15–29.

26. Ian Millhiser, "A New Supreme Court Case Is the Biggest Threat to US Democracy Since January 6," *Vox,* June 30, 2022, https://www.vox.com/23161254/supreme-court-threat-democracy-january-6.

27. *Harper v. Hall,* 2022-NCSC-17, ¶ 51, 380 N.C. 317, 340, 868 S.E.2d 499, 520, *cert. granted sub nom. Moore v. Harper,* No. 21-1271, 2022 WL 2347621 (U.S. June 30, 2022).

28. N.C. Const. art. I, § 10.

29. U.S. Const. art. I, § 4, cl. 1.

30. *Rucho v. Common Cause,* 139 S. Ct. 2484, 2507 (2019) ("Provisions in state statutes and state constitutions can provide standards and guidance for state courts to apply.").

31. Henry P. Monaghan, "Our Perfect Constitution," *N.Y.U. Law Review* 56 (2010): 353–96, 356.

32. *Dred Scott v. Sandford,* 60 U.S. 393 (1857); *Korematsu v. United States,* 323 U.S. 213 (1944); *Hammer v. Dagenhart,* 247 U.S. 251 (1918).

33. Aaron Tang, "Harm-Avoider Constitutionalism," *California Law Review* 109 (2021): 1847–1912, at 1912.

Acknowledgments

Eric Segall, a highly respected scholar and generous mentor to countless young law professors over the years, has often remarked how difficult it is to write something in the field of constitutional law that is both truly novel and intelligent. I fear the same may be true of book acknowledgments. But I would be remorseful if I did not at least try to thank the many people who have been instrumental in bringing this project to fruition.

First, I thank my co-clerks, Fred Smith, Sparkle Sooknanan, and Daniel Winik. So much of what appears in these pages is the product of the intense, year-long experience we shared at the Supreme Court—and the many lessons we learned together. Without their friendship (and editing!), I do not know how I would've survived.

I also want to thank the dozens of colleagues at various law schools who shared feedback and questions on this book and the law review articles that preceded it. Any attempt to list everyone who has shared their time and wisdom will surely leave important people out, so far better for me to express my gratitude en masse. If you are a law professor at an American law school and the ideas in this book sound familiar from conversations we've had—thank you.

I am especially indebted to my old friend, Matt Reagan, for taking the time to read the earliest drafts of each chapter in this book and for sharing his characteristically incisive comments. It is no exaggeration to say that his encouragement, brilliance, and unrelenting honesty were essential to the book, and I owe him more than a few drinks in gratitude.

For tremendous research assistance, I thank Abby Miles, McKenzie Deutsch, Neha Malik, Courtney Patton, and Carmel Wright. I am also grateful to the University of California, Davis Law School, and to Dean Kevin Johnson, for generous research support over the years.

To everyone who has helped care for my young children these past two years, both in and out of school, I thank you, too. I am especially thankful to my parents and my in-laws for all they've done over the years.

To my editor Bill Frucht at Yale University Press, thank you for your keen eye for detail, thoughtful suggestions, and constant support. This book is so much better because of you.

To my agent, Ted Weinstein, I cannot say thank-you enough. We began our relationship just days before the world went on hold in March 2020, and there were many days in the darkest moments of the pandemic when this book felt like an impossibility. All literary agents help unlock doors to publishing a book, but only some agents carry authors on their backs in the process. For this first-time author, Ted was that kind of an agent; he was a craftsman of ideas, an intellectual force, and a steady guide.

I am enormously thankful to the two judges for whom I've clerked, whose influence is borne out in this book in ways big and small. From JHW, I learned so much about the importance of open-mindedness and getting along with those with whom we disagree—which he and I did from time to time. From SS, words cannot express how much I've learned about the law, life, and the incredible force of intellectual humility. As I look ahead with deep concern for our nation's future, her presence is one of the few things that gives me hope.

Finally, and most importantly, I am grateful to my wife, Liz, for making this book—and everything else worthwhile in my life—possible. I love you. Now it's my turn to do the laundry for a year.

Index

Figures are indicated by "f" following the page number.